# The Memoirs of Colonel John S. Mosby

## Southern Classics Series

# SOUTHERN CLASSICS SERIES

# The Memoirs of Colonel John S. Mosby

Foreword by J. O. Tate

J. S. Sanders & Company

NASHVILLE

*Library of Congress Catalog Card Number:*
94-69016

ISBN: 1-879941-27-9

Published in the United States by
J. S. Sanders & Company
P.O. Box 50331
Nashville, Tennessee 37205

J. S. Sanders 1995 Edition

Second Printing May 1997
Manufactured in the United States of America

# Contents

# Foreword

Everything in American history went into the Civil War, and everything since has come out of it. That is what we mean when we say that "the Civil War is the watershed of American history." So we really don't have a choice about the Civil War—we are going to read about it one way or the other. Whatever we say about it is an interpretation of it; the Civil War itself was an interpretation of American history. Perhaps our only choice, then, is in how, not whether, we interpret the past. You must interpret it for yourself, or someone else will do it for you. Today we often see in the papers an interpretation, usually in the degraded form of some distorted rehash, of the Civil War. When, for example, the Soviet Union broke up, the analogy with the Secession of 1861 occurred to a number of editorial writers and cartoonists, and later President Bush's "Chicken Kiev" speech was construed by some to be an endorsement of one tottering empire by another. More recently, in 1993, Senator Carol Moseley-Braun asserted that the refusal of a patent to the United Daughters of the Confederacy would "put a stake through the heart of this Dracula"—meaning the Confederate battle flag. I doubt that the men who fought under that flag would have comprehended any analogy with vampirism or just why insulting an association of ladies would be important to so many U.S. Senators, though certainly they would have understood very well how the demagoguery of Senators can cause bloodshed. Senator Moseley-Braun's less than profound reflections upon an "offensive" flag that stood for slavery omitted many other flags which at one time or another also represented slaveholding nations—the Stars and Stripes, the Union Jack, and even the Tricolor among them. But in 1993, neither the lack of a foreign policy, the worst floods in our history, nor billions of dollars of debt deterred the Senator from her lengthy disquisition. Who would have thought that Senator Bilbo (or Senator Claghorn) would reappear somehow reconstituted as a black woman from Illinois? Or to take another recent example, I thought I detected in the legal theories of Professor Lani Guinier an offbeat echo of Calhoun's doctrine of the concurrent majority—or at least I thought so until Ms. Guinier's nomination was opposed by the nominator, President Clinton. What goes around, comes around. When Marx said that history repeats itself, the first time as tragedy, the second as farce, he effectively prophesied the continued Federal supervision of Southern voting nearly a hundred and thirty years after Appomattox. When we read of contrived controversies about the Confederate flag and Civil War monuments, we must feel that strong sense of *déjà vu* which Walker Percy rendered so powerfully in his second novel, *The Last Gentleman* (1966). There he portrayed definitively that unique historical nausea we sense when the Civil War—our greatest, bloodiest, nastiest, noblest national experience—is re-fought by unlettered yokels who should be changing tires at a gas station and by chicken-hearted politicians who, though incapable of changing a tire or indeed of much of anything else at a gas station or elsewhere, are somehow most passionately sincere when those C-SPAN cameras are on. And yet even this degradation is perversely appropriate, for it is *ours,* ours more than anything else can ever be. It is ours because of those boys and men who collided in the Peach Orchard and the Hornet's Nest and the Cornfield and the Bloody Lane, and because of the Senatorial gasbags who sent them there. The original Civil War beats the present charade hollow—why even the carpetbaggers and the scalawags were made of finer stuff the first-time around.

But of course there are other ways to look at the Civil War, and today Americans look at it with renewed fascination. People want to know about Custer's Civil War days, about Sherman's March, about Lee's character, about Stonewall Jackson's Valley Campaign and Sheridan's Ride and Admiral Farragut damning the torpedoes in Mobile Bay. I should add that they want also to know— and rightly so—about Frederick Douglass, the Underground Railroad, Sojourner Truth, Harriet Beecher Stowe, Andersonville, black regiments, revivalism, music, reenactments, field medicine—you name it. Though all those topics are valid and interesting, I think there is for many a certain quality of fascination that still radiates from the Confederacy—the Lost Cause, the path not taken, the premier alternative vision of our nation—and from the most alluring of its leaders. The Confederates interpreted themselves by their actions, ones which today must seem mysterious, since we are instructed that their cause was exclusively racist. To the sleek contemporary mind, the Southern soldiers' motivation is either a crude reduction or a bafflement. And of all the Confederates, none had then or now more magnetism and mystery than John S. Mosby (1833–1916).

That is the pull that has drawn the reader to this book. It is the story of a "rebel" told by him—one who had no fear of the Yankees during the War, nor indeed of the Southerners afterwards. And it is also of course the story of a renowned cavalryman, one who distinguished himself in that most glamorous of the services among a host of competitors on the Confederate side alone: J. E. B. Stuart, Turner Ashby, Fitz Lee, Rooney Lee, Wade Hampton, John Hunt Morgan, J. O. Shelby, Joseph Wheeler, and Nathan Bedford Forrest, to name only the most salient. But of course, the association of famous cavalrymen with lost causes is a traditional one: Prince Rupert and Joachim Murat spring immediately to mind. Behind them there is all that panoply of horsemen from the late Roman empire and the Germanic tribes extending through the Middle Ages to the Renaissance and to those cognate words *chivalry, chevalier, cavalier,* and *cavalry* which denote the figure of the knight mounted, the image in Western culture of the gentleman as the synthesis of pagan warrior and Christian pilgrim. In that exalted sense, there is something in Mosby of Castiglione's ideal courtier—the Renaissance man, ranger and lawyer, cavalryman and classicist, fighter and writer, warrior and wit.

There is something too in Mosby of the tradition of the citizen-soldier, of Cincinnatus, of the Minute Man. Ethan Allen, Mad Anthony Wayne, "Light-Horse Harry" Lee, and Francis Marion, "the Swamp Fox," would have appreciated Mosby's courage, flair, and flexibility. Defending his community, he spent most of the war behind enemy lines in occupied territory in Northern Virginia, operating as a guerrilla or a "partisan ranger" in what he caused to be called "Mosby's Confederacy." Yet though Mosby wore a plume in his hat, though his cape was lined with red silk, and though his escapades included feats of swashbucking that would have embarrassed Metro-Goldwyn-

Mayer, he was no romantic. His penetrating intelligence included a corrosive modern quality, a skepticism that may surprise some readers.

I think too there is in Mosby a dark quality, a bit of the daredevil, the rogue, the bad boy, that retains a certain permanent charm. In such a case, the worse, the better—but we find upon examination that none of Mosby's excursions into violence are without justification. As a student at the University of Virginia, he shot a man and went to jail for it, but that was as a response to threats. As a soldier, he ordered Union prisoners to be executed—in response to the hanging of his own men by Custer—and the practice stopped. In the War, he did everything he could to make life miserable for the Yankees, which was his duty, his talent, and I suspect even his pleasure. They were, after all, invaders of Virginia, who destroyed community property and killed his comrades. For what he did, he was repeatedly commended by Jeb Stuart and R. E. Lee. Even so, we still read today of how Mosby had the gall to operate "in the shadow of the Dome." Perhaps it is necessary to point out that such a shadow was cast on the sovereign state of Virginia, the home of Washington, Jefferson, Madison, Monroe, Henry, and Randolph. The gall was on the other side, and it still is.

Is any soldier who served below the rank of general on either side in the Civil War better remembered today than Col. John Singleton Mosby, C.S.A.? I doubt that any such person from that conflict has ever been as well known as he was and is—not even "the gallant Pelham." The names Oliver Wendell Holmes, Rutherford B. Hayes, Samuel Langhorne Clemens, and Jesse James are recognized—but they do not immediately evoke service in the War. Mosby's image is bound to horses and pistols, raids in the dark, and an irrepressible spirit. But if anything or anyone could be more interesting than Mosby the soldier, it is Mosby the man. Even so, the nature of Mosby's fame is as problematical as was his own restless nature, for a man's name and reputation can easily become detached from his individual reality. *The Memoirs of Colonel John S. Mosby* are an authentic record of his service in the war, but they are by no means the whole story of his life. His *Memoirs* tell the story of how Mosby made his name immortal, but of course, since they were first published in 1917, they cannot provide a contemporary perspective. Such a view is one I offer here, and I aim ultimately to suggest something about the meaning not only of these memoirs, but also of the man's life. I'd like to begin in reverse chronological order, and then circle back to the present day.

The title of a 1968 collection by the subsequent Nobel Laureate, Saul Bellow—*Mosby's Memoirs and Other Stories*—must, in this context, strike our attention. But the title story seems essentially unrelated to the allusion insisted upon. The portrait of Willis Mosby is, I think, an undistinguished fictional representation of the redoubtable and remarkable political philosopher, Willmoore Kendall. In the only approach to the story's title, I find the ponderous allusion to be a wasted one:

> The real, the original Mosby approach brought Mosby hatred, got Mosby fired. Princeton University had offered Mosby a lump sum to retire seven years early. One hundred and forty thousand dollars. Because his mode of discourse was so upsetting to the academic community. Mosby was invited to no television programs. He was like the Guerilla Mosby of the Civil War. When he galloped in, all were slaughtered.

This prose does as little credit to Bellow as it does to the original Mosby, who was no butcher. The point here must be that Bellow's "Mosby's Memoirs" is not—except perhaps by an unintended ironic point of contrast—meaningfully related to Mosby's *Memoirs*. Even so, one sentence about Willis Mosby may be construed meaningfully about John S. Mosby, as we shall see: "His doom was to live life to the end as Mosby." However that may be, Saul Bellow affirmed in 1968 that knowing a bit even wrongly about Mosby was indeed something that a literate person would do. For my own part, however, I would have preferred that he name his hero Willis Grant, and the story "Grant's Memoirs." In any case, Grant's real, not fictional *Memoirs*—which Mark Twain was instrumental in publishing—pointedly praise the historical Mosby.

On a lesser plane of sophistication, though to be sure one with a certain popular impact, Mosby's name was prominently bandied about in 1957 and later in the syndicated television show "The Gray Ghost," starring Tod Andrews as "Major John Mosby." This show was created and produced by Lindsley Parsons and distributed by CBS Film Sales. Nationally broadcast, the transformation of Mosby and the War into a routine oater or Confederate horse opera is remarkable in itself. Via "The Gray Ghost," a Confederate ranger shared the chivalric role with Hopalong Cassidy and Roy Rogers. The appropriateness of such a juxtaposition today would be debated not upon the point of truth and fiction, but upon a crux of political correctness that no Confederate image could survive. Still, back in the bad old fifties, Mosby achieved more than the share of fame which Andy Warhol allotted to everyone for fifteen minutes, as though the agony of the Civil War was

endured for the sake of questionable entertainment. Today
Mosby has become a post card and even a T-shirt.

But then in some incomparable way, Mosby had entered the popular consciousness during the War itself because of the newspapers and dispatches—the man was
literally a legend in his own time. Such a fame, sinister
from the point of view of the invading Federals, did not
escape the attention of one of America's greatest writers,
who made Mosby the heroic bogeyman and refrain of a
literary ballad of considerable merit. Herman Melville
used Mosby's name toward the close of every stanza of the
longest of his *Battle-Pieces* (1866), "The Scout Toward
Aldie." Those 798 lines were directly inspired by Melville's
own penetration, accompanying Federal troops, into
"Mosby's Confederacy" during the War. Melville's ambivalence toward his cousin, Col. Gansevoort, and his
Shakespearean sense of irony and distance produced a
Northern poem in which the feared enemy, Mosby, is—as
Aaron Kramer has pointed out—"the brilliantly trium-
phant hero of the poem." In Kramer's explication,
". . . Mosby—largely by the constant reminder of his name
and of his genius for ambush—has achieved for the reader
the rank of mythic hero, and the portrait of his followers
in captivity dramatically shifts our sympathy toward
them." I sense too in "The Scout Toward Aldie" the influence of Scott, his dialectical consciousness of cultural dis-
tinctions, and his romantic celebration of the Other.
Melville's Mosby might be at home in one of the Waverley
novels, or in one of Scott's narrative poems—and in that
sense, perhaps Mark Twain had cause to blame the Civil
War on Sir Walter Scott.

However that may be, Professor Kramer was certainly
right—for literary-historical reasons—to point us toward

Melville's neglected poem. But those valid reasons are not necessarily connected to the historical Mosby, or even the Mosby of the War. In Melville's poem, Mosby has become a shadowy figure, a symbolic character, a name—but not a man.

> The morning-bugles lonely play,
>     Lonely the evening-bugle calls—
> Unanswered voices in the wild;
> The settled hush of birds in nest
> Becharms, and all the wood enthralls:
>     Memory's self is so beguiled
>     That Mosby seems a satyr's child.

> They lived as in the Eerie Land—
>     The fire-flies showed with fairy gleam;
> And yet from pine-tops one might ken
> The Capitol Dome—hazy—sublime—
>     A vision breaking on a dream:
>     So strange it was that Mosby's men
>     Should dare to prowl where the Dome was seen.

The mysterious Mosby seems an uncanny force of nature: "As glides in seas the shark, / Rides Mosby through green dark." "Maple and hemlock, beech and lime, / Are Mosby's confederates, share the crime." He foils the arrogance and the plans of the invading Colonel, and dominates the imaginations of the Yankees: "Each eye dim as a sick-room lamp, / All faces stamped with Mosby's stamp." In this poem, the word *Mosby* comes to signify mystery and mortality, but to appreciate that, and Melville's pun on *nutting* and *butternut,* both Melville's poem and the best commentary on it are available in Aaron Kramer's *Melville's Poetry: Toward the Enlarged Heart* (1972). More recently, in his *The Civil War World of Herman*

*Melville* (1993), Stanton Garner has treated Melville's Civil War context in elaborate detail, showing the poem as a "small-scale version of *Moby-Dick*."

Edmund Wilson, in his monumental study of the literature of the Civil War, *Patriotic Gore* (1962), also focussed on Melville's "The Scout Toward Aldie." He saw the poem as related to other and better known works of Melville:

> What we recognize, of course, in this story is Melville's familiar theme: the pursuit or the persecution by one being of another, with an ambivalent relation between them which mingles repulsion and attraction but which binds them inescapably together: Captain Ahab and Moby-Dick, Claggart and Billy Budd, Babo and Don Benito. For though the death of the young colonel is a tragedy and though Mosby plays the role of menace, the whole poem, in a way characteristic of Melville, involves a glorification of Mosby. We are made to feel that the colonel has a fatal rendezvous with the sinister ranger, that he is drawn to his opponent by a kind of spell that is somehow a good deal more powerful than the attraction which has drawn him to his bride.
>
> Yet the story, though so personal a product of Melville's imagination, has also its historical significance in its insight into one aspect of the Civil War. What Melville has revealed in the fanciful tale inspired by his visit to his cousin is a mutual fascination of each of the two camps with the other, the intimate essence of a conflict which, though fratricidal, was also incestuous.

Wilson had a point not so much about the War as about Melville, for though everyone was fascinated with Mosby, it does not follow that many were fascinated by Custer or Sheridan or Grant.

There is no need for me to say anything about Mosby's adventures, but perhaps I can say a word about his recounting of them. In the first place, it is traditional, at least in literature, for the hero to recite his own tale—it is not sufficient for the bard to do so! Odysseus, Aeneas, and Beowulf—each takes up the telling of his own story, at least at some point. In that sense, it is appropriate for Mosby to let us have the thing straight from the horseman's mouth, though he did not finish the job—the book was edited and published after his death by his brother-in-law, Charles W. Russell. Second, the book is replete with a wealth of classical, literary, and historical allusions that say much not only about Mosby's particular intelligence but also about the possibilities if not the state of education and literacy in the South in his day. It is well to remember that Mosby made himself a lawyer before the War, and that he understood that deeds can be done with words as well as with bullets. And thirdly I will merely note at this point something of the relish with which Mosby spins his narrative. His sense of humor and of drama is as operative as is his lawyerly logic and disputatiousness. The doer of the deed as well as the teller of the tale, Mosby knows how to cap an adventure with a flourish of bravado. When he captures General Stoughton in bed, he does not neglect to draw down the bedclothes, pull up the General's nightshirt, and give that unfortunate a whack on the backside. As with many another of Mosby's coups, the emphasis is on laughter rather than on violence.

And we should remember also that although John S. Mosby really was the Gray Ghost of legend and even television, he was also the Virginia lawyer who endorsed U. S. Grant for his second term, and who was appointed consul to Hong Kong by President Hayes. He worked in the West for the Union Pacific Railroad, worked for the Land Office, and was appointed assistant attorney in the Department of Justice by Theodore Roosevelt. He was forced out in 1910 at the age of 77. The Mosby who worked on these *Memoirs* was an impoverished one-eyed widower, a cantankerous old geezer who walked the streets of Washington in his carpet slippers and remembered his impetuous youth.

The reader of these pages should know of other books by and about the elusive, contradictory, and fascinating Mosby. *Mosby's War Reminiscences and Stuart's Cavalry Campaigns* (1887) includes material that Mosby had used on the lecture platform. *Ranger Mosby* (1944) by Virgil Carrington Jones remains a good biography that emphasizes the War years. *Rebel: The Life and Times of John Singleton Mosby* by Kevin H. Siepel (1983) much more thoroughly explores Mosby's post bellum life. *Mosby's Rangers* by Jeffrey D. Wert (1990) recounts the activities of the 43rd Battalion of Virginia Cavalry. *Mosby and His Rangers* by Susan Provost Beller (1992) retells the story for young readers. Because he was one of the greatest guerrilla leaders of history, the books about Mosby keep on coming—but not for that reason alone.

Mosby's behavior after the War continued his path of independence, a course that was then in his context what we might call today "politically incorrect." His endorsement of Grant anticipated the modern Southern politics we have known since World War II; and his argument in favor of a two-party South was enlightened and ahead of his time. Though Mosby made the "right" noises many times, memorializing the Lost Cause, he also at other times pointedly refused to do so. At one time or another, he denounced the evils of slavery, asserted that the Confederates were guilty of treason, and even endorsed the Reconstruction. If his views were not logically consistent, they were fairly earned, and he felt free to speak them.

The last paragraph of his *Memoirs* declares Mosby's undying attachment to the Lost Cause, even at that late hour, in language that is a perfect illustration of Southern *Romanitas*—the citation of Virgil and Aeneas says as much about the Southern sense of community and fidelity as it does about a classical education. Mosby is careful to show his own awareness of the ambivalence of politics, for Washington's suppression of the Whiskey Rebellion suggests an analogy to the Civil War in which Virginia was, in effect, on the other side. His recountal of Lee's resignation from the Army and his opposition to secession is, I think, intended to justify Mosby's own involvement in the Confederacy, and indeed the Confederacy itself. Mosby thought that such an example was a powerful one, and some of the rest of us still do.

"The visions we have cherished of a free and independent country have vanished, and that country is now the spoil of the conqueror." So Mosby defined the conflict in his Farewell Address to his Command, April 21, 1865. Since the war was over, Mosby felt free to respond to tremendous changes as he thought fit. Later on, he became both a progressive and a reactionary. As an old man, he despised "buzz wagons" (horseless carriages), for example. This was the same Mosby who had ridiculed the cavalry sabre in favor of a pair of Colt's revolvers. The old man attacked college football, saying that mind and honor and courage were the manly qualities to be developed in higher education, not muscle. I sometimes wonder what Mosby would say about the Beltway around Washington, D.C. and about the University of Virginia's athletic program,

and I think I know the answer. I also believe I know what
he would say and indeed did say about the charge that the
South stood merely for racism and slavery. The irony of
Mosby, like that of Henry Adams, would be useful as we
consider contemporary "race-norming," racial quotas, racial gerrymandering, and Professor Leonard Jeffries's theory of "neural melanin," taught for college credit today.
Who is the racist, after all?

Ultimately, to say "American History" is to say "the
Civil War." Who says "the Civil War," must say "the
Confederacy." And who says "the Confederacy" must
sooner or later say "Mosby." Those who want to revise
our history must exclude so much reality that the "new"
history gives us a head without a body, and Confederates
without a cause. That's only one reason why we need
Mosby today—and there are others remaining to be delivered in his own narrative.

The *Memoirs* represent an individual achievement, but
one associated with a larger cause. That cause was not
ultimately lost because, as T. S. Eliot indicated, no cause is
ever finally won. Though politically correct Senators today
distort history for cynical purposes, the Confederate flag
stood in its immediate context for an effort to maintain
independence. Later such an image had a memorial quality, of sorrow perhaps but never of shame. Still later, mass
reproduced as an automobile tag, a beach towel, or worse,
the flag was taken up not by old ladies who wished to
decorate cemeteries but by young hooligans who wanted
to make trouble. Even so, in the former territories of the
Soviet empire today, the Confederate battle flag is thought
of as an image of freedom, and not its opposite—and for
good reason. Perhaps there too those people will have reason to remember their own Civil War, and a great man

such as Baron Wrangel, in a new and enhancing way, just as there is something to be gained for us in remembering Lee—and Mosby—and even their flag.

That was the flag that for four years Mosby fought under, and fought for. He understood what we seem to have forgotten—namely, that such an image denoted armies of the Confederate States *of America*. Later he served the U.S. government with all the devotion he had given to another one. Such virtues as Lee and Stuart and Mosby possessed remain accessible today to all Americans—to whoever admires them. The courage, the cunning, the high spirits, and the fierce love of liberty that Mosby always demonstrated were as remarkable in peacetime as in war, and as visible on the page as in his life. As long as we continue to admire those qualities, and before our children are finally taught not to, there will always be a place for Mosby in the national, not only the regional, gallery of heroes; and for his book on the short shelf of the best memoirs of the most American of wars.

*Oakdale, Long Island, N.Y.*                    J. O. TATE

# The Memoirs
# of Colonel
# John S. Mosby

Southern Classics Series

# CHAPTER I

## EARLY LIFE

I WAS born December 6, 1833, at the home of my grandfather, James McLaurine, in Powhatan County, Virginia. He was a son of Robert McLaurine, an Episcopal minister, who came from Scotland before the Revolution. Great-grandfather McLaurine lived at the glebe and is buried at Peterville Church in Powhatan. After the church was disestablished, the State appropriated the glebe, and Peterville was sold to the Baptists. My grandfather McLaurine lived to be very old. He was a soldier of the Revolution, and I well remember his cough, which it was said he contracted from exposure in the war when he had smallpox. My grandfather Mosby was also a native of Powhatan. He lived at Gibraltar, but moved to Nelson County, where my father, Alfred D. Mosby, was born. When I was a child my father bought a farm near Charlottesville, in Albemarle, on which I was raised.  I recollect that one day I went with my father to our peach orchard on a high ridge, and he pointed out Monticello, the home of Thomas Jefferson, on a mountain a few miles away, and told me some of the history of the great man who wrote the Declaration of Independence.

At that time there were no public and few private schools in Virginia, but a widow opened a school in Fry's Woods, adjoining my father's farm.  My sister Victoria and I went as her pupils.  I was seven years old when I learned to read, although I had gone a month or so to a country school in Nelson, near a post office called Murrell's Shop, where I had learned to spell.  As I was so young my mother always sent a negro boy with me to the schoolhouse, and he came for me in the evening.  But once I begged him to stay all day with me, and I shared my dinner with him.  When playtime came, some of the larger boys put him up on a block for sale and he was knocked down to the highest bidder.  I thought it was a *bona fide* sale and was greatly distressed at losing such a dutiful playmate.  We went home together, but he never spent another day with me at the schoolhouse.

The first drunken man I ever saw was my schoolmaster.  He went home at playtime to get his dinner, but took an overdose of whiskey. On the way back he fell on the roadside and went to sleep. The big boys picked him up and carried him into the schoolhouse, and he heard our lessons. The school closed soon after; I don't know why.

It was a common thing in the old days of negro slavery for a Virginia gentleman, who had inherited a fortune, to live in luxury with plenty of the comforts of life and die insolvent, while his overseer retired to live on what he had saved. Mr. Jefferson was one example of this. I often heard that Jefferson had held in his arms Betsy Wheat, a pupil at the school where I learned to read. She was the daughter of the overseer and, being the senior of all the other scholars, was the second in command. She exercised as much authority as the schoolmistress.

As I have said, the log schoolhouse was in Fry's Woods, which adjoined my father's farm. To this rude hut I walked daily for three sessions, with my eldest sister — later with two — often through a deep snow, to get the rudiments of an education. I remember that the schoolmistress, a most excellent woman, whipped her son and me for fighting. That was the only blow I ever received during the time I went to school.

A few years ago I visited the spot in company

with Bartlett Bolling, who was with me in the war. There was nothing left but a pile of rocks — the remains of the chimney. The associations of the place raised up phantoms of the past. I am the only survivor of the children who went to school there. I went to the spring along the same path where I had often walked when a barefooted schoolboy and got a drink of cool water from a gourd. There I first realized the pathos of the once popular air, "Ben Bolt"; the spring was still there and the running brook, but all of my schoolmates had gone.

The "Peter Parley" were the standard schoolbooks of my day. In my books were two pictures that made a lasting impression on me. One was of Wolfe dying on the field in the arms of a soldier; the other was of Putnam riding down the stone steps with the British close behind him. About that time I borrowed a copy of the "Life of Marion", which was the first book I read, except as a task at school. I remember how I shouted when I read aloud in the nursery of the way the great partisan hid in the swamp and outwitted the British. I did not then expect that the time would ever come when I would have escapes as narrow as that of Putnam and take part in adventures that have been compared with Marion's.

When I was ten years old I began going to school in Charlottesville; sometimes I went on horseback, and sometimes I walked. Two of my teachers, — James White, who taught Latin and Greek, and Aleck Nelson, who taught mathematics — were afterwards professors at Washington and Lee, while General Robert E. Lee was its president. When I was sixteen years old I went as a student to the University of Virginia — some evidence of the progress I had made in getting an education.

In my youth I was very delicate and often heard that I would never live to be a grown man. But the prophets were wrong, for I have outlived nearly all the contemporaries of my youth. I was devoted to hunting, and a servant always had coffee ready for me at daylight on a Saturday morning, so that I was out shooting when nearly all were sleeping. My father was a slaveholder, and I still cherish a strong affection for the slaves who nursed me and played with me in my childhood. That was the prevailing sentiment in the South — not one peculiar to myself — but one prevailing in all the South toward an institution [1] which we now

---

[1] Colonel Mosby never had a word to say favorable to slavery — a fact which may be attributed to the influence of Miss Abby Southwick, afterwards Mrs. Stevenson, of Manchester, Massachusetts, who was employed to teach his sisters. She was a strong and outspoken abolitionist and a friend of Garrison and Wendell Phillips. All the Mosby

thank Abraham Lincoln for abolishing. I had no taste for athletics and have never seen a ball game. My habits of study were never regular, but I always had a literary taste. While I fairly recited Tacitus and Thucydides as a task, I read with delight Irving's stories of the Moors in Granada.

[Colonel Mosby's career at the University of Virginia, where he graduated in Greek and mathematics, was not so serene throughout as that of the ordinary student. One incident made a lasting impression upon his mind and affected his future course. He was convicted of unlawfully shooting a fellow student and was sentenced to a fine and imprisonment in the jail at Charlottesville. It was the case of defending the good name of a young lady and, while the law was doubtless violated, public sentiment was indicated by the legislature's remitting the fine and the governor's granting a pardon.

The Baltimore *Sun* published an account of this incident, by Mr. John S. Patton, who said

family were, and remained, devoted to Miss Southwick. She and young Mosby had numerous talks on the subject of slavery and other political topics. At the close of the war she immediately sent money and supplies to the family and told how anxiously she had read the papers, fearing to find the news that he had been killed.

that Mosby had been fined ten dollars for assaulting the town sergeant. The young Mosby had been known as one not given to lawless hilarity, but as a "fighter." "And the Colonel himself admits," continues Patton, "that he got the worst of these boyish engagements, except once, when the fight was on between him and Charles Price, of Meachem's, — and in that case they were separated before victory could perch. They also go so far as to say that he was a spirited lad, although far from 'talkative' and not far from quiet, introspective moods. . . . His antagonist this time was George Turpin, a student of medicine in the University. . . . Turpin had carved Frank Morrison to his taste with a pocket knife and added to his reputation by nearly killing Fred M. Wills with a rock. . . .

"When Jack Mosby, spare and delicate — Turpin was large and athletic—received the latter's threat that he would eat him 'blood raw' on sight, he proceeded to get ready. The cause of the impending hostilities was an incident at a party at the Spooner residence in Montebello, which Turpin construed as humiliating to him, and with the aid of some friends who dearly loved a fisticuff, he reached the conclusion that John Mosby was to blame and that it was his duty to chastise him. Mosby was due at Mathematics lecture room and thither he went and met Professor Courtnay and did his problems first of all. That over, he thrust a pepper-box pistol into his jacket and went forth to find his enemy. He had not far to go; for by this time the Turpins were keeping a boarding house in the building then, as now, known as the Cabell House, about the distance of four Baltimore blocks from the University. Thither went the future partisan leader, and, with a friend, was standing on the back porch when Turpin approached. He advanced on Mosby at once — but not far; the latter brought his pepper-box into action with instant effect. Turpin went down with a bullet in his throat, and was taken up as good as dead. . . . The trial is still referred to as the *cause célèbre* in our local court. Four great lawyers were engaged in it: the names of Robertson, Rives, Watson, and Leach adorn the legal annals of Virginia."

The prosecutor in this case was Judge William J. Robertson, of Charlottesville, who made a vigorous arraignment of the young student. On visiting the jail one day after the conviction, much to his surprise Robertson was greeted by Mosby in a friendly manner. This was followed by the loan of a copy of Blackstone's "Commentaries" to the prisoner and a lifelong friendship between the two. Thus it was that young Mosby entered upon the study of law, which he made his profession.

Colonel Mosby wrote on a newspaper clipping

giving an account of the shooting incident: "I did not go to Turpin's house, but he came to my boarding house, and he had sent me a message that he was coming there to 'eat me up.'"

Mosby's conviction affected him greatly, and he did not include an account of it in his story because — or at least it would seem probable — he feared that the conclusion would be drawn that he was more like the picture painted by the enemy during the war, instead of the kindly man he really was. However this may be, nothing pleased him more than the honors paid to him by the people of Charlottesville and by the University of Virginia. He spoke of these things as "one of Time's revenges."

In January, 1915, a delegation from Virginia presented Colonel Mosby with a bronze medal and an embossed address which read as follows:

To Colonel John S. Mosby, Warrenton, Virginia.

Your friends and admirers in the University of Virginia welcome this opportunity of expressing for you their affection and esteem and of congratulating you upon the vigor and alertness of body and mind with which you have rounded out your fourscore years.

Your *Alma Mater* has pride in your scholarly application in the days of your prepossessing youth; in your martial genius, manifested in a career singularly original and romantic; in the forceful fluency of your record of the history made by yourself and your comrades in the army of Northern Virginia; and in the dignity, diligence, and sagacity with which you have served your united country at home and abroad.

Endowed with the gift of friendship, which won for you the confidence of both Lee and Grant, you have proven yourself a man of war, a man of letters, and a man of affairs worthy the best traditions of your University and your State, to both of which you have been a loyal son.]

# CHAPTER II

## THE WAR BEGINS

I WENT to Bristol, Virginia, in October, 1855, and opened a law office. I was a stranger and the first lawyer that located there.

When attending court at Abingdon in the summer of 1860 I met William Blackford, who had been in class with me at the University and who was afterwards a colonel of engineers on General Stuart's staff. Blackford asked me to join a cavalry company which he was assisting to raise and in which he expected to be a lieutenant. To oblige him I allowed my name to be put on the muster roll; but was so indifferent about the matter that I was not present when the company organized. William E. Jones was made captain. He was a graduate of West Point and had resigned from the United States army a few years before. Jones was a fine soldier, but his temper produced friction with his superiors and greatly impaired his capacity as a commander.

There were omens of war at this time, but nobody realized the impending danger. Our first drill was on January Court Day, 1861. I borrowed a horse and rode up to Abingdon to take my first lesson. After the drill was over and the company had broken ranks, I went to hear John B. Floyd make a speech on the condition of the times. He had been Secretary of War and had lately resigned. Buchanan, in a history of his administration, said that Floyd's resignation had nothing to do with secession, but he requested it on account of financial irregularities he had discovered in the War Department.

But to return to the campaign of 1860. I never had any talent or taste for stump speaking or handling party machines, but with my strong convictions I was a supporter of Douglas [1] and the Union.

Whenever a Whig became extreme on the slave question, he went over to the opposition party. No doubt the majority of the Virginia Democrats agreed with the Union sentiments of Andrew Jackson, but the party was controlled

[1] Colonel Mosby was almost the only Douglas Democrat in Bristol; that is to say he was in favor of recognizing the right of a territory belonging to the United States to vote against slavery within its borders. The Breckinridge Democrats believed, especially after the decision of the Supreme Court in the Dred Scott case, in the right of the slaveholders to take their slaves into the territories and hold them there in slavery against the wishes of the inhabitants.

by a section known as "the chivalry", who were disciples of Calhoun, and got most of the honors. It was for this reason that a Virginia Senator (Mason), who belonged to that school, was selected to read to the Senate the dying speech of the great apostle of secession and slavery (Calhoun). It proved to be a legacy of woe to the South.

I met Mr. Mason at an entertainment given him on his return from London after the close of the war. He still bore himself with pride and dignity, but without that *hauteur* which is said to have characterized him when he declared in the Senate that he was an ambassador from Virginia. He found his home in the Shenandoah Valley desolate. It will be remembered that, with John Slidell, Mason was captured when a passenger on board an English steamer and sent a prisoner to Fort Warren (in Boston Harbor), but he was released on demand of the English government. Mason told us many interesting things about his trip to London — of a conversation with Lord Brougham at a dinner, and the mistake the London post office had made in sending his mail to the American minister, Charles Francis Adams, and Mr. Adams's mail to Mason. Seeing him thus in the wreck of his hopes and with no future to cheer him, I was reminded of Caius Marius brooding among the ruins of Carthage.

William L. Yancey, of Alabama, did more than any other man in the South to precipitate the sectional conflict. In a commercial convention, shortly before the campaign of 1860, he had offered resolutions in favor of repealing the laws against the African slave trade. Yancey attacked Thomas Jefferson as an abolitionist, as Calhoun had done in the Senate, and called Virginia a breeding ground for slaves to sell to the Cotton States. He also charged her people with using the laws against the importation of Africans to create for themselves a monopoly in the slave market. Roger A. Pryor replied to him in a powerful speech.

Yancey was more responsible than any other man for the disruption of the Democratic Party and, consequently, of the Union. He came to Virginia to speak in the Presidential canvass. I was attending court at Abingdon, where Yancey was advertised to speak. A few Douglas men in the county had invited Tim Rives, a famous stump orator, to meet Yancey, and I was delegated to call on the latter and prepare a joint debate. Yancey was stopping at the house of Governor Floyd — then Secretary of War.

I went to Floyd's home, was introduced to Yancey, and stated my business. He refused the joint debate, and I shall never forget the arrogance and contempt with which he treated me. I heard his speech that day; it was a strong one for his side. As the Virginia people had not yet been educated up to the secession point, Yancey thinly veiled his disunion purposes. That night we put up Tim Rives, who made a great speech in reply to Yancey and pictured the horrors of disunion and war. Rives was elected a member of the Convention that met the next winter, and there voted against disunion.

Early in the war, the company in which I was a private was in camp near Richmond, and one day I met Rives on the street. It was the first time I had seen him since the speech at Abingdon. I had written an account of his speech for a Richmond paper, which pleased him very much, and he was very cordial. He wanted me to go with him to the governor's house and get Governor Letcher, who had also been a Douglas man the year before, to give me a commission. I declined and told him that as I had no military training, I preferred serving as a private under a good officer. I had no idea then that I should ever rise above the ranks.

A few days before the presidential election, I was walking on the street in Bristol when I was attracted by a crowd that was holding a Bell and Everett meeting. Some one called on me to make a Union speech. I rose and told the meeting that I saw no reason for making a Union speech at a Bell and Everett meeting; that it was my mission to call not the righteous, but sinners, to repentance. This "brought down the house." I little thought that in a few months I should be regarded as one of the sinners.

I was very friendly with the editor of the secession paper in my town. One day he asked me what I intended to do in the case of a collision between the Government and South Carolina. I told him I would be on the side of the Union. He said that I should find him on the other side. "Very well," I replied, "I shall meet you at Philippi." Some years after the war he called upon me in Washington and jokingly reminded me of what I had said to him. As he was about my age and did not go into the army, I was tempted to tell him that I did go to Philippi, but did not meet him there.[1]

[1] The editor in question, Mr. J. A. Sperry, of the *Bristol Courier*, has told the story in a somewhat different way. In writing his reminiscences of Mosby he said:

"Mosby pursued the even tenor of his way until the memorable

In April, 1861, came the call to arms. On the
day after the bombardment by South Carolina
and the surrender of Fort Sumter that aroused
all the slumbering passions of the country, I was

Presidential Campaign of 1860. So guarded had been his political
utterances that but few of the villagers knew with which of the parties
to class him, when he suddenly bloomed out as an elector on the Douglas ticket. This seemed to fix his status as a Union Democrat. I
say seemed, for I am now inclined to think his politics was like his
subsequent fighting, — independent and irregular.

"We saw little of him in the stirring times immediately succeeding
the election. One morning about the middle of January, 1861, I met
him in the street, when he abruptly accosted me, 'I believe you are a
secessionist *per se.*'

"'What has led you to that conclusion?'

"'The editorial in your paper to-day.'

"'You have not read it 'carefully,' said I. 'There is nothing in it
to justify your inference. In summing up the events of the week, I
find that several sovereign States have formally severed their connection
with the Union. We are confronted with the accomplished fact of
secession. I have expressed no opinion either of the right or the expediency of the movement. I am not a secessionist *per se,* if I understand the term; but a secessionist by the logic of events.'

"'I am glad to hear it,' he rejoined. 'I have never coveted the
office of Jack Ketch, but I would cheerfully fill it for one day for the
pleasure of hanging a disunionist *per se.* Do you know what secession
means? It means bloody war, followed by feuds between the border
States, which a century may not see the end of.'

"'I do not agree with you,' I said. 'I see no reason why secession
should not be peaceable. But in the event of the dreadful war you
predict, which side will you take?'

"'I shall fight for the Union, Sir, — for the Union, of course, and you?'

"'Oh, I don't apprehend any such extremity, but if I am forced
into the struggle, I shall fight for my mother section. Should we meet
upon the field of battle, as Yancey said to Brownlow the other day, I
would run a bayonet through you.'

"'Very well, — we'll meet at Philippi,' retorted Mosby and stalked
away.

"'Several months elapsed before I saw him again, but the rapid and
startling events of those months made them seem like years. I was

again attending court at Abingdon, when the telegraph operator told me of the great news that had just gone over the wire. Mr. Lincoln had called on the States for troops to suppress the rebellion.

In the preceding December, Floyd had ordered Major Anderson to hold Sumter against the secessionists to the last extremity. Anderson simply obeyed Floyd's orders. When the news came, Governor Floyd was at home, and I went to his house to tell him. I remember he said it would be the bloodiest war the world had ever seen. Floyd's was a sad fate. He had, as Secretary of War, given great offense to the North by the shipping of arms from the northern arsenals to the South, some months before secession. He was charged with having been in collusion with the enemies of the Government under which he held office, and with treachery. At Donelson he was the senior officer in command. When the

sitting in my office writing, one day in the latter part of April, when my attention was attracted by the quick step of some one entering and the exclamation, 'How do you like my uniform?'

"It was a moment before I could recognize the figure pirouetting before me in the bob-tail coat of a cavalry private.

"'Why, Mosby!' I exclaimed, 'This isn't Philippi, nor is that a Federal uniform.'

"'No more of that,' said he, with a twinkle of the eye. 'When I talked that way, Virginia had not passed the ordinance of secession. She is out of the Union now. Virginia is my mother, God bless her! I can't fight against my mother, can I?'"

other brigadiers refused to fight any longer, he brought off his own men and left the others to surrender to Grant. This was regarded as a breach of discipline, and Jefferson Davis relieved him of his command.

When Lincoln's proclamation was issued, the Virginia Convention was still in session and had not passed a secession ordinance, so she was not included with States against which the proclamation was first directed. With the exception of the northwestern section of the State, where there were few slaves and the Union sentiment predominated, the people of Virginia, in response to the President's call for troops to enforce the laws, sprang to arms to resist the Government. The war cry "To arms!" resounded throughout the land and, in the delirium of the hour, we all forgot our Union principles in our sympathy with the pro-slavery cause, and rushed to the field of Mars.

In issuing his proclamation, Lincoln referred for authority to a statute in pursuance of which George Washington sent an army into Pennsylvania to suppress the Whiskey Insurrection. But the people were persuaded that Lincoln's real object was to abolish slavery, although at his inaugural he had said:

There has never been any reasonable cause for such apprehension that by the accession of the Republican administration their property and their peace and personal security were endangered. Indeed, the most ample evidence to the contrary has all the while existed and been open to their inspection. It is found in nearly all the published speeches of him who now addresses you. I do but quote from one of those speeches when I declare that "I have no purpose, directly or indirectly, to interfere with the institution of slavery in the States where it exists." I believe I have no lawful right to do so, and I have no inclination to do so.

The South had always been solid for slavery and when the quarrel about it resulted in a conflict of arms, those who had approved the policy of disunion took the pro-slavery side. It was perfectly logical to fight for slavery, if it was right to own slaves. Enforcing the laws was not coercing a State unless the State resisted the execution of the laws. When such a collision came, coercion depended on which was the stronger side.

The Virginia Convention had been in session about two months, but a majority had opposed secession up to the time of the proclamation, and even then a large minority, including many of the ablest men in Virginia, voted against it.

Among that number was Jubal Early, who was prominent in the war. Nobody cared whether it was a constitutional right they were exercising, or an act of revolution. At such times reason is silent and passion prevails.

The ordinance of secession was adopted in April and provided that it be submitted to a popular vote on the fourth Thursday in May. According to the States' Rights theory, Virginia was still in the Union until the ordinance was ratified; but the State immediately became an armed camp, and her troops seized the United States Armory at Harper's Ferry and the Norfolk Navy Yard. Virginia went out of the Union by force of arms, and I went with her.

## CHAPTER III

### A Private in the Cavalry

In that fateful April, 1861, our local company, with other companies of infantry and cavalry, went into camp in a half-finished building of the Martha Washington College in the suburbs of Abingdon. Captain Jones allowed me to remain in Bristol for some time to close up the business I had in hand for clients and to provide for my family. A good many owed me fees when I left home, and they still owe me. My last appearance in court was at Blountville, Tennessee, before the Chancellor.

My first night in camp I was detailed as one of the camp guards. Sergeant Tom Edmonson — a gallant soldier who was killed in June, 1864—gave me the countersign and instructed me as to the duties of a sentinel. For two hours, in a cold wind, I walked my round and was very glad when my relief came and I could go to rest on my pallet of straw. The experience of my first night in camp rather tended to chill my military ardor and was far more distasteful than picketing near the enemy's lines on the Potomac, which I afterwards did in hot and cold weather, very cheerfully; in fact I enjoyed it. The danger of being shot by a rifleman in a thicket, if not attractive, at least kept a vidette awake and watching. At this time I was the frailest and most delicate man in the company, but camp duty was always irksome to me, and I preferred being on the outposts. During the whole time that I served as a private — nearly a year — I only once missed going on picket three times a week. The single exception was when I was disabled one night by my horse falling over a cow lying in the road.

Captain Jones had strict ideas of discipline, which he enforced, but he took good care of his horses as well as his men. There was a horse inspection every morning, and the man whose horse was not well groomed got a scolding mixed with some cursing by Captain Jones. Jones was always very kind to me. He drilled his own company and also a company of cavalry from Marion, which had come to our camp to get the benefit of his instruction in cavalry tactics.

In the Marion company was William E. Peters, Professor at Emory and Henry College, who had graduated in the same class in Greek with me at the University. When he and I were students reading Thucydides, we did not expect ever to take part in a greater war than the Peloponnesian. Peters had left his literary work to be a lieutenant of cavalry. He was made a staff officer by General Floyd in his campaign that year in West Virginia. For some reason Peters was not with Floyd when the latter escaped from Fort Donelson in February, 1862. Peters was a strict churchman, but considered it his duty to fight a duel with a Confederate officer. He became a colonel of cavalry. Peters's regiment was with McCausland -when he was sent by General Early in August, 1864, to Chambersburg, and his regiment was selected as the one to set fire to the town. Peters refused to obey the order, for which he is entitled to a monument to his memory. Reprisals in war can only be justified as a deterrent. As the Confederates were holding the place for only a few hours, while the Northern armies were occupying a large part of the South, no doubt, aside from any question of humanity, Peters thought it was bad policy to provoke retaliation. General Early ordered a reprisal in kind on account of the houses burned in the Shenandoah Valley a few months before by General Hunter. As General Early made no mention of Peters in his book, I imagine it was because of his refusal to apply the torch to Chambersburg. On his return from this expedition, McCausland was surprised by Averill at Moorefield, and Peters was wounded and captured. He told me that he had expected to be put under arrest for disobedience as soon as he got back to Virginia.

Hunter was a member of an old Virginia family, but he showed no favor to Virginians. At Bull Run he commanded the leading division that crossed at Sudley and was badly wounded, but there was no sympathy for him in Virginia. A relative of his told me that when Hunter met a lady who was a near relative, he offered to embrace her, but was repelled. She thought that in fighting against Virginia he was committing an unnatural act and that he had the feelings, described by Hamlet, of one who "would kill a king and marry with his brother." On Hunter's staff was his relative, Colonel Strother, who had won literary distinction over the pen name of "Porte Crayon." Both men seemed to be animated by the same sentiments towards their kin. Hunter presided over the court that condemned Mrs. Surratt as an accessory to the assassination of President Lincoln. He closed his life by suicide.

But to return to our company of cavalry and my first days as a soldier. We were sent, within a few days, to another camping ground, where we had plank sheds for shelter and where we drilled regularly. Several companies of infantry shared the camp with us. Once I had been detailed for camp guard and, having been relieved just as the company went out to drill, I saddled my horse and went along. I had no idea that it was a breach of discipline to be doing double duty, until two men with muskets came up and told me that I was under arrest for it. I was too proud to say a word and, as my time had come, I went again to walking my rounds. Once after that, when we were in camp on Bull Run, I was talking at night with the Colonel in his tent and did not hear the bugle sounded for roll call. So a lieutenant, who happened to be in command, ordered me, as a penalty, to do duty the rest of the morning as a camp guard. He knew that my absence from roll call was not wilful but a mistake. I would not make any explanation but served my tour of duty. These were the only instances in which I was punished when a private.

Our Circuit Judge, Fulkerson, who had served in the Mexican War, was appointed a colonel by

Governor Letcher, and took command of the camp at Abingdon. But in a few days we were ordered to Richmond. Fulkerson, with the infantry, went by rail, but Jones preferred to march his company all the way. As he had been an officer in the army on the plains, we learned a good deal from him in the two weeks on the road, and it was a good course of discipline for us. I was almost a perfect stranger in the company to which I belonged, and I felt so lonely in camp that I applied to Captain Jones for a transfer to an infantry company from Bristol. He said that I would have to get the approval of the Governor and forwarded my application to him at Richmond. Fortunately the next day we were ordered away, and I heard nothing more about the transfer.

On May 30, in the afternoon, our company — one hundred strong — left Abingdon to join the army. In spite of a drizzling rain the whole population was out to say farewell; in fact a good many old men rode several miles with us. We marched ten miles and then disbanded to disperse in squads, under the command of an officer or of a non-commissioned officer, to spend the night at the country homes. I went under Jim King, the orderly sergeant, and spent the night at the house of Major Ab. Beattie, who gave us the best of everything, but I was so depressed at parting with my wife and children that I scarcely spoke a word. King had been a cadet at West Point for a short time and had learned something of tactics, He was afterwards transferred to the 37th Virginia Infantry and was killed in Jackson's battle at Kernstown.

When the roll was called the next morning at the rendezvous at old Glade Spring Church, I don't think a man was missing. The men were boiling with enthusiasm and afraid that the war would be over before they got to the firing line. I remember one man who was conspicuous on the march; he rode at the head of the column and got the bouquets the ladies threw at us; but in our first battle he was conspicuous for his absence and stayed with the wagons. Our march to the army was an ovation. Nobody dreamed of the possibility of our failure and the last scene of the great drama at Appomattox. We made easy marches, and by the time we got to Wytheville, all of my depression of spirits had gone, and I was as lively as anybody. It took us two weeks to get to Richmond, where we spent a few days on the Fair Grounds. We were then sent to a camp of instruction at Ashland, where we remained a short time or until we, with a cavalry company from Amelia County, were ordered to join Joe Johnston's army in the Shenandoah.

I well remember that we were in Ashland when news came to us that Joe Johnston, on June 15, had retreated from Harper's Ferry to Winchester. To begin the war by abandoning such an outpost, when there was no enemy near and no necessity for it, was a shock for which we were not prepared, and it chilled our enthusiasm. I couldn't understand it — that was all — but my instinct told me at the time what was afterwards confirmed by reason and experience — that a great blunder had been committed.

At Wytheville, on our third day's march to Richmond, we got the papers which informed us that the war had actually begun in a skirmish at Fairfax, where Captain Marr had been killed. We were greatly excited by the news of the affair. Our people had been reading about war and descriptions of battles by historians and poets, from the days of Homer down, and were filled with enthusiasm for military glory. They had no experience in the hardships of military service and knew nothing, had no conception, of the suffering it brings to the homes of those who have left them. In all great wars, women and children are the chief sufferers.

Our company joined the First Virginia Cavalry, commanded by Colonel J. E. B. Stuart, in the Shenandoah Valley. At Richmond, Captain Jones, who stood high with those in authority, had procured Sharp carbines for us. We considered this a great compliment, as arms were scarce in the Confederacy. We had been furnished with sabres before we left Abingdon, but the only real use I ever heard of their being put to was to hold a piece of meat over a fire for frying. I dragged one through the first year of the war, but when I became a commander, I discarded it. The sabre and lance may have been very good weapons in the days of chivalry, and my suspicion is that the combats of the hero of Cervantes were more realistic and not such burlesques as they are supposed to be. But certainly the sabre is of no use against gunpowder. Captain Jones also made requisition for uniforms, but when they arrived there was almost a mutiny. They were a sort of dun color and came from the penitentiary. The men piled them up in the camp, and all but Fount Beattie and myself refused to wear them.

We joined Joe Johnston's army in the Shenandoah Valley at his headquarters in Winchester and rested there for a day. Then we went on to join Colonel J. E. B. Stuart's regiment at Bunker

Hill, a village about twelve miles distant on the pike leading to Martinsburg, where Patterson's army was camped.  We were incorporated into the First Virginia Cavalry, which Stuart had just organized, now on outpost to watch Patterson.  I had never seen Stuart before, and the distance between us was so great that I never expected to rise to even an acquaintance with him.  Stuart was a graduate of West Point and as a lieutenant in Colonel Sumner's regiment, the First Cavalry, had won distinction and had been wounded in an Indian fight.  At the beginning of the war he was just twenty-eight years old.  His appearance — which included a reddish beard and a ruddy complexion — indicated a strong physique and great energy.

In his work on the outposts Stuart soon showed that he possessed the qualities of a great leader of cavalry.  He never had an equal in such service.  He discarded the old maxims and soon discovered that in the conditions of modern war the chief functions of cavalry are to learn the designs and to watch and report the movements of the enemy.

We rested a day in camp, and many of us wrote letters to our homes, describing the hospitable welcome we had met on our long march and our anxiety to meet the foe who was encamped a few miles away. On the following day, to our great delight, Captain Jones was ordered to take us on a scout towards Martinsburg. My first experience was near there—at Snodgrass Spring—where we came upon two soldiers who were out foraging. They ran across the field, but we overtook them. I got a canteen from one—the first I had ever seen—which I found very useful in the first battle I was in. It was a trophy which I prized highly. We got a good view of Patterson's army, a mile or so away, and returned that evening to our bivouac, all in the highest of spirits. Nearly every man in the company wrote a letter to somebody the next day.

# CHAPTER IV

## JOHNSTON'S RETREAT FROM HARPER'S FERRY

THE first great military blunder of the war was committed by Johnston in evacuating Harper's Ferry. Both Jackson and General Lee, who was then in Richmond organizing the army and acting as military adviser, were opposed to this. They wanted to hold it, not as a fortress with a garrison, but to break communication with the West, and a salient for an active force to threaten the flank of an invading army.

On April 27, Stonewall Jackson was ordered to the command of Harper's Ferry, which the militia had seized a few days before. Harper's Ferry is situated in a gap in the Blue Ridge through which flow the waters of the Potomac and the Shenandoah. John Brown had seized the place in his rebellion. The fact that he tried to start a slave insurrection in a region where there were few slaves is proof that he was a monomaniac. But Harper's Ferry was a place of great strategic value for the Confederates, as the railroad and canal on the Potomac from Washington, fifty miles below, passed through the gap. It was a salient position; its possession by the Confederates was a menace to the North and broke direct communication between the Capital and the West. A strategic offensive on the border was the best policy to encourage Southern sentiment in Maryland and defend the Shenandoah Valley from invasion.

A Virginian lieutenant, Roger Jones, had been stationed at Harper's Ferry with a small guard to protect the property of the Government. He remained until the force coming to capture the place was in sight, then set fire to the buildings, and retreated. His example in holding the position to the last extremity was not followed by the Confederates.

When Jackson arrived at the scene of his command, without waiting for instructions, he prepared to hold it by fortifying Maryland Heights. "I am of the opinion," he wrote to General Lee, "that this place should be defended with the spirit that actuated the defenders of Thermopylæ and if left to myself such is my determination." General Lee was in accord with Jackson's sentiments. Now Jackson did not mean that Harper's Ferry should be held as a fortress to stand a siege; nor that he would stay there and die like the Spartans in the Pass, but that he would hold it until a likelihood of its being surrounded by superior numbers was imminent. There was no prospect of this being the case, for no investing force was near. The best way to defend the Shenandoah Valley was to hold the line of the Potomac as a menace to Washington.

Major Deas, who had been sent to Harper's Ferry as an inspector of the Confederate War Department, thought that the troops showed an invincible spirit of resistance. On May 21 he wrote: "I have not asked Colonel Jackson his opinion on the subject, but my own is that there is force enough here to hold the place against any attack which, under the existing state of affairs, may be contemplated." And on May 23, the day before McDowell's army at Washington crossed into Virginia, he reported that there were "about 8000 troops at Harper's Ferry and the outposts, including five companies of artillery and a naval battery, and that 7300 were then able to go into battle well-armed. The Naval Batteries," he said, "under Lieutenant Fauntleroy, are placed on the northern and southern salients of the village of Harper's Ferry and envelop by their fire the whole of the town of Bolivar and the approaches of the immediate banks of the Potomac and Shenandoah rivers. The cavalry under Lieutenant-Colonel J. E. B. Stuart is in very good condition and quite effective. All the infantry regiments are daily drilled in the school of the soldier and company, and valuable assistance is received in this respect from the young men who have been instructed at the Military School at Lexington." Neither Jackson nor Major Deas knew of any immediate danger of Harper's Ferry being invested.

On May 24, in accordance with orders from the Confederate Government at Montgomery, General Joseph E. Johnston assumed command at the Ferry, and in a few days Jackson was given a brigade of five Virginia regiments. The outposts at the Ferry then extended from Williamsport on the Potomac to Point of Rocks on the river below. Johnston at once submitted a memorandum to Richmond on the conditions at Harper's Ferry, which displayed the caution for which he became distinguished. He seemed to have little confidence in his troops and thought the position could be easily turned from above or below, taking no account of the fact that he might turn the flank of an enemy who was flanking him. Johnston asked instructions from General Lee in relation to the manner in which the troops he commanded should be used. And on May 28 he again wrote in the same tone of despair: "If the Commander-in-Chief has precise instructions to give I beg to receive them early. I have prepared means of transportation for a march. Should it be decided that the troops should constitute a garrison this expense can be recalled," which shows he was getting ready for a retreat. With this letter Johnston enclosed a memorandum from a staff officer, Major Whiting, in which the latter spoke of troops that were gathering at Carlisle and Chambersburg, intimating that in the event of the advance of this force it might be necessary to move out to prevent being shut up in a *cul-de-sac*. But such a thing was too remote and contingent to constitute a danger of investment at that time. No place is absolutely impregnable; Gibraltar has been captured. The answer Johnston should have received to this request for orders was that he did not command a garrison to defend a fortress, but an active force in the field; and that Harper's Ferry might be held as a picket post.

The discipline of Johnston's troops ought to have been as good as that of the three months' men that Patterson was collecting at Chambersburg, fifty miles away. In addition to the cadets of the Virginia Military Institute, who were drilling his regiments, Johnston had in his army at least ten officers who had lately resigned from the U. S. Army. Nearly all of the field officers of Jackson's brigade had been educated at the Military Institute, and several had been officers in the Mexican War. Their conduct in battle a few weeks afterwards shows how much Johnston had underrated them. The men were volunteers full of enthusiasm for a cause and rendered cheerful obedience to orders; it was not necessary to drill such material into machines to make them soldiers.

Johnston complained of the want of discipline of his army and the danger of being surrounded by a superior force. The force that was coming to surround the Ferry was a spectre. McDowell's and Patterson's armies were fifty miles away and a hundred miles apart. At the request of Governor Pierpont a few regiments had crossed the Ohio, but McClellan's headquarters were still at Cincinnati. Any movement from that direction would naturally be through central Virginia — towards Richmond — in coöperation with Mc-Dowell. Johnston continued to show great anxiety about his position and wrote about it several times to General Lee. But neither Lee nor President Davis could see the danger as he saw it, and on June 7 General Lee — to calm his fears — wrote him: "He (the President) does not think it probable that there will be an immediate attack by troops from Ohio. General N. J. Garnett, C. S. Army, with a command of 4000 men, has been dispatched to Beverly to arrest the progress of troops. . . . Colonel McDonald has also been sent to interrupt the passage of troops over the Baltimore and Ohio Railroad. It is hoped by these means you will be relieved from an attack in that direction, and will have merely to meet an attack in front from Pennsylvania."

In the meantime reinforcements were going to Beauregard and Johnston almost daily. Wise and Floyd had been sent to the Kanawha Valley to counteract any movement there, and Garnett, with four thousand troops, had been sent to northwest Virginia. Patterson's was the only force from which Johnston could expect an attack, and as he would have to make detachments from it to guard his communications, Patterson could not be much superior in numbers when the collision should come.

General Lee, as adviser to the War Department,

was really the *de facto* Secretary of War and directed all operations in the field. He had selected Manassas Junction as a strategic point for the concentration of troops, on account of its being in connection with the Valley. On return from Manassas Junction, to relieve Johnston of anxiety about his flank being turned, Lee wrote to him that he had placed Colonel Ewell in advance at Fairfax Court House and Colonel Eppa Hunton at Leesburg on the Potomac, each with a force of infantry and cavalry in reservation, who would inform him of any movement to his rear. But Johnston continued uneasy and, although he was receiving reinforcements, he again wrote that he had heard that Patterson had 10,000 troops at Chambersburg, that some of McClellan's troops had reached Grafton, and he apprehended a junction of all of those forces against him. He should at least have waited for the development of such a plan and then, instead of retreating, have taken the offensive to defeat it. Johnston's suggestion meant the abandonment of the Valley.

Patterson, who was organizing the force at Chambersburg, was a political general, only remembered for having allowed the force he commanded in the Shenandoah Valley to render no service at a critical time. Patterson proposed to capture Harper's Ferry, which, of course, General Scott was very willing to do. But the only support Scott could promise from Washington was to make a demonstration towards Manassas to prevent reinforcements going to the Valley and to send a force of 2500 on a secondary expedition up the Potomac. As the Ferry was of great strategic value as an outpost, Scott warned Patterson of the desperate resistance he might expect from the Confederates. He did not suspect that the Confederates were then packing up to leave.

On June 14 the Confederates began the evacuation of Harper's Ferry and retreated ten or twelve miles to Charles Town. No movement had been made against them from any direction. Several regiments had just arrived — there were about 3000 militia at Winchester, and a force of the enemy had retreated from Romney.

On June 13, after repeated requests for instructions about holding Harper's Ferry, which showed clearly a desire to shift the responsibility for it, the War Department wrote him the conditions on which the place should be evacuated: "You have been heretofore instructed to use your own discretion as to retiring from your position at Harper's Ferry and taking the field to check the advance of the enemy. . . . As you seem to desire, however, that the responsibility of your retirement should be assumed here, and as no reluctance is felt to bear any burden which the public interest may require, you can consider yourself authorized, whenever the position of the enemy shall convince you that he is about to turn your position and thus deprive the country of the services of yourself and the troops under your command, to destroy everything at Harper's Ferry."

Johnston seems to have met this letter at Charles Town while it was on the way, and did not wait for it at the Ferry. Johnston's report says he met a courier from Richmond with a despatch authorizing him to evacuate Harper's Ferry at his discretion. The dispatch he received had no such instructions; the conditions on which he was authorized to abandon the place had not arisen; no enemy was threatening to turn his position.

On June 15 Patterson crossed the Maryland line. His leading brigade was commanded by Colonel George H. Thomas, a Virginian, who was an officer in the Second Cavalry under Lee. It had been expected that he would go with the people of his native State. On the sixteenth his brigade waded the Potomac. When Patterson heard that Harper's Ferry had been abandoned, he was incredulous and thought it was a ruse, giving Joe Johnston a credit he himself never claimed.

The evacuation of Harper's Ferry before it was compelled by the presence of an enemy was not approved at Richmond, nor was it done to act in concert with any other force, as was then supposed. The victory at Bull Run a few weeks afterwards confirmed the impression that the movement had been made in coöperation with Beauregard. The latter knew nothing of such a purpose until he heard that the Confederates had lost their advantage, and that the enemy held the key to the Shenandoah Valley. In plain words it was a retreat.

The evacuation of the post before there was any pressure to compel it made Johnston the innocent cause of a comedy at Washington. General Scott could not comprehend what could be the motive for it, except on the theory of its being a feigned retreat to capture Washington by a stratagem. No other reason could be conceived why the Confederates should surrender, without making a defense, the advantage of Harper's Ferry as a base.

After a part of his force had crossed the Potomac, to his surprise, Patterson received a telegram from

General Scott, on June 16, ordering him to send at once to Washington all the regular troops, horse and foot, and Burnside's Rhode Island regiment. And on the 17th of June, Scott repeated the order and said : "We are pressed here. Send the troops I have twice called for without delay." Where the pressure could come from was a mystery to Patterson, as he knew that Johnston was still in the Shenandoah Valley, but the order was imperative, and he obeyed. "The troops were sent," he said, "leaving me without a single piece of artillery, and for the time with but one troop of cavalry, which had not been in service over a month." So the hostile armies retreated in opposite directions. Patterson recrossed the Potomac, and Johnston, unconscious of the alarm which his retreat had given in Washington, went on to Winchester.

There was another amusing episode on June 16 as a result of the Harper's Ferry operations. In anticipation of the demonstration he was to make in favor of Patterson's predicted attack on Harper's Ferry, McDowell had sent General Schenck on the Loudoun railroad as an advance guard. When turning a curve near Vienna, a fire was opened on the train by what Schenck called a "masked battery." The engine was in the rear, and as the engineer could not draw the train out of the range of fire, he detached the engine and disappeared under a full head of steam. So Schenck and his men had to walk back. Under a flag of truce he asked permission to bury the dead and take care of the wounded. Schenck afterwards gained notoriety as U. S. Minister at London and was recalled. The only distinction he won in the war was as the inventor of the term "masked battery." The battery that did so much damage was commanded by my schoolmate, Del Kemper.

The whole country was greatly surprised by the news of the evacuation of Harper's Ferry. If Johnston had waited a day longer for the answer to his request for instructions, his retreat would have been a disobedience of orders. The conditions did not exist, in the opinion of the War Department, which would justify the evacuation. Johnston sent a reply in which he disclaimed a desire to shift responsibility — which was clearly inconsistent with his request for instructions.

Harper's Ferry should have been held until danger was imminent. It must have been a position of strategic value as well as of tactical strength since it was held by 11,000 men against the Confederates and used as a base in the

Gettysburg campaign and also when Early invaded Maryland. When the Ferry was evacuated, McDowell's army was fifty miles below, defending Washington, and Beauregard, in his front, fully occupied his attention. Patterson was at Hagerstown, had not crossed the Potomac, and had given no sign of doing so.

# CHAPTER V

## RECOLLECTIONS OF BATTLE OF MANASSAS [1]

THE First Virginia Cavalry remained in the Shenandoah Valley until the eighteenth of July when, by forced marches, it was sent to join the army and take its part in the Battle of Manassas. When we left the Valley, Stuart sent Captain Patrick's company to watch Patterson, whose army was in camp at Charles Town, and to screen the transfer of the army to the east of the Blue Ridge. It was well known that in a few days the most of Patterson's regiments would be mustered out of service and would go home. It was evident that his prime object had been not to divert Johnston's army but to avoid a collision. Patterson no doubt thought that he had effected his purpose and was content to rest where he was.

Stuart's regiment arrived at the scene of the approaching battle on the evening of July 20 and went into bivouac near Ball's Ford. The armies

[1] This, the first battle of the war, was known in the North as the Battle of Bull Run, and in the South as the Battle of Manassas.

were so close together that there was a great deal
of picket firing, and I remember very well the
foreboding I felt when I lay down under a pine
tree to rest beside Fount Beattie. When the
bugle sounded on the morning of the twenty-first,
in counting off, I was Number 1 in the first set of
fours and rode at the head of the squadron that
day. Nothing afterwards occurred in my military career that gives me more satisfaction to
remember. A few days before six Colt pistols
had been sent to our company, and Captain
Jones had selected the men who were to have
them. I was one of the six — I don't know why.
But to reconcile those who got no pistols, Jones
told them that the six should be selected for the
most dangerous work. Shortly after breakfast
on the morning of the battle, Stuart sent Jones to
make a reconnaissance over Bull Run. When we
reached the woods where he thought the enemy
might be, Jones called for the six men. We all
responded and rode off into the woods to reconnoitre, but we didn't find an enemy. So the
company recrossed the Run.

Our regiment was divided during the battle,
and the squadron to which I belonged was placed
under a Major Swan, a Marylander. Late in
the day when the enemy was in retreat, Swan

halted us in a field within fifty yards of Kemper's guns, which were firing on the retreating troops. That was the very time for us to have been on the enemy's flank. I was near Captain Jones. He rose in his stirrups and said indignantly, "Major Swan! You can't be too bold in pursuing a flying enemy." But he made no impression on Swan. After dark Swan marched us back over Bull Run, and I slept in a drenching rain in a fence corner. Swan did not get a man or a horse scratched. He did a life insurance business that day. Instead of Swan supporting the battery, the battery supported Swan. Afterwards my last official act as adjutant of the company was to carry an order from Jones who had become colonel, for Swan's arrest. We lay all the next day near the battlefield, and I rode over it, carrying a despatch to Stuart at Sudley. But the first thing I did in the morning was to make a temporary shelter from the rain in a fence corner and write a letter to my wife.

Monday, July 22d, Battlefield of Manassas.

My dearest Pauline:

There was a great battle yesterday. The Yankees are overwhelmingly routed. Thousands of them killed. I was in the fight. We at one time stood for two hours under a perfect storm of shot and shell — it was a miracle that none of our company was killed. We took all of their cannon from them; among the batteries captured was Sherman's — battle lasted about 7 hours — about 90,000 Yankees, 45,000 of our men. The cavalry pursued them till dark — followed 6 or 7 miles. Genl. Scott commanded them. I just snatch this moment to write — am out doors in a rain — will write you all particulars when I get a chance. We start just as soon as we can get our breakfast to follow them to Alexandria. We made a forced march to get here to the battle — travelled about 65 miles without stopping. My love to all of you. In haste.

Yours devotedly,

Early on Tuesday morning (July 23) Stuart's regiment and Eley's brigade moved to Fairfax Court House and camped near there on opposite sides of the Alexandria pike. Stuart's dispatch to General Johnston, who was still at Manassas, says we got there at 9.30 A.M. The country looked very much like Egypt after a flood of the Nile —it was strewn with the debris of McDowell's army. I again wrote to my wife and used paper and an envelope which the Zouaves had left behind. On it was a picture of a Zouave charging with a fixed bayonet and an inscription — "Up guards and at them"—which is said to have been Wellington's order at Waterloo. The Zouaves were then charging on New York.

Fairfax Court House, July 24th, 1861.

My dearest Pauline:

I telegraphed and wrote you from Manassas early the next morning after the battle. We made a forced march from Winchester to get to Manassas in time for the fight, — travelled two whole days and one night without stopping (in the rain) and getting only one meal. We arrived the morning before the fight. It lasted about ten hours and was terrific. When we were first brought upon the field we were posted as a reserve just in rear of our artillery and directly within range of the hottest fire of the enemy. For two hours we sat there on our horses, exposed to a perfect storm of grapeshot, balls, bombs, etc. They burst over our heads, passed under our horses, yet nobody was hurt. I rode my horse nearly to death on the battlefield, going backward and forward, watching the enemy's movements to prevent their flanking our command. When I first got on the ground my heart sickened. We met Hampton's South Carolina legion retreating. I thought the day was lost and with it the Southern cause. We begged them, for the honor of their State, to return. But just then a shout goes up along our lines. Beauregard arrives and assures us that the day will be ours. This reanimated the troops to redouble their efforts. Our regiment had been divided in the morning; half was taken to charge the enemy early in the action and the remaining part (ours and Amelia Co.) were held as a reserve, to cover the retreat of our forces, if unsuccessful, and to take advantage of any favorable moment.

When, late in the evening, the Yankees gave way, they seemed overwhelmed with confusion and despair. They abandoned everything — arms, wagons, horses, ammunition, clothing, all sorts of munitions of war. They fled like a flock of panic-stricken sheep. We took enough arms, accoutrements, etc. to equip the whole army. They were splendidly equipped, had every imaginable comfort and convenience which Yankee ingenuity could devise.

The fight would not have been half so long had it been an open-field one, but the Yankees were protected by a thick pine woods, so that it was almost impossible to get at them with the cavalry. They never once stood to a clash of the bayonet — always broke and ran. In the evening, when they gave way, the order was given to charge them. We were then in the distant part of the field. In a moment we were in full pursuit, and as we swept on by the lines of our infantry, at full speed, the shouts of our victorious soldiers rent the air. We pursued them for six or eight miles, until darkness covered their retreat. The whole road was blocked up with what they abandoned in their flight. All our regiment (in fact, nearly all the soldiers) now have splendid military overcoats which they took. I have provided myself very well. We took every piece of their artillery from them — 62 pieces — among them, one of the finest batteries in the world. Their total loss cannot be less than 5000. Our company is now equipped with Yankee tents, (I am writing under one). We are also eating Yankee provisions, as they left enough to feed the army a long

time. . . . All of the Northern Congress came out
as spectators of the fight. A Senator was killed by a
cannon ball — Foster. All of our troops fought well,
but the Virginia troops bore the brunt of the battle,
especially Jackson's brigade. A Washington paper
says they were scarce of ammunition — a lie, for we
took enough from them to whip them over again.
Our Captain (who you know is an old army officer)
complimented our company very much for their coolness and bravery in standing fire, — said that we stood
like old veterans. We were placed in the most trying
position in which troops can be placed, to be exposed
to a fire which you cannot return. . . . There was
scarcely a minute during the battle that I did not think
of you and my sweet babes. I had a picture of May
[his daughter] which I took out once and looked at.
For a moment the remembrance of her prattling inno-
cence almost unfitted me for the stern duties of a soldier, — but a truce to such thoughts. We are now
marching on to bombard Washington City.

Fairfax Court House, July 27, 1861.

Dearest Pauline :

We are here awaiting for the whole army to come
up. . . . Several of our men got scared into fits at
the battle. A Dr. —— put a blister on his heart as an
excuse not to go into battle; one named —— was so
much frightened when the shells commenced bursting
around us that he fell off his horse — commenced
praying; the surgeon ran up, — thought he was shot;

examined him, told him he was only scared to death. He got up and left the field in double-quick time. I could tell you of a good many such ludicrous incidents.

# CHAPTER VI

## THE STRATEGY OF THE BATTLE OF MANASSAS

ON May 24, 1861, the day after Virginia ratified the Secession Ordinance, McDowell's army crossed the Potomac on three bridges. McDowell made his headquarters at Arlington, General Lee's home, and it should be recorded to his credit that he showed the highest respect for persons and property.

One regiment of the New York Zouaves, commanded by Colonel Ellsworth, went on a steamer to Alexandria and landed under the guns of the *Pawnee*. A Confederate flag was flying from the top of a house which was owned by a citizen named Jackson. Ellsworth went up and pulled down the flag. As he descended the stairs, Jackson shot him and was himself shot by a Union soldier.

On June 26, McDowell's total strength present for duty was 153,682 men and twelve guns; Patterson's was 14,344 men. Of McDowell's twenty regiments, seventeen were three months' men. With the exception of one infantry regiment, four companies of cavalry, and three artillery companies, Patterson's force was composed of three months' men.  Johnston's force at the same time was 10,654 men and five or six batteries.

General Lee had selected Manassas Junction as the point for the concentration of the Confederate troops on account of its being in connection with the Valley.  Beauregard was in command here, while Jackson and Johnston with their forces were across the Blue Ridge in the Shenandoah Valley.  On June 15, Johnston retired towards Winchester, because, as he said, Patterson's army had reached the Potomac twenty miles above, and he wanted to be in a position to repel an invasion of the Valley, or quickly to reinforce Beauregard at Manassas.  Johnston thought, so he said, that Patterson was making a combined movement with McDowell, who was expected to move from Washington on Richmond. If so, Johnston at Harper's Ferry had the interior line and the choice of reinforcing Beauregard or striking Patterson.  As Patterson hesitated, it showed that he was afraid to cross the Potomac with Johnston on his flank.

Johnston's movement to Winchester, which, as I have said, was really a retreat, about doubled the distance between him and Beauregard. If he had really wanted to join Beauregard, his quickest way to do it would have been to march directly from Harper's Ferry to Bull Run. The distance would have been shorter than his march from Winchester to the railroad station, on his way to Manassas. There he left nearly half of his army for want of transportation. It is remarkable, however, that Jackson's biographers, Dabney, Cook, and Henderson, regarded the retreat to Winchester as only a strategic move. Jackson did not think so.

Jackson's brigade and Stuart's regiment of cavalry were sent to observe Patterson on the upper Potomac. Patterson had no cavalry for outpost duty, while Johnston had the regiments of Stuart and Ashby. Jackson's orders were to feel out the enemy, but to avoid an engagement. On July 2 Patterson crossed the Potomac, and Jackson showed sufficient resistance to compel him to display his force and retired as his orders required. He was sure that Patterson had no aggressive purpose, but was only making a feint to create a diversion and retain Johnston in the Valley, when McDowell moved against Beauregard at Manassas. Jackson thought that a blow at Patterson would have been the best way to co-operate with Beauregard. As Jackson had strict ideas of military discipline, he would not criticise his superiors, and, although the order to fall back was a disappointment, he did not, like Achilles, sulk in his tent. But a letter he wrote at the time to his wife, read between the lines, shows the chagrin he felt.

Colonel Henderson, in his "Life of Jackson", said:

The Federal army crawled on to Martinsburg. Halting seven miles southwest, Jackson was reinforced by Johnston's whole command and here for four days the Confederates drawn up in line of battle awaited attack. But the Federals stood fast in Martinsburg and on the fourth day Johnston withdrew to Winchester. The Virginia soldiers were bitterly dissatisfied.

At first even Jackson chafed. He was eager for action. His experience at Falling Waters had given him no exalted notion of the enemy's prowess and he was ready to engage them singlehanded. "I want my brigade," he said, "to feel that it can itself whip Patterson's whole army and I believe that we can do it."

The truth is that the numerical difference in the strength of the two armies was inconsiderable, but Johnston's had a great advantage in morale and a superior force of cavalry.

On July 15, in obedience to General Scott's orders, Patterson moved up the Valley, threw some shells at Stuart's regiment, and then turned squarely around and retreated towards Harper's Ferry. The movement was so timid that it was more a farce than a feint. Patterson was not seeking a fight; his movement was only a blind. If the Confederates had then taken the offensive, there would have been a footrace towards the Potomac, and McDowell would not have moved against the troops at Manassas.

The most effective way to aid Beauregard was to strike Patterson. The next year Jackson did what should have been done in 1861. He turned on Banks and swept him out of the Shenandoah Valley, creating such alarm in Washington that McDowell, who was moving from Fredericksburg to join McClellan at Richmond, was recalled to save the Capital.

The following dispatch to McClellan from Mr. Lincoln shows what Jackson did in 1862 and what he would have done in 1861, if he had been in command:

May 24th, 1862.

In consequence of General Banks's critical position I have been compelled to suspend General McDowell's movements to join you. The enemy are making a desperate push on Harper's Ferry and we are trying to throw General Fremont's force and a part of McDowell's in their rear.

The next that was heard of Jackson, he had defeated Fremont and Shields in the Valley and then turned off on McClellan's flank at Cold Harbor.

In July 1861, the larger part of the troops at Manassas should have gone to Johnston, instead of his reinforcing Beauregard. That is, if Johnston was willing to take the offensive and cross the Potomac. That was the best way to defend Richmond.

On July 17, McDowell began his movement towards the Confederate Capital. Mr. Davis telegraphed to Johnston aᵗ Winchester to join Beauregard, if practicable. He said:

General Beauregard is attacked. To strike the enemy a decisive blow a junction of all your effective force will be needed. If practicable make the movement, sending your sick and baggage to Culpeper Court House either by railroad or by Warrenton. In all arrangements exercise your discretion.

President Davis endorsed on Johnston's report of the battle that his order, or rather request to Johnston to join Beauregard gave him discretion because Johnston's letters of July 12 and 13 "made it doubtful whether General Johnston had the power to effect the movement."

In the letters Johnston said that he had to "defeat Patterson or elude him." It would have been impossible for him to defeat Patterson as the latter was running; as Patterson was trying to elude Johnston, the latter had no trouble in eluding Patterson.

On July 13 General Johnston telegraphed to President Davis: "Unless he (Patterson) prevents it, we shall move toward Beauregard to-day." Up to that time Johnston does not seem to have contemplated, nor was there any plan for, any concerted action between Johnston and Beauregard.

The march to Manassas did not begin until noon of the eighteenth. Jackson's brigade was in the advance. It waded the Shenandoah, climbed the Blue Ridge, and arrived at Manassas by rail on the next day. When the troops left Winchester, they could not have been expected to join Beauregard at Manassas before a battle, because McDowell's delay of three days at Centreville could not have been anticipated. On the seventeenth General Scott telegraphed Patterson that McDowell would take Manassas the next day, which probably would have been done if

Scott's program to cross the Occoquan and turn the Confederate right had been carried out. But McDowell changed the plan, waited to make a reconnaissance on the Confederate left, and decided to cross Bull Run at Sudley. Beauregard was not expecting aid from Johnston, for in a telegram to the War Department he said, "I believe this proposed movement of General Johnston is too late. Enemy will attack me in force to-morrow morning."

When Johnston left the Valley, Patterson was in camp at Charles Town. As late as the nineteenth Patterson insisted that Johnston was at Winchester receiving reinforcements; but on the twentieth he acknowledged that Johnston had gone. It was then too late for him to give assistance to McDowell in the battle the next day. When Patterson was reproached for what he had *not* done, he consoled Scott by telling him that if he had attacked Joe Johnston, he (Scott) would have had to mourn the loss of two battles instead of one.

Johnston arrived at Beauregard's headquarters at Manassas at noon on July 20, but nearly half of his army was left behind him. Beauregard's army was posted on Bull Run at five or six fords stretching from Stone Bridge to Union Mills, a distance of eight miles. Bull Run is a creek running through a largely wooded country, and is passable anywhere but for its steep banks. Johnston's troops were posted behind Beauregard's at the fords, and Jackson was placed in the rear of Bonham. McDowell's headquarters were in plain view six miles distant at Centreville and also in view of the signal station Captain Alexander had established on the Manassas plain.

Beauregard proposed an offensive plan which Johnston approved, but no attempt was made to execute it. The battle was defensive on the Confederate side. Early on the morning of the twenty-first the signal officers discovered McDowell's column marching towards Sudley to turn our left at Stone Bridge. They reported the movement to General Evans, who commanded there, and to headquarters. Johnston's brigades were in the rear of the fords as reserves ready to be moved to any point on the line. As Bull Run presented no defensive advantages, it is hard to discover why that line was selected. No matter whether Beauregard intended to act on the offensive or defensive, his army should have been concentrated at one or two fords, instead of being distributed at several.

Long afterwards Beauregard claimed that Johnston accepted his plan of battle, waived his rank, and consented to act as his chief of staff. As there was no emergency that required such an abdication of authority, and as there was ample time for Johnston to learn the conditions and get all the topographical knowledge necessary, it would have been shirking responsibility for him to have done so. His objective, McDowell's army, was in sight; he was near Bull Run, and he could easily learn from maps where the fords were and the roads that led to them. Beauregard and his staff officers could have easily told him how the troops were disposed. With such explanation Johnston might, in an hour or so, have taken in the whole situation. Very few commanders were ever on the ground more than a few hours before a battle; it is not their business to act as guides — the country furnishes plenty of them. Of course, generals must utilize other men's knowledge.

But the inconsistency is that Beauregard claims the credit as commander-in-chief for winning the victory, but makes Johnston responsible for the failure to reap the fruit of it. He contradicts his own report, written a few days after the battle, which says that the army, after the hard day's fighting, was in no condition to pursue.

He did not seem to know that he had 15,000 fresh men on the field and that the remainder of Johnston's men arrived next morning. In his "Military Memoirs", General Alexander, who was chief signal officer and also in the evening carried orders on the field, said:

Not far off Stonewall Jackson, who had been shot through the hand but had disregarded it until victory was assured, was now having his hand dressed by Doctor Hunter McGuire. Jackson did not catch the President's (Davis) words and Doctor McGuire repeated them to him. Jackson quickly shouted, "We have whipped them! They ran like sheep! Give me 5000 men and I will be in Washington City tomorrow morning."

Doctor Edward Campbell, a surgeon in Jackson's brigade, told me soon after the war that he heard Jackson make that speech.

But Johnston's endorsement on Beauregard's order of battle shows that so far from waiving he asserted his rank as commander. Here it is:

4.30 A.M., July 21st.

The plan of battle given by General Beauregard in the above order is approved and will be executed accordingly.

(Signed) J. E. Johnston,
General, C. S. Army.

As Beauregard submitted his program to Johnston's approval, he recognized Johnston as his superior officer. Orders are not submitted to the approval of subordinates. As a worse plan of operations could hardly have been devised, Johnston might have given Beauregard credit for it if he had adopted it. As there was no attempt to execute it, however, it is immaterial who was the author. The battle was fought on McDowell's plan. What was most remarkable was that instead of directing its immediate execution by an advance of his columns on Centreville, it instructed brigade commanders to hold themselves in readiness to advance but to wait orders. None but D. R. Jones received such an order to cross the Run that morning, and his was soon revoked. As the enemy was in their front, old soldiers like Jackson, Longstreet, and Ewell, ought to have been presumed to be ready for combat without instructions. If the Confederates were to assume the offensive to turn McDowell, their movement should have been begun, as McDowell's was, before daybreak; and as they would have had to move through a wooded country, their columns should have been as much as possible in sight of and in supporting distance of each other. But what is stranger

still is that Beauregard's order of battle, although
it contemplated the offensive, is dated at 4.30
A.M., July 21, long after McDowell's army was
in motion. McDowell issued his order of battle
on the twentieth.

McDowell saw the danger of keeping the wings
of his army so far apart and said :

I had felt anxious about the road from Manassas
by Blackburn's Ford to Centreville along this ridge,
fearing that while we should be in force to the front
and endeavoring to turn the enemy's position, we ourselves should be turned by him by this road. For if
he should once obtain possession of this ridge, which
overlooks all the country to the west to the foot of the
spurs to the Blue Ridge, we should have been irretriev-
ably cut off and destroyed. I had, therefore, directed
this point to be held in force, and sent an engineer to
extemporize some field works to strengthen the position. . . . The divisions were ordered to march at
2.30 o'clock A.M., so as to arrive on the ground early
in the day and thus avoid the heat which is to be expected at this season.

If the Confederates had moved in two columns
from the lower fords, while Evans and Cocke
attracted the attention of the enemy above,
they would have reached Centreville before Mc-
Dowell reached Sudley, and they would have
been between McDowell and Washington. In

that event McDowell said his army would have been destroyed. McDowell saw more clearly than the Confederate generals what they ought to do, but he trusted to their not doing it. Beauregard's first plan for a simultaneous advance from all the Bull Run fords to Centreville was impracticable in the wooded country, and it was well that no attempt was made to execute it. His line of battle would have been several miles long.

Beauregard commanded that day under Johnston as Meade commanded the Army of the Potomac under Grant. Beauregard's report said:

General Johnston arrived here about noon of the 20th of July, and being my senior in rank he necessarily assumed command of the forces of the Confederate States then concentrating at this point. Made acquainted with my plan of operations and dispositions to meet the enemy, he gave them his entire approval and generously directed their execution under my command.

Beauregard must have forgotten, when he wrote afterwards and claimed that he was commander-in-chief at Bull Run, that he had ever written that Johnston was.

Beauregard said that, being informed at 5.30 A.M. that a strong force was deployed in front of Stone Bridge, he ordered Evans and Cocke to maintain their positions to the last extremity, and that he thought the most effective method of relieving his left was by making a determined attack by his right. No doubt that was so. He knew, long before McDowell reached Sudley, that Ewell, Holmes, Jones, and Early had not advanced on Centreville, and there was then abundance of time for them to have reached Centreville before McDowell reached Sudley.

But he said that the news from the left afterwards changed his plan. As it was clear that McDowell was making only a feeble demonstration in our front and none on our right, he must have known early in the morning that the main portion of his army was moving against our left. He could not have expected McDowell to stand still; nor does he give a satisfactory reason for a change of plan, but the reverse. McDowell was doing what he ought to have wanted him to do.

At 7.10 A.M., D. R. Jones, whose brigade was at McLean's Ford near headquarters, said he received the following order:

Brigadier-General D. R. Jones,

General :

General Ewell has been ordered to take the offensive upon Centreville. You will follow the movement at once by attacking him in your front.

July 21st, 1861.

[Signed] G. T. Beauregard,
Brigadier.

Ewell was at the next ford below, with Holmes's brigade in support. It was not pretended that any such orders were sent to the brigades at the fords above. Longstreet, who was at Blackburn's Ford, with Early in support, said that in obedience to orders of the twentieth to assume the offensive, he crossed Bull Run early on the morning of the twenty-first, but as he immediately came in contact with the enemy and ordered his men to lie down under cover from the artillery fire, he does not seem to have been ordered to move on Centreville, and does not refer to any such order. He must have been waiting for further orders.

It is clear that Bonham received no orders to cross the Run, as he did not attempt it, although the enemy opened fire on him early in the morning. He said that before daylight one of his aides, General McGowan, brought intelligence that the enemy was moving on his left, and that he arose and with a field glass discovered the enemy moving on the pike to Stone Bridge. He said that he immediately communicated the news to headquarters and directed his command to prepare for action, as he supposed "an assault would be made early along our whole line." But no such assault was ordered.

Early, who was near McLean's farm in support of Longstreet, did not mention receiving any order to move on Centreville; neither did Jackson, who was supporting Bonham at Mitchell's Ford. He simply got an order to place himself in position where he could reinforce either Cocke or Bonham. In the meantime Jackson ascertained that Bee, who had been sent with his own and Bartow's brigades to reinforce Evans, was hard pressed. He seems to have moved, in the exercise of his own discretion, where the sound of the cannon indicated that the real conflict was. When he reached the plateau where the Henry house stood, he met the shattered brigades of Bee and Bartow retreating. Jackson formed his brigade on the crest of the ridge, which will forever be associated with his name.

General Alexander described the scene as follows:

A fresh brigade was drawn up in line on the elevated ground known as Henry House Hill and its commander, till then unknown, was henceforth to be called Stonewall. Bee rode up to him and said: "General, they are driving us!" "Then, Sir," said Jackson, "we must give them the bayonet." Bee galloped among his retreating men and called out to them: "See Jackson standing like a stone wall — rally behind the Virginians." It was at this moment when Jackson's and Hampton's were the only organized troops opposing the Federal advance and Bee and Bartow were attempting to rally their broken forces, that Johnston and Beauregard reached the field.

This was the crisis of the battle, as Jackson's heroic bearing electrified the troops and saved the day. Jackson selected this place as a battleground, and the great struggle was for the possession of the plateau. This was crescent shaped, the ridge forming a cover which protected his men from artillery fire.

Jones said that after getting the order from Beauregard to cross the Run and follow Ewell, he sent a message to Ewell but crossed and took a position on the road from Union Mills to Centreville and waited for Ewell. In the meantime he received the following order directing him to return:

10.30 A.M.

General Jones:

On account of the difficulties in our front it is thought preferable to countermand the advance of the right wing. Resume your position.

Beauregard said that as early as 5.30 A.M. the enemy opened fire on Evans at Stone Bridge, and that by 8.30 A.M. he discovered that it was a mask to cover a movement around his flank, and Evans promptly moved to meet it. So it was then clear that the enemy would be on the left. Instead of a change of plans and a retrograde movement, when this was discovered, it was the opportune moment to order our right to advance. Only four companies were left to hold Stone Bridge against Tyler's division; they held it all day.

The sound of the battle now informed our generals where the main effort of the enemy would be made. The "difficulties" in his front, of which Beauregard spoke in his note to Jones as the cause for revoking the order to advance, instead of deterring should have encouraged him to take the offensive. It was now clear that there was only a small force between him and the enemy's rear at Centreville. Hunter's and Heintzelman's divisions reached Sudley Ford, at least eight miles away, about 9.30 A.M. They halted for rest and for the men to fill their canteens from the stream. The main body of the Confederate army was then about half the distance from Centreville that Sudley is. The three brigades of Miles that were in reserve on the road to Blackburn's and McLean's fords could easily have been brushed aside before any reinforcements could have reached them. Then one of his brigade commanders, Richardson, reported that Colonel Stevens, who commanded a regiment there, said, "We have no confidence in Colonel Miles, because Colonel Miles is drunk;" all of which was in our favor. It was much better for the Confederates if Ewell's and Jones's forward movements were delayed until nine o'clock by a miscarriage of orders, for by that time McDowell had progressed too far to turn back when he heard of it.

When at Austerlitz Napoleon saw the allies marching towards his rear, he told his marshals to be quiet, not to interrupt them. After their movement had developed sufficiently, he struck such a blow as Johnston and Beauregard might have repeated at Centreville. McDowell dreaded such a counterstroke, and in the morning on the road to Sudley he halted Howard and kept his brigade in reserve near the pike until noon to meet such a contingency. On the field McDowell saw what he might do; and reports from the signal stations and heavy firing told Johnston and Beauregard what they could do — that the enemy had exposed his rear. But "in my judgment," said Beauregard, "it was now (10.30 A.M.) too late for the contemplated movement." Napoleon would have thought it was the hour for it to begin. It is a mystery why the Confederate generals abandoned their plan — if they ever had such a plan.

Alexander said, "About 8 A.M. Johnston and Beauregard, accompanied by their staffs and couriers, rode to the vicinity of Mitchell's Ford, where they left their party under cover and took position on an open hill some 200 yards to the left of the road."

Richardson was in their front, making a feint by shelling the woods. If he had intended a real attack, he would not have halted. The resistance made by Evans's small force on the Sudley road showed that, with reinforcement of Cocke's brigade at the ford below, McDowell's turning column could have been held in check until ours took Centreville. The fact is that the roaring guns and the despairing cry for help from Centreville would have stampeded McDowell.  General Johnston said the news from our left made their plan *impracticable*.  I think it showed not only that it was practicable, but a dead sure thing if they had attempted to execute it.  McDowell thought so too.  I am not judging the Confederate generals by the lights that are now before me, but by what their reports say was before them then.

Again quoting Alexander :

As he rode out in the morning, Beauregard directed me to go with a courier to the Wicoxen signal station and remain in general observation of the field, sending messages of all I could discover.  I went reluctantly as the opportunity seemed very slight of rendering any service.  There were but two signal stations on our line of battle — one in rear of McLean's Ford and one near Van Pelt's house on a bluff a few hundred yards to the left and rear of Stone Bridge.  Beyond the latter the broad, level valley of Bull Run for some miles with its fields and pastures as seen through the glass was foreshortened into a narrow band of green.  While watching the flag of this station with a good glass, when I had been there about half an hour, the sun being in the east behind me, my eye was caught by a glitter in this narrow band of green.  I recognized it at once as the reflection of the morning sun from a brass field piece.  Closer scrutiny soon revealed the glittering of bayonets and masked barrels.  It was about 8.45 A.M., and I had discovered McDowell's turning column the head of which at this hour was just arriving at Sudley, eight miles away.  I appreciated how much it might mean and thought it best to give Evans immediate notice, even before sending word to Beauregard.  So I signalled Evans quickly, "Look out for your left, you are turned."  Evans afterwards told me that a picket, which he had at Sudley, being driven in by the enemy's advanced guard, had sent a courier, and the two couriers, one with my signal message and one with the report of the picket, reached him together.  The simultaneous reports from different sources impressed him, and he acted at once with sound judgment.  He left four companies of his command to watch the bridge and the enemy in his front — Tyler and his three brigades.  With the remainder of his force (six companies of the 4th S. C. and Wheat's La. Battalion) he marched to oppose and delay the turning column, at the same time notifying Cocke, next on his right, of his movement. . . . Having sent Evans notice of his danger, I next wrote to Beauregard as follows: "I see a body of troops crossing Bull Run about two miles above the Stone Bridge.  The head of the column is in the woods on this side.  The rear of the column is in the woods on the other side.  About half a mile of its length is visible in the open ground between.  I can see both infantry and artillery."

This message reached Beauregard in a few minutes.  Johnston's report said :

About 8 o'clock General Beauregard and I placed ourselves on a commanding hill in rear of Gen. Bonham's left (Mitchell's Ford). Near nine o'clock the signal officer, Captain Alexander, reported that a large body of troops was crossing the Valley of Bull Run some two miles above the bridge. General Bee, who had been placed near Col. Cocke's position, Col. Hampton with his legion, and Colonel Jackson from a point near Gen. Bonham's left were ordered to hasten to the left flank.

Alexander continued his account:

For a long time there was little change and the battle seemed to stand still. When Evans and Bee were broken by Sherman's attack on the flank, their retreat was specially pressed by the Federal artillery. On reaching the Warrenton pike they were met by the Hampton Legion and Hampton made an earnest effort to rally the retreating force upon his command. The ground, however, was unfavorable and though Hampton made a stubborn fight (losing 121 out of 600 men) and delaying the advance near two hours before leaving the pike, our whole line then fell back under the enemy's fire.

Jackson now came to the rescue. He had 2611 men and with the remnants of Hampton's 600, they were the only organized troops opposing the enemy's advance. Bee, Bartow, and Evans were engaged in rallying their troops as Johnston and Beauregard appeared. Johnston took up his headquarters a short distance in the rear to direct reinforcements, while the immediate conduct of the battle was left to Beauregard. His task was to hold the line until fresh troops could be brought upon the scene. McDowell's last chance was to crush Beauregard's line at once before any reinforcements arrived. Some of his brigades were absent — Burnside's had drawn off for rest and ammunition — and his partial attacks only consumed time.

About three o'clock Kirby Smith's brigade arrived, and it was closely followed by Early's brigade and Beckham's battery. Kirby Smith was severely wounded just as he was extending his line on our left, and Elzey took command. Kirby Smith was the first man I ever saw carried from the field on a stretcher. About four o'clock Beauregard advanced his whole line, and the 18th Virginia under Colonel Withers, the 8th Virginia under Colonel Hunton, and the Hampton Legion with Jackson's brigade swept the field and turned the enemy's guns on them. Early, with Beckham's battery and Stuart's cavalry, crossed the Warrenton pike and opened on the flank and rear of a new line which McDowell had formed. This force had no artillery to reply

to ours, and it soon broke. McDowell said,
"The retreat soon became a rout and this soon
degenerated into a panic."

Heintzelman said, "Such a rout I never witnessed before."

Stuart's cavalry had charged and routed the
Ellsworth Zouaves on the Sudley road as they
were coming to the support of the Federal batteries. Heintzelman led the Zouaves. His account of this was as follows.

In the meantime I sent orders for the Zouaves to move
forward to support Ricketts' battery on its right. As
soon as they came up I led them forward against an
Alabama regiment, partly concealed in a clump of small
pines in an old field. At the first fire they broke and
the greater portion fled to the rear, keeping up a desultory fire over the heads of their comrades in front. At
the same time they were charged by a company of Secession cavalry on their rear, who had come by a road
through two strips of woods on our extreme right.

Stuart's charge was not on the rear of the
Zouaves but on their front, when they were
advancing to the support of the batteries. Heintzelman said the regiment dispersed and did not
appear on the field again; the greater portion
kept on to New York.

Porter said:

The evanescent courage of the Zouaves prompted them to fire perhaps a hundred shots, when they broke and fled, leaving the batteries open to a charge of the enemy's cavalry, which took place immediately. . . . Soon the slopes behind us were swarming with our retreating and disorganized forces, whilst riderless horses and artillery teams ran furiously through the flying crowd.

As McDowell, with the larger part of his army, had moved in a circle by Sudley, and as they retreated by the same route, if our troops on the field had moved on the straight line on the pike leading over Stone Bridge to Centreville, they would have cut off their retreat. This is what Jackson wanted to do.

After the battle had shifted, Alexander joined Beauregard. He said that Jackson alone of the Confederate leaders on the field gave any evidence of his appreciation of the victory. After the war Doctor Edward Campbell, a surgeon of Jackson's brigade, told me that Jackson said to him, "I wonder if General Johnston and General Beauregard know how badly they (the enemy) are whipped. If they will let me, I will march my brigade into Washington to-night."

Alexander said he heard Jackson tell President Davis the same thing. His account concludes:

Jackson's offer to take Washington City the next morning with 5000 men had been made to the President as he arrived upon the field; probably about five o'clock. It was not sunset until 7.15 and there was nearly a full moon. But the President himself and both Generals spent these precious hours in riding over the field where the conflict had taken place. . . . Johnston and Beauregard both sent orders to different commands to make such advances, *but neither went in person to supervise or urge forward the execution of the order, though time was of the essence.* [The italics are Alexander's.]

Kershaw with two South Carolina regiments, Kemper with two guns, and some cavalry were all the troops that pursued over Stone Bridge, although there were several brigades near that had not been much engaged — some not at all. Alexander carried the first order from Beauregard about 6 P.M. in checking pursuit. It directed Kershaw to advance over Bull Run carefully, but not to attack. Alexander, surprised at his ill-timed caution, asked if he forbade any attack. Beauregard replied that Kershaw must wait for Kemper and pursue cautiously. It would have been as easy to send half a dozen batteries as one. Alexander overtook Kershaw just as Kemper's two guns opened on the retreating column and upset a wagon on Cub Run bridge that created a blockade by which a good deal of artillery was lost. On his way back to Beauregard, Alexander met a staff officer carrying an order for all the troops to return.

Alexander was at the council of Mr. Davis and the generals that night at Manassas. The conclusion was reached to make a reconnaissance the next morning. Some cavalry scouting parties were sent, who saw nothing but the wreck of McDowell's army. It would have been as easy to have found that out before midnight as in the morning, if they had tried, as no attempt was made to rally the retreating army.

McDowell sent a dispatch from Fairfax Court House:

The larger part of the men are a confused mob, entirely demoralized. It was the opinion of all the commanders that no stand could be made this side of the Potomac. . . . They are now passing through this place in a state of utter disorganization.

Edwin M. Stanton, afterwards Secretary of War, on July 26, five days after the battle, wrote to ex-President Buchanan:

The capture of Washington now seems to be inevitable; during the whole of Monday and Tuesday it might have been taken without resistance. The rout, overthrow, and demoralization of the army is complete.

General Johnston afterwards said as an excuse for not pursuing that his army was as much demoralized by victory as the enemy's by defeat. Nobody suspected it then. We had about 15,000 troops on the field who had not been engaged, and a good many arrived the next morning.

On the caisson attached to one of Kemper's guns, when it swept over Bull Run, was an old Virginian, whose long white hair hung over his shoulders and gave him the look of a patriarch. When Kemper unlimbered near Cub Run, he claimed the privilege of firing the first gun. He had done the same when Beauregard opened his batteries on Sumter. When the curtain was let down on the last scene at Appomattox, he blew out his brains and ended life's fitful fever.

In his report General Johnston said that "our victory was as complete as one gained by infantry and artillery can be." He took no account of Stuart's charge at a critical moment when the Zouaves were coming upon Jackson's flank; nor of the fact that his army exceeded McDowell's in numbers, and had three or four times as much cavalry. The returns show that in Beauregard's army that day there were 1468 cavalry, and that Stuart, who had come from the Shenandoah Valley, had twelve companies. Besides, Ashby arrived the day after the battle with a cavalry regiment. Johnston and Beauregard had a total of effectives that day of 31,982 men and fifty-five guns, although they sent only two guns over the Run in pursuit. McDowell's total was 29,862 men and but seven companies of cavalry. Cavalry is needed as much to cover a retreat as to pursue.

We had enough cavalry to have taken Washington. It is true, as General Johnston said, that the city is situated on an unfordable river; but less than twenty miles above is a ford at Seneca where Stuart crossed going to Gettysburg, and I often afterwards crossed there. Our cavalry were nearer Seneca than McDowell's army was to Washington when the retreat began, and ought to have crossed the Potomac that night. The next day it could have easily moved around towards Baltimore, broken communications, and isolated Washington.

It is paradoxical but true that the Confederate cause was lost at Bull Run. Yet the victory reflected on those who won it all "the glory that was Greece and the grandeur that was Rome." And no matter now what men may speculate as to what might have been, cold must be the heart that can read that glorious record and not —

"Feel sympathy with suns that set."

# CHAPTER VII

## ABOUT FAIRFAX COURT HOUSE

UNTIL the spring of 1862 we did picket duty on the Potomac, a more agreeable duty than the routine of a camp. There were some skirmishes and many false alarms. A hog rooting or an old hare on its nocturnal rounds would often draw the fire of a vidette. My company went three times a week on picket and remained twenty-four hours, when we were relieved by another company.

[The following letters from Colonel Mosby to his wife and his sister give the most interesting events of the time between the Battle of Manassas and the campaign of 1862.]

Fairfax Court House, July 29, 1861.

Dearest Pauline:

We have made no further advance and I know no more of contemplated movements than you do. . . . A few nights ago we went down near Alexandria to stand as a picket (advance) guard. It was after dark. When riding along the road a volley was suddenly poured into us from a thick clump of pines. The balls whistled around us and Captain Jones' horse

fell, shot through the head. We were perfectly helpless, as it was dark and they were concealed in the
bushes. The best of it was that the Yankees shot
three of their own men, — thought they were ours.
. . . Beauregard has no idea of attacking Alexandria.
When he attacks Washington he will go about Alexandria to attack Washington. No other news. For one
week before the battle we had an awful time, — had
about two meals during the whole time, — marched two
days and one night on one meal, in the rain, in order
to arrive in time for the fight. . . . We captured a
great quantity of baggage left here by the Yankees;
with orders for it to be forwarded to Richmond.

Fairfax Court House, August 18, 1861.

My dearest Pauline:

    . . . I was in a little brush with them one day
last week. A party of ten of us came upon about
150. We fired on them and of course retreated before
such superior numbers. We jumped into the bushes
to reload and give it to them again when they came
up, but instead of pursuing us they put back to their
own camp. . . . When I was last on picket I was
within about four miles of Georgetown and could
distinctly hear the enemy's morning drum beat.
Some of the Yankees came to my post under a flag of
truce, — stayed all night, — ate supper with me; and
we treated each other with as much courtesy as did
Richard and Saladin when they met by the Diamond
of the Desert. . . . Our blister plaster doctor affords

us a good deal of fun. He is one of the most pompous fellows you ever saw. He went with us on picket one night, — got scared, — ran to us and swore he had ridden through a whole regiment of the enemy's infantry. The whole truth was there was not a Yankee in three miles of him.

Fairfax Court House, September 2, 1861.

My dearest Pauline:

. . . I received a fall from my horse one day last week, down at Falls Church, which came near killing me. I have now entirely recovered and will return to camp this morning. I was out on picket one dark rainy night; there were only three of us at our post; a large body of cavalry came dashing down towards us from the direction of the enemy. Our orders were to fire on all. I fired my gun, started back toward where our main body were, my horse slipped down, fell on me, and galloped off, leaving me in a senseless condition in the road. Fortunately the body of cavalry turned out to be a company of our own men who had gone out after night to arrest a spy. When they started they promised Captain Jones to go by our post and inform us of the fact, in order to prevent confusion, — this they failed to do and their own culpable neglect came near getting some of them killed. . . . Our troops are gradually encroaching on the Federals, — now occupying a position in full view of Washington, — *a brush is looked for there to-day.* . . . I rode out one day about a week ago with our wagon after hay,

— came to where our pickets were stationed, — they were in full view of the Yankees, a few hundred yards off on the opposite hill. The Yankees were firing at our men with long range guns, but ours could not return it, as they have only old muskets. I have a splendid Sharp's carbine, which will kill at a thousand yards. I dismounted . . . and turned loose on them. . . . I had to fire at them most of the time in a thick field of corn, — of course, could not tell the effect, — but once, when a fellow ran out into the road (in which I stood) to shoot at me, it took several to carry him back.

Camp near Fairfax Court House,

September 17, 1861.

Dear Liz: [Mosby's sister]

. . . Beauregard and Johnston are expected to move their headquarters up to Fairfax to-day. . . . Although Captain Jones is a strict officer he is very indulgent to me and never refuses me any favor I ask him. I think he will be made a Colonel very soon. Aaron [Mosby's negro servant] considers himself next in command to Captain Jones. . . . Nobody thinks the war will continue longer than a few months. We will clean them out in two more battles.

Camp near Fairfax Court House,

September 14, 1861.

My dearest Pauline:

. . . To-day we go on picket at the Big Falls on the Potomac. One hill we occupy commands a full view of the Capitol. I went to take a view of it with Lloyd. We could see it distinctly, with all their fortifications and the stars and stripes floating over it. I thought of the last time I had seen it, for you were there with me, and I could not but feel some regrets that it was no longer the Capitol of my Country, but that of a foreign foe.

Camp near Fairfax,

September —, 1861.

My dearest Pauline:

. . . The Enemy had come up with three thousand men, artillery, etc. to Lewisville, one of our picket stations; when we got there they were still there. Three men of our Company (including myself) were detached to go forward to reconnoitre. Col. Stewart [sic] was with us. While standing near the opening of a wood a whole regiment of Yankees came up in full view, within a hundred yards of me. Their Colonel was mounted on a splendid horse and was very gaily dressed. I was in the act of shooting him, which I could have done with ease with my carbine, when Col. Stewart told me not to shoot, — fearing they were our men. . . . I never regretted anything so much in my life as the glorious opportunity I missed of winging their Colonel. We went back and brought up our artillery, which scattered them at the first shot. I never enjoyed anything so much in my life as standing by the cannon and watching our shells when they burst over them.

Camp Cooper, November 21, 1861.

My dearest Pauline:

On Monday I participated in what is admitted to have been the most dashing feat of the war. Col. Lee took about 80 men out on a scout, — hearing where a company of about the same number of Yankees were on picket, we went down and attacked. They were concealed in a pine thicket, where one man ought to have been equal to ten outside. We charged right into them and they poured a raking fire into our ranks. Fount Beattie and myself, in the ardor of pursuit, had gotten separated some distance from our main body, when we came upon two Yankees in the woods. We ordered them to surrender, but they replied by firing on us. One of the Yankees jumped behind a tree and was taking aim at Fount when I leveled my pistol at him, but missed him. He also fired, but missed Fount, though within a few feet of him. I then jumped down from my horse and as the fellow turned to me I rested my carbine against a tree and shot him dead. He never knew what struck him. Fount fired at one with his pistol, but missed. A South Carolinian came up and killed the other. . . . The man I killed had a letter in his pocket from his sweetheart Clara. . . . They were of the Brooklyn Zouaves and fought at Manassas.

— 1862.

My dearest Pauline:

Get Aaron to give you a full account of his adventure, — his memorable retreat from Bunker Hill,

— his doctoring the sick men [1] during the battle. He is a good deal thought of in the company.

At the end of 1861 occurred an event which greatly disappointed Southern hopes. Mason and Slidell had been sent as ambassadors to England and France. They escaped through the blockading fleet at Charleston and arrived at Nassau, where they took passage on the English steamer *Trent.* The vessel was stopped on the high seas by Captain Wilkes of the *San Jacinto,* and the ambassadors were taken off and confined in Fort Warren, Boston. This action was hailed with as much joy in the South as in the North. The Confederates thought their ambassadors would be held as prisoners and conceived it to be impossible that they would be surrendered on the demand of England after the Secretary of the Navy had approved the conduct of Wilkes, and Congress had given him a vote of thanks. Fortunately for the Union cause, neither Mr. Lincoln nor Mr. Seward had committed himself to an approval of it, but both had kept a judicious silence until they could hear from England. In the South we all felt sure that England would

[1] The story of the "sick" men concerns the Battle of Manassas. They covered themselves with heavy blankets and shivered when the shells were flying. When they were not, they would recover and raise up and ask Aaron, "Haven't you got a few more of those corn cakes?"

never submit to such an indignity and breach of neutrality.

War between England and the United States was considered inevitable, and we could almost hear the roar of English guns dispersing the fleets which were blockading our coasts. With England as an ally of the South our success was certain. But the Administration wisely yielded to England's demand and surrendered the captives. Mr. Seward, in a letter to Lord Lyons, ingeniously maintained that he was consistent in so doing, and that in demanding their release England had at last claimed for neutrals the rights for which the United States had always contended. Mason and Slidell were transferred to an English gunboat lying off Cape Cod, and thus withered our hopes of having England as an ally. There was no longer a *casus belli*.

The *Richmond Examiner*, January 1, 1862, said of this affair: "The year which has just begun opens with evil tidings. We fear there is no doubt of the fact that the Northern Union has consented to the surrender of Mason and Slidell, and with that event all hopes of an immediate alliance between the Southern Confederacy and Great Britain must cease."

It happened that I brought to the camps in

Fairfax the first news of the capture of Mason and Slidell. Fitzhugh Lee took a part of my regiment on a scout and we came upon the Brooklyn 14th that was doing picket duty. They wore red breeches, so we called them the red-legged Yankees. As soon as we got in sight of them we charged. A portion of them were in a dense thicket, which we couldn't penetrate on horseback, and so a few of us dismounted and charged on foot, with carbines, to the point where the reserve had a fire. We took a number of prisoners and I picked up a newspaper. It was about sundown; the paper was a copy of the *Washington Star* of that evening, and had an account of the capture of Mason and Slidell. When we brought the prisoners to Fitz Lee, I said, "Colonel, here's a copy of to-day's paper." Fitz Lee replied, "The ruling passion strong in death," referring to my reputation of always being the first man in the company to get hold of a newspaper. Colonel Jones sent the paper to General Johnston's headquarters at Centreville.

A popular notion has prevailed that a great benefit would have resulted to the South if England and France had received our ministers and established diplomatic relations with the Southern Confederacy. I never thought so, unless they had gone further and intervened in our behalf, as France did with the Colonies, and sent their fleets to break the blockade. In that event they would have become parties to the war. When they proclaimed their neutrality and accorded us belligerent rights and the hospitality of their ports to Confederate cruisers, they just as much recognized the independence of the South as if they had officially received its ministers. The human mind cannot conceive of belligerent rights except as attached to a supreme independent power.

There was a great deal of complaint against England for her haste in proclaiming neutrality and thus recognizing the belligerent character of the contest. But the Congress called by Mr. Lincoln, in July, 1861, before Bull Run had been fought, as Webster said about Bunker Hill, elevated an insurrection into a public war. It passed an act forbidding commercial intercourse between persons living north and south of the Potomac, and declaring the forfeiture of goods caught in transit and also the seizure of vessels on the high seas as enemy property, if the owners lived in the South. It also declared that such seizures and intercourse should be governed, not by the municipal law of the country, but by the law of nations. It thus recognized our sectional conflict as a public territorial war and not, like the Wars of the Roses, a contest of factions.

The law of nations regulates the relations of alien enemies in war and can have no application to citizens of the same country. This act of Congress was a declaration of a war *inter gentes*, as much so as that between France and Prussia. The *Amy Warwick*, owned in Richmond, sailed from Rio without notice of the blockade. She was seized on the voyage and condemned as a prize of war. It was contended that there was no proof that her owner was in rebellion. But the Supreme Court held that international law took no notice of the personal sentiments of individuals, but that their domicile determined their legal status.

In the opening of the year 1862 there was a great deal of depression in the Southern Confederacy. A considerable amount of this was due to the failure of our hopes of having England as an immediate ally, but most of it was on account of the expiration, in the coming spring, of the terms of enlistment of most of the regiments and the reluctance of the men to reenlist before going to their homes. General Joe Johnston issued an address urging the twelve-months' volunteers to reenlist, but it had little or no effect. He said:

The Commanding General calls upon the twelve-months' men to stand by their brave comrades who have volunteered for the war, to revolunteer at once and thus show the world that the patriots who engaged in this struggle do not swerve from the bloodiest path they may be called to tread.

The fear that the army would disappear like a morning mist is shown in the farewell address of General Beauregard, dated January 30, 1862, when he was about to leave to take command in the West. He said:

Above all I am anxious that my brave countrymen here in arms fronting the haughtily arrayed master of Northern mercenaries should thoroughly appreciate the exigency, and hence comprehend that this is no time for the Army of the Potomac — the men of Manassas — *to stack their arms and quit, even for a brief period, the standards they have made glorious by their manhood.*

The fact that Beauregard italicized the latter part of this sentence was an omen of impending danger. Mr. Davis also sent a message to Congress in which he said, "I therefore recommend the passage of a law declaring that all persons residing within the Confederate States between the ages of eighteen and thirty-five years and rightfully subject to military duty shall be held to be in the military service of the Confederate States."

The conscription law increased the numbers but impaired the *esprit de corps* of the volunteer army that won the victory of Manassas, — the flower of Southern manhood had been gathered there. But the law saved the Confederacy from the danger of collapse without another battle through the disbandment of its army. After the war I heard severe criticism of the Conscription Act which, in fact, saved the Confederacy — for a time.

# CHAPTER VIII

## CAMPAIGNING WITH STUART

THE last time I went on picket was on the 12th of February (1862). By this time Stuart had been made a brigadier-general, and Jones was colonel of the regiment. The road from our camp to the outpost passed through Centreville, where General Joe Johnston and Stuart had their headquarters. On that February day Stuart joined us, and I observed that an empty carriage was following, although I did not understand the reason. When we arrived at Fairfax Court House, Stuart asked Captain Blackford to detail a man to go in the carriage with some ladies. There was a fine family in the place, who always gave me my breakfast when I was on picket and, as one of the ladies in the party was a member of the family, I was detailed to go as an escort several miles inside our lines. They did not like being on the picket line where there were frequent skirmishes. So I left my horse for my messmate, Fount Beattie, to bring back to camp the next day, and took my seat in the carriage with the ladies. It was a raw, cold morning, and it soon began to snow. We arrived at our journey's end in the evening, and I then started for Stuart's headquarters. When I reached there it was dark, and the snow was still falling. Although I had been in Stuart's regiment from the beginning of the war, I had no acquaintance with him and no reason to suppose that he had ever heard of me. So I went into the house, reported to him that I had left the ladies at their destination, and asked him for a pass, as my camp on the Bull Run was several miles away. The sentinels would not let me go back without one.

Now the weather would not have been any more severe on me if I had walked back to camp that night than if I had stayed on picket. I never dreamed of Stuart's inviting me to spend the night at headquarters, or that I should ever rise to intimacy with him. There could have been nothing prepossessing in my general appearance to induce him to make an exception of me, for I was as roughly dressed as any common soldier. But he told me the weather was too bad and to stay there that night. Of course I obeyed and took my seat before a big, blazing fire. Both of the generals were sitting there, but I felt so small in their presence that I looked straight into the fire and never dared to raise my head. I would have felt far more comfortable trudging back to camp through the snow. Presently a boy announced that supper was ready. The generals arose and, as Stuart walked into the supper room, he told me to come in and get some supper. I was astonished and kept my seat. Stuart observed my absence from the table and sent for me. So I obeyed, went in, and took a seat with the generals. I do not think I raised my eyes from my plate, although they chatted freely. When it was time to go to sleep Stuart had some blankets spread on the floor, and I was soon snoring. The same thing happened in the morning — a boy announced breakfast — Stuart told me to come in, and I again stayed behind — and he had to send for me.

It has always been a mystery to me why Stuart made me his guest that night and did not put me with his couriers — which would have been more agreeable to me. After breakfast Stuart sent me, mounted, to my camp, with a courier to bring back the horse I rode. So here began my friendship for Stuart which lasted as long as he lived. It is a coincidence that it began on the very day I received my first promotion. I had scarcely reached our camp when a message came from the commander of the regiment, Colonel Jones, to come to his tent. I went, and he offered me the position of adjutant. I was as much astonished as I had been the night before to be asked to sit at the table with the generals. Of course I was glad to accept it, and Jones wrote to the War Department requesting my appointment. The Journal of the Confederate Senate shows that I was confirmed to take rank from February 17, 1862. I have always had a repugnance to ceremonials and was not half so much frightened in the battle of Bull Run as I was on the first dress parade I conducted. On such occasions the adjutant is the most conspicuous figure. I never could repeat the formulas of the regulations, and for this reason I remember the few weeks I served as an adjutant with less satisfaction than any other portion of my life as a soldier.

[Undated fragment of a letter to Mrs. Mosby.]

We are suffering the most intense anxiety to hear the final result from Donelson, — if we are defeated there it will prolong the war, I fear, but the idea of giving up or abandoning the field now should never enter a Southern man's head. To be sure there must be a costly sacrifice of our best blood, but the coward dies a thousand deaths, the brave man dies but one.

When news came to Richmond that Grant's attack on Fort Donelson had been repulsed, Confederate hopes of final success were raised to a high pitch. But they sank to zero the next day when a dispatch came announcing the fall of Donelson and the surrender of most of the garrison. Kentucky was now lost to us and most of middle Tennessee.

A greater blunder was never committed in war than when General Albert Sidney Johnston sent Floyd, Buckner, and Pillow down the Cumberland River, with about 17,000 troops, to hold a fort situated in the angle made by the confluence of the Cumberland and a deep, unfordable creek. There was no line of retreat open by land and no transportation provided for escape by water, in case of defeat. The Confederates were caught in a trap, and their surrender was, of course, inevitable. The first attacks of the gunboats under Commodore Foote were repulsed, and in the evening the situation was about the same as it had been in the morning. But Buckner and Pillow seemed to think that their men would not fight any longer, although they had an abundance of rations, and Floyd swore that he would not surrender either himself or his brigade. Floyd was the senior officer, and it was agreed that he should turn over the command to Pillow, who was next in rank, and that he, in turn, should turn it over to Buckner. Floyd with his brigade escaped at night on two steamboats that happened to come down with supplies from Nashville that evening. Pillow in some way got to the opposite bank of the river and left his troops behind him. It has never been explained why a few boats were not on hand to set the Confederates over the river, when resistance became hopeless, or why the two which Floyd took were not used during the night to convey the army to the other bank.

At daybreak Buckner ordered a parley to be sounded and capitulated to Grant without conditions. He did not even get as good terms as General Lee got for the fragment of his army at Appomattox. Mr. Davis relieved both Floyd and Pillow of command, but with strange inconsistency he praised General Johnston for putting them in a hole where they fought for two days to get out. The affair of Donelson was a most discreditable thing to our side of the war.

Camp of 1st Cavalry,

March 1, 1862.

Dear Pauline :

Nobody here is the least discouraged at our late reverses; that they will prolong the war I have no doubt. But they have not made the first step towards subjugation. Nothing can reverse my own decision to stay in the foremost ranks, "where life is lost or freedom won." I want to see in Southern women some of that Spartan heroism of the mother who said to her son, when she buckled on his armor: "Return with your shield or return upon it." Our army is now falling back from Centreville, but whether to Manassas or Gordonsville I don't know. We haven't moved our camp.

When Johnston retired from Centreville, in the spring of 1862, our regiment was the rear-guard of the army. Johnston fell back leisurely; first to the Rappahannock and then to the Rapidan, where he waited for McClellan to develop his campaign. In December, 1864, I had dinner with General Lee at his headquarters near Petersburg, and he told me that Johnston should never have moved from the Rapidan to Richmond; that when it was discovered that McClellan was moving down the Potomac, he wrote Johnston and urged him to move back against Washington. Lee was confident that such a menace of the capital would recall McClellan to defend it.

A considerable Union force followed our regiment as we withdrew along the railroad, and when it got near our picket line on Cedar Run, it deployed in an open field and made a great display.

Jones was on the picket line that day, and I was with him and witnessed the exhibition. The pickets withdrew, and the enemy occupied the ground on which we had been for several days. That night my regiment camped near Bealeton Station.

The next morning I rode there and met Stuart. The enemy was already in sight and advancing. I had become pretty well acquainted with Stuart after I became an adjutant and had already conducted several scouting expeditions for him. As we met that morning, he said to me very earnestly, — he seemed puzzled, — "General Johnston wants to know if McClellan's army is following us, or if this is only a feint he is making." Evidently Stuart wanted me to find out for him, but did not like to order me. I saw the opportunity for which I had longed and said in a self-confident tone, "I will find out for you, if you will give me a guide." He gave me one who knew the road, and with two others of my party I started around the flank of the hostile column and got in its rear while it was advancing to the Rappahannock. As the enemy moved south and we went north, my party was in its rear when the Union column reached the Rappahannock and began shelling the Confederates who had just crossed.

As we were behind the enemy, we soon discovered that an isolated body was following Johnston, and that it kept up no line of communication with Washington. It was clear that the movement was a mask to create a diversion and cover some operation. Of course, I was proud to have made the discovery, and I rode nearly all night to report it to Stuart. When we got near the river, we halted at a farmhouse, for there was danger of being shot by our own pickets if we attempted to cross the river in the dark. As soon as it was daylight, I started, leaving my companions asleep. A picket halted me when I got halfway across the river, and it was with great difficulty that I could persuade him not to fire. At last I made him ashamed of himself when I told him I was only *one* man and asked him if he was afraid of *one* Yankee. He told me to come on, but he kept his gun levelled at me.

I went on at a gallop and found Stuart with General Ewell, whose division was in line of battle expecting the enemy to attempt to cross the river — a heavy fog concealed their backward movement. I told Stuart that there was no support behind the force in front, and that it was falling back. A curtain of cavalry had been left behind to cover the retreat. Our cavalry was immediately ordered in pursuit, and I went with it. In the rapture of the moment Stuart told me I could get any reward I wanted. His report confirms this statement about the information that was obtained — but I got no reward.

Culpeper Co.,

April 1st, 1862.

My dearest Pauline:

. . . Although I do not belong to that Company (Blackford's), being on the regimental staff, I went with them into the fight. . . . The appearance of the enemy when they crossed Cedar Run was the most magnificent sight I ever beheld. . . . We let them [advance guard of cavalry] cross, when, dismounting, we delivered a volley with our carbines which sent them back across the deep stream in the wildest confusion. One fellow was thrown into the water over his head; and scrambling out ran off and left his horse; another horse fell, rose, and fell again, burying his rider with him under the water. We ceased firing, threw up our caps, and indulged in the most boisterous laughter. . . . Col. Jones speaks of some service I have recently rendered. At one time, with four men, I passed around, got to the rear of the enemy, discovered that they were making a feint movement on the railroad, while they were really moving in another direction. I rode nearly all night to give the information, which resulted in General Stuart's ordering our regiment in pursuit and the capture of about 30 prisoners, 16 horses, arms, etc. General Stuart was so much pleased with my conduct that he wrote a report to General Johnston commending me very highly and also recommending my promotion.

When our regiment got to the vicinity of Yorktown, it was reorganized, and Fitz Lee, who had been a lieutenant-colonel, was elected colonel. Stuart invited me to come to his headquarters and act as a scout. I got no commission and stayed with his couriers. In this ambiguous condition I remained for a year, or until I took up my independent command.

April 25, 1862.

My dearest Pauline:

Our regiment was reorganized day before yesterday. Col. [Fitzhugh] Lee was elected over Col. Jones. Col. Jones left immediately for Richmond. He expects to be a Brigadier-General. Immediately after the election I handed in my resignation of my commission. The President had commissioned me for the war, but I would not be adjutant of a Colonel against his wishes or if I were not his first choice. General Stuart told me yesterday that he would see that I had a commission.

Richmond, June 2, 1862.

My dearest Pauline:

The papers will give you about as much as I know of the fight [Battle of Fair Oaks, or Seven Pines].

I went down over the battlefield yesterday. Our men were all among the enemy's tents, which were still standing, their camp kettles on the fire, etc. We whipped them in their fortifications. . . . General Lee is now in command, General Johnston being wounded. . . . There is so much confusion in Richmond that I do not know whether I can get your memorandum filled to-day. There is nothing like a panic, everybody being engaged in preparing to take care of the wounded.

In June (1862) McClellan was astraddle of the Chickahominy; his right rested on the Pamunkey, but there was a gap of several miles between his left and the James. The two armies were so close to each other that the cavalry was of little use, and it was therefore kept in the rear.

One morning I was at breakfast with Stuart, and he said that he wanted to find out if McClellan was fortifying on the Totopotomy, a creek that empties into the Pamunkey. I was glad to go for him and started off with three men. But we found a flag of truce on the road and turned off to scout in another direction — I did not want to go back without doing something. We did not get the information for which we were sent, but we did get intelligence of even more value.

We penetrated McClellan's lines and discovered that for several miles his right flank had only cavalry pickets to guard his line of communication with his depot at the White House on the Pamunkey. Here, it seemed to me, was an opportunity to strike a blow. McClellan had not anticipated any such move and had made no provision against it.

On discovering the conditions, I hastened back to Stuart and found him sitting in the front yard. It was a hot day — I was tired and lay down on the grass to tell him what I had learned. A martinet would have ordered me to stand in his presence. He listened to my story and, when I had finished, told me to go to the adjutant's office and write it down. At the same time he ordered a courier to get ready to go with him to General Lee's headquarters. I did as he requested and brought him a sheet of paper with what I had written. After reading it, Stuart called my attention to its not being signed. I signed it, although I had thought he only wanted a memorandum of what I had said — General Lee had never heard of me. Stuart took the paper and went off with a courier at a gallop. As soon as he returned, orders were issued to the cavalry to be ready.

General Lee's instructions authorizing the expedition were dated June 11. I had reported the day before. On the morning of the twelfth, with 1200 cavalry and two pieces of artillery, Stuart passed through Richmond and took the road towards Ashland. I was at headquarters when Stuart was leaving. The officer in charge asked him when he would be back. His answer was, "It may be for years, it may be forever." His spirits were buoyant.

The column moved on to Old Church in Hanover where two squadrons of U. S. regular cavalry were stationed under the command of Captain Royall. When the pickets were chased in, Royall heard the firing and went to their support. He had no cause to suspect the numbers he was meeting, for McClellan had never even considered the possibility of a force breaking through his lines and passing around him. A squadron of the Ninth Virginia Cavalry led our column. Captain Latané was in command. A charge was ordered, and in the combat Royall was wounded and routed, and Latané was killed. We could not stay to give him even a hasty burial. Our forces soon had possession of the abandoned camp and, as the enemy had had no time to pack up, there was a festival.

We were now on the flank of the enemy but nine miles from the railroad which was his line of communication. The question which Stuart had to determine was whether to go on or turn back. We were near the Pamunkey, and if we kept on, the road would soon be closed behind us. The only way of return would then be to pass around McClellan. I felt great anxiety for fear that Stuart would halt, for I realized that there was a chance for him to do something that had never been done. His decision to go on showed that he possessed true military genius.

Just before Stuart gave the order for us to move, he turned to me and said, "I want you to go on some distance ahead." "Very well," said I, "but give me a guide." Two soldiers who knew the roads were ordered to go with me. I was proud to be selected for such a duty and was full of enthusiasm. We had not gone far before Stuart sent one of his staff to tell me to go faster and increase the distance between us. As we jogged along two miles in advance of the column, we came upon a sutler's wagon. It was filled with so many tempting things which we had not seen for nearly two years that we felt as if the blockade had been raised. We exercised the belligerent right of search. At the same time I could see, about a mile away in the Pamunkey River, a forest of masts of schooners which were unloading supplies into a train of wagons ready to carry them to the army. So I sent one man back to tell Stuart to hurry and capture the prizes and put the other as a guard over the sutler. I then went on alone. When Stuart came up, he sent a squadron to burn the schooners and the wagon train. Capturing watercraft was a novel experiment in cavalry tactics. At a bend in the road, I came upon a vidette and a sutler's wagon; they submitted quietly. Just then a bugle sounded, and I saw a body of cavalry a few hundred yards away. Fugitives from the camp we had captured had given the alarm, and the second troop was getting ready to leave. As soon as the head of our column appeared, the enemy's force at once disappeared.

A Confederate newspaper described my part as follows:

Appreciating the public interest in the recital of everything connected with the recent exploit of General Stuart's cavalry in his reconnaissance through the enemy's lines, we have gathered, from reliable participants in the affair, these additional particulars. After destroying the enemy's camp near the old church,

Lieutenant John S. Mosby, aid to General Stuart and who had been most daring and successful as a scout, was sent on in advance, with a single [sic] guide, towards Tunstall Station, to reconnoitre and ascertain the position and force of the enemy. On his way he met two Yankees whom he took prisoners and sent to the rear in charge of his guide. Alone he pushed on and overtook a cavalryman and an artilleryman of the enemy's forces, having in charge a quartermaster's wagon and stores. Lieutenant Mosby dashed up and, drawing his pistols, demanded their surrender. The New Yorker surrendered at once, but the Pennsylvanian, beginning to fumble for his pistol, the lieutenant made a more emphatic demand for his surrender, and at the same moment compelled him to look quite closely into the muzzle of his pistol. All this time there was drawn up, not four hundred yards distant, a company of Yankee cavalry in line of battle. In a moment a bugle sounded as for a movement on him, when, anxious to secure his prisoners and stores, Lieutenant Mosby put spurs and galloped across the field, at the same time shouting to his imaginary men to follow him, when none of the Confederate cavalry were in sight and the swiftest more than a mile in the rear. The Yankees, hearing the word of command and apprehending the descent of an avalanche of Confederate cavalry upon them, broke line, each man galloping off to take care of himself. The wagon, prisoners, and stores were then secured and among them were found forty splendid Colt's pistols with holsters, besides boots, shoes, blankets, etc., etc.

About sundown we reached the York River Railroad, and the column still went on. The only way to get back to Richmond was now to recross the Chickahominy near its mouth and pass by McClellan's left flank. As some evidence of the consternation that prevailed among the Union troops, I remember that, after we left the camp, a sergeant and twenty-five men of the regular cavalry followed on under a flag of truce and surrendered to the rearguard. That night was a feast for Stuart's cavalry. On all the roads were burning trains with supplies and sutlers' goods. Champagne and Rhine wine flowed copiously.

A force was sent in pursuit of us under the command of General St. George Cooke — Stuart's father-in-law. Although the march of our column was slow, we never saw an armed foe after we left Royall's camp, except a small guard at the railroad. General Warren, who commanded a brigade behind us, said, "It was impossible for the infantry to overtake him and as the cavalry did not move without us, it was impossible for them to overtake him." Fitz-John Porter regretted that "When General Cooke did pursue, he should have tied his legs with the infantry command." As there were six cavalry regiments, including all the regulars, with a battery, on our track, it is hard to see why they wanted infantry.

Although more than forty-eight hours elapsed between the time when we passed McClellan's right flank and back around his left, he made no attempt to intercept us. In making the circuit of his army, the Confederate column was at all times within five or six miles of his headquarters, with two navigable rivers enclosing it, and another river over which we had to build a bridge in order to cross. McClellan was a soldier of great organizing ability and trained in the science of war — I mean in those operations that can be regulated by rules. But he had none of the inspiration that decides and acts instantly, and he was now confronted by a condition without a precedent. So he was helpless.

About daylight we reached a ford of the Chickahominy, a narrow crooked stream which meanders between the Pamunkey and the James. We had crossed it on the morning before. Stuart had expected to be able to ford this stream, but at this point it was overflowing. A guide told us of a bridge a mile below — or where one had been — so the column was headed for that point.

When we got there, we found that the bridge was gone, although the piles were standing. Near by were the remains of an old warehouse, which furnished material for building another. It was soon constructed — it seemed to rise out of the water by magic. It may not have been so good a bridge as Cæsar threw over the Rhine, but it answered our purpose. While the bridge was building, Stuart showed no anxiety and was in as gay a humor as I ever saw him. During the night I had provided for our commissary department a lot of stores from the sutlers' wagons, and these were soon spread about on the grass. We had not been disturbed on the night march, but just as the bridge was finished a body of lancers came in sight and halted. They had captured one of our men, a German, whom we had to leave behind, as he was too full of Rhine wine to travel. When we reached Westover, the command was halted to rest and get forage, for we knew that the road to Richmond was open. Stuart now left Fitz Lee in command and rode on to report to General Lee. The column moved on by moonlight and at daybreak was in sight of Richmond. The game was won.

I had ridden several miles ahead of the column and met Stuart returning. Of course, he was delighted to hear that the cavalry was safe.

To excuse himself for what he had not done, McClellan, in a dispatch, tried to belittle this affair by saying that Stuart's cavalry did nothing but gain a little *éclat;* but it can be said with more truth that he himself lost a good deal. It was the first blow at his reputation.

The Comte de Paris, one of McClellan's staff officers, said with more truth, "They had, in point of fact, created a great commotion, shaken the confidence of the North in McClellan, and made the first experiment in those great cavalry expeditions which subsequently played so novel and important a part during the war."

Richmond, Monday,

June 16, 1862.

My dearest Pauline:

I have just received your letter this morning. I returned yesterday with General Stuart from the grandest scout of the war. I not only helped to execute it, but was the first one who conceived and demonstrated that it was practicable. I took four men, several days ago, and went down among the Yankees and found out how it could be done. The Yankees gave us a chase, but we escaped. I reported to General

Stuart, — suggested his going down, — he approved, — asked me to give him a written statement of the facts, and went immediately to see General Lee, who also approved it. We were out nearly four days, — rode continuously four days and nights, — found among the Yankee camps and sutlers' stores every luxury of which you ever conceived. I had no way of bringing off anything. General Stuart gave me the horses and equipments I captured. What little I brought off is worth at least $350. Stuart does not want me to go with Floyd, — told me before this affair that I should have a commission, — on returning yesterday he told me that I would have no difficulty in doing so now. I met Wyndham Robertson on the street to-day. He congratulated me on the success of the exploit, and said I was the hero, and that he intended to write an account of it for the papers, — made me promise to dine with him to-day. I send you some captured things, — the carpet was in an officer's tent. . . . There is no prospect of a battle here, — heavy reinforcements have been going to Jackson. . . . I got two splendid army pistols. Stuart's name is in every one's mouth now. I was in both cavalry charges, — they were magnificent. . . . I have been staying with General Stuart at his head-quarters. . . . The whole heavens were illuminated by the flames of the burning wagons, etc. of the Yankees. A good many ludicrous scenes I will narrate when I get home. Richmond in fine spirits, — everybody says it is the greatest feat of the war. I never enjoyed myself so much in my life. . . .

Headquarters Cavalry Brigade,

June 20, 1862.

Hon. Geo. W. Randolph,
  Secretary of War.

General :

Permit me to present to you John S. Mosby, who for months past has rendered time and again services of the most important and valuable nature, exposing himself regardless of danger, and, in my estimation, fairly won promotion.

I am anxious that he should get the Captaincy of a Company of Sharpshooters in my brigade, but the muster rolls have not yet been sent in.   I commend him to your notice.

Most respectfully, General,
Your obedient servant,
J. E. B. Stuart,
Brigadier General Commanding Cavalry.

# CHAPTER IX

## The Campaign Against Pope

Richmond, July 4, 1862.

My dearest Pauline:

I reached our wagon camp near Richmond about twelve o'clock Tuesday and as the battle [Malvern Hill] was raging below did not go to Richmond. I came up to get my horse shod. McClellan has retreated about thirty-five miles and is now under cover of his gun-boats on James River. . . . McClellan is badly whipped.

Richmond, July 7, 1862.

My dearest Pauline:

I came up to Richmond yesterday from our camp below. Our army has now fallen back near Richmond, as we could not attack McClellan under his gun boats, it was no use keeping our army so far off from supplies. . . . I have just returned from an expedition down James River where I succeeded, with half a dozen men, in breaking up an assemblage of negroes and Yankees. They were armed.

It is an open secret that in August, 1862, the disobedience of two Confederate generals saved

Pope's army in Virginia from ruin and nearly resulted in the capture of the Confederate Chief of Cavalry. But historians have been strangely silent about it. I had a part in the play, and I take more pleasure in telling about it now than I did when I was an actor in the great drama. In war there are lights mingled with shadows. In the retrospect we see a great deal of the comedy where once all seemed to be tragedy.

After the Seven Days' Battles around Richmond, that closed on July 1, several weeks of calm succeeded. McClellan had shifted his base from the Pamunkey to the James, and both armies rested for another collision. If McClellan had possessed the intuition of Grant, he would not have halted on the bank of the river, but would have crossed and seized the communications of the Confederate Capital. General John Pope had been called from the West to take command of an army in front of Washington. This army was organized mostly from fragments which Jackson had overlooked in the Shenandoah Valley. Pope came East with some reputation, but he soon lost it.

Pope opened his campaign in northern Virginia with a bombastic manifesto that, by an invidious comparison, gave offence to his own side and amusement to ours. He was, however, unjustly

criticised for declaring that his army should subsist on the country it occupied. That is a right as
old as war — to live on the enemy. I did the
same thing whenever I could. Pope declared that
in the West he had seen only the backs of his
enemies, and that he would look only to his front
and let his rear take care of itself. But he must
be acquitted of the charge, so often repeated, of
having said that his headquarters would be in the
saddle. I know that it is no use to deny it now —
it is a part of our mythology, and the people of
Virginia believe it as religiously as they do the
legend of Pocahontas. It is said that even so
grave a person as General Lee made humorous
remarks about this proclamation.

But what interested me most in this proclamation was the following :

I hear constantly of taking strong positions and
holding them, of lines of retreat and bases of supplies.
Let us dismiss such ideas, . . . let us study the probable lines of retreat of our opponents and leave our
own to take care of themselves. Let us look before
us and not behind.

At this time I was at cavalry headquarters, in
Hanover County, about ten miles from Richmond.
When I read what Pope said about looking only
to his front and letting his rear take care of itself,

I saw that the opportunity for which I had longed had come. He had opened a promising field for partisan warfare and had invited, or rather dared, anybody to take advantage of it. The cavalry at Richmond was doing nothing but picket duty, and "quiet to quick bosoms is a hell." So I asked Stuart for a dozen men to make the harvest where the laborers were few, and do for Pope what he would not do for himself, take care of his rear and communications for him. Stuart was, of course, well-disposed to me. He had spoken well of me in his report of his ride around McClellan on the Chickahominy, and General Lee had also mentioned me in his general order announcing it to the army.

I really thought that there was a chance to render effective service. I had served the first year of the war in a regiment of cavalry in the region which was now in Pope's department and had a general knowledge of the country. I was sure then — I am surer now — that I could make Pope pay as much attention to his rear as his front, and that I could compel him to detail most of his cavalry to guard his long line of communications, or turn his commissary department and rear over to me — which would have been perfectly satisfactory to me. There never was afterwards such a field for partisan war in Virginia. Breaking communications is the chief work for a partisan — it defeats plans and starts confusion by destroying supplies, thus diminishing the offensive strength of an army.

Judged in the light that is before us now, it looks strange that I was refused. Stuart told me that he was getting his cavalry ready for the active campaign soon to begin, but that he would give me a letter to Jackson, who, no doubt, would give me the men I wanted. I had to beg for the privilege of striking the enemy at a vulnerable point. If the detail had been given me, I would have started directly to cross the Rapidan to flank Pope, and my partisan war would have begun then.

I accepted the letter to Jackson — the best I could get — and with a club-footed companion, an exempt from military service, I started off. I was so anxious to be at work that I concluded to go by rail and arrange with Jackson for the cavalry to go with me. We spent the night with a farmer near Beaver Dam station on what is now the Chesapeake and Ohio Railroad. I sent my companion on to lead my horse to Jackson's headquarters and went to the depot. I laid down my pistols and haversack that had the letter to Jackson — the man leading my horse had scarcely gotten out of sight — when somebody exclaimed, "Here they are!" A regiment of Northern cavalry was not a hundred yards away, coming up at a trot. I ran, but they caught me and got my pistols and haversack. This capture apparently blasted my hopes, especially when I was sent to the Old Capitol Prison in Washington, but an exchange of prisoners was agreed upon the next day.

I was captured by a New York regiment — the Harris Cavalry. It had ridden all night to break the communications between Lee and Jackson. The men did not wait for my train, although I told them it could be taken with impunity. It was not true, but I suppose I was justified by the code of war. I was taken to General King's headquarters at Fredericksburg and very kindly treated. He let me write a letter to my family, which he sent through the lines. Some letters were captured at the depot. General King read one aloud — everybody laughed. It was from a Richmond girl to her country cousin. I remember four lines. I hope they won't shock people who read them now:

> "Jeff Davis is our President,
>     Lincoln is a fool.
> Jeff Davis rides a white horse,
>     Lincoln rides a mule."

A history of the Harris Cavalry says:

At six o'clock on the evening of July 19th the Harris Light was set in rapid motion almost directly south. By means of a forced march through the night, at gray dawn of morning we descended upon Beaver Dam depot on the Virginia Central, like so many ravenous wolves. During an affray we captured a young Confederate, who gave his name as Captain John S. Mosby. By his sprightly appearance and conversation he attracted considerable attention. He is slight but well formed; has a keen blue eye and a blond complexion, and displays no small amount of Southern bravado in his dress and manners. His gray plush hat is surmounted by a waving plume, which he tosses, as he speaks, in real Prussian style. He had a letter in his possession from General Stuart commending him to the kind regards of General Jackson.

Old Capitol Prison,

Washington, July 23, '62.

My dearest Pauline:

I wrote you from Falmouth [opposite Fredericksburg], announcing my capture by the enemy's cavalry at Beaver Dam. I was going up to see General Jackson for Stuart. I had a young man with me. I concluded to let him lead my horse and I would take the train and pay you a flying visit. I had just arrived at the depot, — had pulled off my arms and placed them in a storehouse and was sitting down outdoors waiting for a train, which was due in the course of an hour, — when the cavalry suddenly appeared and I had no time to escape. The Colonel and Captain treated me with the greatest courtesy. General King, before whom I was carried, ordered my arms to be restored to me. In my haversack was a letter from General Stuart introducing me to General Jackson. You need feel no uneasiness about me. . . . Colonel Davis, who captured me, offered to lend me Federal money. I thanked him, but declined.

I had been a prisoner about ten days when I was taken, with a good many prisoners, down the Potomac to Fortress Monroe. Here we waited four days for others to arrive, that we might go up the James River to the place of exchange. When we arrived at Hampton Roads, I saw a large number of transports with troops lying near. As a prisoner I kept up my habits as a scout and soon learned that they were Burnside's troops who had just come from North Carolina. If they were reinforcements for McClellan, it would indicate that he would advance again on Richmond from his new base on the James. On the other hand, if they sailed up the Chesapeake, it would show that they were going to join Pope, and that McClellan would be withdrawn from the peninsula.

This was the problem that I had to solve. It was

a pivotal point in the campaign. There were several officers of high rank among the prisoners, but I did not communicate my purpose to any one, for fear my secret work might leak out, with the result that we should be detained. I was, however, much surprised that none of them seemed to regard what was before their eyes as of any significance.

On the fourth day, several steamers with prisoners from their places of confinement in the North anchored near us, and I was told that we were to start that evening up the James River, to the point where the commissioners would meet for the exchange. During the day, I saw the transports with Burnside's troops weighing anchor and passing out by the fort. I had become pretty well acquainted with the captain of the steamer that brought us down from Washington, and found out that he was a Confederate in sympathy; so when he was going ashore for his orders, I asked him to find out where the transports were going.

When he returned, he whispered to me that Aquia Creek, on the Potomac, was the point. That settled it — McClellan's army would not advance, but would follow the transports northward.

I was feverish with excitement and anxiety to

carry the news to General Lee, but nobody suspected what I had discovered, nor did I hear any
comment on the movement of Burnside's troops.
I was so restless that I sat nearly all night on the
deck of the steamer, watching for the day star.

Early in the morning we arrived at the landing,
and I was the first to jump ashore. As I was in
a hurry, and afraid of being detained by some
formality in exchanging, I whispered to the Confederate Commissioner that I had important information for General Lee, and asked him to let
me go. He made no objection.

It was a hot day in August, and I set out alone
to walk twelve miles to headquarters. Some one
in Washington had given me a patent-leather
haversack and a five-dollar greenback. The latter
I had invested in lemons at Fortress Monroe,
for the blockade kept them out of Virginia.
After trudging several miles I was so exhausted
and footsore that I had to lie down by the roadside; but I held on to my lemons. A horseman
— one of Hampton's legion — came along, and
I told him how anxious I was to get to General
Lee. He proved a benefactor indeed, for he put
me on his horse, walked to his camp with me, got
another horse, and rode to General Lee's headquarters with me. I wish I knew his name, for

I have always thought his conduct was one of the most generous deeds of the war.

When we reached headquarters, I dismounted and told a staff officer, who was standing on the porch, that I had important information for General Lee and wished to see him. As I was roughly dressed and unkempt, no doubt the officer thought I was presumptuous to ask the privilege. In the imperious tone customary with staff officers, he said that I could not see the General. I protested that I must, but he would accept no explanation. So I turned to leave, but another officer, who had overheard what I had said, told me to wait. He went inside the house, but soon came out and told me to go inside. I did so and found myself in, what was then to me, the awful presence of the Commander-in-Chief.

We had never met before, but I was soon relieved of embarrassment; General Lee's kind, benevolent manner put me at ease. I found him looking over a map on the table. As quickly as I could, I told him that Burnside's troops had been sent to Pope. I then said that he did not know what confidence he could put in my report and told him my name and that I was on Stuart's ride around McClellan. "Oh," he said, "I remember."

After I had finished my story, he asked me a few questions. I remember very well that he inquired on what line I thought the next movement against Richmond would be made, and that I considered it a high compliment that he should ask my opinion on such an important matter. He then called one of his staff into the room and told him to have a courier ready to go to General Jackson. At that time Jackson was about eighty miles west of Richmond, on the railroad near Gordonsville, but ever since the affair at Beaver Dam, Lee had been afraid to trust the telegraph, and kept a relay line of couriers. As soon as Jackson got the news about Burnside, he hastened to strike Pope at Cedar Mountain before reinforcements could reach him.

Richmond, August 6, '62.

My dearest Pauline:

I arrived here yesterday evening. I came by flag of truce steamer, — landed twelve miles below Richmond and had to walk all the way up. My feet were so sore I could scarcely stand. As soon as I got here I went out to see General Lee, as I had a good deal of very important information to give him. . . . I brought information of vital importance.

The Comte de Paris said in his "History of the Civil War in America":

So long as Burnside and the fleet of transports which lay in readiness to ship his troops remained at the mouth of the James, whence they could proceed either to Harrison's Landing or to Aquia Creek, it was evident to Lee that the movement of the Federals had not yet been determined upon. Accordingly he sought with particular care for every item of intelligence calculated to enlighten him as to the design of his adversaries.

Finally, one evening, on the 4th or 5th of August, a small steamer bearing a flag of truce was seen coming up the James, passing the Confederate outposts and approaching Aiken's Landing, a place designated for the exchange of prisoners. In the midst of the soldiers, whose gray coats were worn out by long confinement, and the sick and wounded, to whom the thought of freedom restored both strength and health, an officer was making himself conspicuous by his extreme anxiety to land. His face was well known to every Virginian, and his name to all his companions in arms; it was the celebrated partisan, Colonel John Mosby.

His eagerness, which everybody attributed to his ardent temperament, was very natural, for he had news of the greatest importance to communicate to Lee. A few hours later he was at the headquarters of his chief, to whom he made known the fact that at the very moment when he was leaving Hampton Roads, that same morning, the whole of Burnside's corps was being embarked, and that its destination, as he knew positively, was Aquia Creek.

Lee lost no time in availing himself of this information, which chance had opportunely thrown into his hands.

When I rose to leave General Lee at this my first meeting with him, I opened my haversack and put a dozen lemons on the table. He said I had better give them to some of the sick and wounded in the hospitals; but I left them and bade him good-by. I had little expectation of ever seeing him again.

I went to see Stuart, who was still in Hanover, and then went home to get my horse. I reached the army again on August 17, just in time to meet Stuart who had come by rail from Richmond, leaving Fitz Lee to bring up the cavalry. By this time it was plain that McClellan was about to leave the peninsula, so that General Lee was concentrating on the Rapidan. Stuart had just had a conference with General Lee and had received his final instructions. He did not say what they were, but the coming event cast its shadow before. Stuart was to meet Fitz Lee at Verdiersville, and I went with him. I had no arms — I had lost my pistols when I was captured at Beaver Dam — but trusted to luck to get another pair.

On the way to meet Fitz Lee, we passed Longstreet's camp. The soldiers knew instinctively that a movement was on foot; they were cooking their rations for a march and singing "Annie Laurie." We reached the appointed rendezvous that night but found a deserted village. There were no signs of the cavalry, and Stuart was greatly disappointed and worried, for the operation, which had been planned for the next morning, depended on the cavalry. I did not then suspect how much depended on meeting the cavalry and how much was lost by its absence. It was the crucial point of the campaign.

A staff officer, Major Fitzhugh, went in search of Fitz Lee, and Stuart and I tied our horses and lay down to sleep on the porch of a house by the road. Before sunrise I was awakened by a young man, Gibson, who had just come with me, unarmed, from prison. He said that he heard the tramp of cavalry down the plank road; that it was probably Fitz Lee, but it might be Yankee cavalry. Although we were near the Rapidan, we thought we were inside of Longstreet's picket line, but I did not want to be caught napping again. So I awoke Stuart and told him what we had heard and that Gibson and I would ride down the road to see what was there. We soon saw a body of cavalry that had stopped at a house a few hundred yards away. A heavy fog made it impossible to distinguish friends from foes. But we were soon relieved of doubt — two cavalry-men saw us and rode forward. When they got in pistol range, they opened fire — that settled it. We knew they were not our friends. As Gibson and I had no arms, there was nothing for us to do but wheel and run — which we did — and used our spurs freely. The firing gave the alarm and saved Stuart. He mounted his horse, bare-headed, leaped a fence in the back yard, and got away. But he left his hat!

Before Gibson and I got to the house where we had slept, a Prussian on Stuart's staff dashed through the front gate and went down the road ahead of us as fast as his horse could carry him. We never overtook him. After the war he published a lot of fables in which he described an encounter he had with the Yankees that morning as more wonderful than the feat of St. George and the Dragon. Our ambition was to escape. We ran as fast as we could, but the Prussian ran faster. That was all the distinction he won.

Pope had advanced to the line of the Rapidan, with his army stretched across the Orange and Alexandria Railway, which was his line of supply. His forces were massed near the river. Lee, with

Jackson and Longstreet, was in Orange County, a few miles in his front. Our cavalry picketed the south bank of the river. As late as the seventeenth Pope did not know — and this was the evening before he retreated in such a hurry — that Lee had arrived with Longstreet. He thought Jackson was at Gordonsville, twenty miles south. Pope spoke of crossing the river and making a demonstration towards Richmond; he told Halleck "our position is strong and it will be very difficult to drive us from it." A worse position for an army could not have been selected for Pope by an enemy. He urged Halleck to let him cross the river and take the offensive, but the latter would not consent.

General Lee never again had such an opportunity to destroy an army. It would have been easy, on that day, to pass around under cover of Clarke's Mountain — that is on the south bank of the Rapidan — cross at the fords below, and strike Pope both in flank and rear at the same time. It was particularly so, as Pope had said he would look only to his front. The fact is, the railroad turns east at such an angle in Culpeper that, after crossing the river below Pope, Lee's army would have been nearer the Rappahannock bridge than Pope's army was. His railroad communications with Washington would have been seized, and reinforcements from McClellan cut off. According to Pope's dispatches of that day to Halleck, there was no sign of a movement to cross the Rapidan. He was anxious to attack Jackson. By an accident Pope was rudely awakened from his dream of security.

John C. Ropes, the historian, wrote:

Hence, when he saw him (Pope) quickly occupying the line of the Rapidan, Lee at once saw his opportunity. He ordered Longstreet and Jackson to cross the river at Raccoon and Somerville fords and to move on Culpeper Court House, while the cavalry of Stuart, crossing further to the east at Morton's Ford, was to make Rappahannock Station, destroying the bridge there and then turning to the left, form the right of Longstreet's corps. Pope would have been attacked in the rear and flank and his communications severed in the bargain. Doubtless, he would have made a strenuous fight, but he could hardly have escaped defeat, and defeat under such circumstances might well have been ruin. From this disaster fortune saved Pope through the capture of Stuart's staff officer.

Stuart had sent Major Fitzhugh to look for Fitz Lee, whose orders required him to be at Verdiersville the night of the seventeenth. The place is a few miles south of the Rapidan. Daybreak on the eighteenth was the time fixed for crossing the river. But Fitz Lee, as appears from Stuart's report, after leaving Hanover, instead of marching directly to the vicinity of Raccoon Ford, as he was ordered, changed his course and turned back to follow his wagons that had been sent by Louisa Court House for provisions. By this detour he was a day late in reaching his destination. The delay was fatal to General Lee's plan and saved Pope. General Lee would not make the movement without his cavalry, but Jackson wanted to go on without it. Major Fitzhugh, while looking for Fitz Lee, was captured on the night of the seventeenth by a body of cavalry that had been sent over the river on a scout. It was the same body that came so near getting us the next morning. They got Lee's letter to Stuart that disclosed his plan to cross on the morning of the eighteenth and flank Pope. The dispatch was sent in hot haste to headquarters and created a panic.

General Pope, in his report, spoke of the capture of this letter as the cause of his hasty and unpremeditated retreat. He said the cavalry expedition he sent out captured the Adjutant General of Stuart and was near capturing that officer himself. Among the papers taken from him was an autograph letter of General Lee to General Stuart "which made manifest the disposition and force of the enemy, and their destination to overwhelm the army and my command before it could be reinforced by any portion of the Army of the Potomac."

But Fitz Lee was not alone responsible for General Lee's failure to envelop Pope. General Longstreet said that, as the cavalry had not come up on the seventeenth, he ordered two regiments of Toombs's brigade to be sent to guard the Rapidan fords. Toombs had ridden from his headquarters to have dinner with a farmer. When the order came, his next in rank ordered the detail to be sent. When Toombs learned what had been done without asking him, he ordered the regiment back to their camp. So the fords were unguarded, and Pope's cavalry crossed without giving any alarm, captured Stuart's staff officer with General Lee's order, and saved Pope's army. Longstreet put Toombs under arrest, but Fitz Lee was not relieved of his command. In the midst of the battle of Manassas, a few days later, Toombs rode up to Longstreet and begged to lead his brigade. Longstreet relented, and Toombs led his men into battle. So it seemed that General Pope was saved by a comedy of errors. General Lee had to wait for his cavalry to come up, but when they came the opportunity was gone.

If Toombs had not withdrawn the picket from the Rapidan, the Union cavalry could not have crossed; if Fitz Lee had obeyed orders, even if the cavalry had crossed, they would have been caught. By this combination of errors, Pope got warning and lost no time in getting away.

I rode with Stuart to the signal station on Clarke's Mountain where we could see Pope's army retreating and his trains scudding back to the Rappahannock.

General George Gordon, who was with Pope, said: "Without delay the retreat began. By rail and along the roadways, in cars and in baggage wagons, from Mitchell's Station and Culpeper (Court House) vast stores of subsistence, forage, and ammunition streamed out for the left bank of the Rappahannock. . . . The Confederates were disappointed; many of them scolded bitterly. Rarely had a better opportunity offered for the destruction of an army."

Dabney, Jackson's staff officer and biographer, in an account of the campaign written when it was fresh in memory, said that the plan of the commander-in-chief was for the movement to begin at dawn on the eighteenth, but was defeated by dilatory subordinates, and that he overruled the eagerness of Jackson and postponed it until the twentieth. "It was then," he wrote, "most fortunate that Jackson was not in command."

A few days afterwards Stuart went on a raid around Pope. As he galloped by me, he said, "I am going after my hat." Sure enough, he captured Pope's headquarters wagons, with the hat and plume and full-dress uniform, besides his money chest. Stuart was now at least even with Pope.

Dranesville, September 5, '62.

My dearest Pauline:

Our arms have been crowned with a glorious victory [Second Battle of Manassas and Chantilly]. Our army is now marching on toward Leesburg, and we all suppose it will cross into Maryland. I have escaped unhurt, though I got my horse slightly shot in the shoulder and had a bullet through the top of my hat, which slightly grazed my head. . . . I have a very good Yankee horse, also two fine saddles and two pistols I captured. With one man I captured seven cavalry and two infantry.

[Colonel Mosby accompanied Stuart on the fall campaign which culminated in the battle of Antietam. Of this campaign Mosby noted two incidents as follows:

I rode just behind Jackson when he marched at the head of his columns through Frederick City, Md., in September, 1862, with his band playing "My Maryland." But I never heard the story of Barbara Frietchie shaking the Stars and Stripes in his face until I read Whittier's poem. I am sorry the story is a myth, for, as the poet tells it, the respect which the Confederates showed her was a great contrast with the treatment an order of a certain general required to be shown to a woman who by word, sign, or gesture should be disrespectful to the U. S. soldier or flag.

I only once saw Stonewall Jackson in battle. At Antietam I rode with Stuart by some batteries where Jackson was directing their fire on the flank of a column that was advancing against him, and I stopped a minute to look at the great soldier who was then transfigured with the joy of battle. In a quiet way he was giving orders. McClellan had sent three corps in succession against him — Hooker's, Mansfield's, and Sumner's — and each in turn was repulsed. While I was near him, the last onset was made, but Jackson held the same ground at sunset that he held in the morning.

I rode on and overtook Stuart, but the killed and wounded were strewn on the ground "like leaves of the forest when autumn hath blown", and I had to be careful not to ride over them. Whole ranks seemed to have been struck down by a volley. Although hundreds were lying all around me, my attention was in some way attracted to a wounded officer who was lying in an uncomfortable position and seemed to be suffering great agony. I dismounted, fixed him more comfortably, and rolled up a blanket on which he rested his head, and then got a canteen of water for him from the body of a dead soldier lying near him. As I passed a wounded soldier, I held the canteen toward him so that he could drink. He said, "No, take it to my Colonel, he is the best man in the world." [This was a speech worthy of Sidney, the model of chivalry.]

# CHAPTER X

## FIRST EXPLOITS AS A PARTISAN

Near Culpeper, November 24, '62.

My dearest Pauline:

I have been on another big scout since I wrote. General Stuart sent me with nine men down to reconnoitre in the vicinity of Manassas. There was a Yankee regiment there. We came upon ten. We charged them with a yell. The Yankees ran and stampeded their whole regiment, thinking all of Stuart's cavalry were on them. . . . Jackson is in the Valley. I will join Stuart in a day or so. I stayed behind on a scout and have just returned.

Tuesday, December 2nd, '62.

My dearest Pauline:

I am now with the 1st regiment near Spottsylvania Court House, but it is uncertain how long we will be here. Jackson has arrived. I reckon you saw the account in the Richmond papers of my scout and stampede of the Yankees near Manassas. . . . Several of my old company have been shot lately.

December 9.

My dearest Pauline :

Enclosed I send a copy of my report to General Stuart of my scout down to Manassas when with nine men I stampeded two or three thousand Yankees. I see the Richmond papers give Col. Rosser [Fifth Va. Cavalry] the credit of it. He had nothing to do with it, and was not in twenty-five miles of there. . . . General Lee sent me a message expressing his gratification at my success. I believe I have already written of my trip around McClellan at Catlett's Station, when I saw him leave his army at the time he was superseded by Burnside. The courier by whom I sent the dispatch to General Stuart announcing it passed five Yankee cavalry in the road. Not dreaming there was a rebel army in their rear, they passed on by him, merely saying "Good morning." We did not go in disguise, as spies, but in Confederate uniform and with our arms. Had a slip from a Northern paper, which I lost, giving an account of a squad of rebel cavalry having been seen that day in their rear. Aaron thinks himself quite a hero, though he does not want to come again in such disagreeable proximity to a bombshell.

I want you to send me some books to read. Send Plutarch, Macaulay's "History" and "Essays," "Encyclopedia of Anecdotes," Scott's Works, Shakespeare, Byron, Scott's Poems, Hazlitt's "Life of Napoleon," — if you can get me a copy of "My Novel," send it, also "Memoirs of an Irish Gentleman" (for Fount Beattie), "Corinne," and "Sketch Book."

The situation is now changed. McClellan and Pope have been driven from Virginia, and Burnside has met a bloody repulse at Fredericksburg. The two hostile armies are in winter quarters on the Rappahannock, and the pickets on opposite banks have declared a truce and are swapping coffee and tobacco. Occasionally a band on the Northern bank plays a favorite Southern air and soon, in response, the strain of the Star Spangled Banner comes from our side. The cavalry is not used for picketing and has been sent to the rear to be more convenient to forage.

To relieve the monotony Stuart resolved to take his cavalry on a Christmas raid to Dumfries on Burnside's line of communication with Washington. A good many wagons with supplies were captured, and we chased a cavalry regiment through their own camp and got all their good things. There is a dispatch in the history of the telegraph in the war from an operator in Fairfax, which says, "The 17th Pennsylvania Cavalry just passed here, furiously charging to the rear."

When he returned, Stuart let me stay behind a few days with six men to operate on the enemy's outposts. He was so satisfied with our success that he let me have fifteen men to return and begin my partisan life in northern Virginia —

which closed with the war. That was the origin of my battalion. On January 24, 1863, we crossed the Rappahannock and immediately began operations in a country which Joe Johnston had abandoned a year before. It[1] looked as though I was leading a forlorn hope, but I was never discouraged. In general my purpose was to threaten and harass the enemy on the border and in this way compel him to withdraw troops

[1] [A Confederate newspaper described the Mosby of this time as follows. "His figure is slight, muscular, supple, and vigorous; his eye is keen, penetrating, and ever on the alert."

Another description of his appearance during the war:—

"He was thin, wiry, and I should say about five feet nine or ten inches in height. A slight stoop in the back was not ungraceful. His chin was carried well forward; his lips were thin, and wore a somewhat satirical smile; the eyes, under the brown felt hat, were keen, sparkling, and roved curiously from side to side. He wore a gray uniform, with no arms but two revolvers, — the sabre was no favorite with him. His voice was low, and a smile was often on his lips. He rarely sat still ten minutes. Such was his appearance at that time. No one would have been struck with anything noticeable in him except his eyes. These flashed at times, in a way which might have induced the opinion that there was something in the man, if it only had an opportunity to come out. . . . The face of this person is tanned, beardless, youthful looking, and pleasant. He has white regular teeth, which his habitual smile reveals. His piercing eyes flash out from beneath his brown hat, with its golden cord; and he reins his horse with the ease of a practised rider. A plain soldier, low and slight of stature, ready to talk, to laugh, to ride, to oblige you in any way, — such was Mosby in outward appearance. Nature had given no sign but the restless, roving, flashing eyes, that there was much worth considering beneath. The commonplace exterior of the partisan concealed one of the most active, daring, restless minds of an epoch fruitful in such. . . . His activity of mind and body, — call it, if you choose, restless, eternal love of movement, was something wonderful."]

from his front to guard the line of the Potomac and Washington. This would greatly diminish his offensive power. General "Joe" Hooker said before a committee of Congress that we created so much anxiety that the planks on the bridge across the Potomac were taken up every night to prevent us from carrying off the Government.

Recruits came to us from inside the enemy's lines, and they brought valuable information. Then, I had picketed for some time in Fairfax the year before and had acquired considerable local knowledge. The troops attached to the defence of Washington, south of the Potomac, were distributed in winter quarters through Fairfax County and extended in an arc of a circle from the upper to the lower Potomac. The headquarters of General Stoughton, who commanded them, were at the Court House. In a day or so after I arrived in Loudoun, we began operations on the outposts of Fairfax. The weak points were generally selected for attack. Up to that time the pickets had passed a quiet life in their camps or dozing on the picket posts, but now they were kept under arms and awake all night by a foe who generally assailed them where he was least expected. At first they accounted for our attacks on the theory that the farmers and cripples they saw in the

daytime ploughing their fields and taking care of
their flocks collected in bands at night, raided
their camps, and dispersed at daybreak. But
when they went around at night searching the
homes for these invisible foes, they generally
found the old farmers in bed, and when they
returned to camp, they often found that we had
paid them a visit in their absence. The farmers
could prove an alibi.

An English officer, Colonel Percy Wyndham, a
soldier of fortune who had been with Garibaldi in
Italy, commanded the cavalry brigade and had
charge of the outposts. He was familiar with the
old rules of the schools, but he soon learned that
they were out of date, and his experience in war
had not taught him how to counteract the forays
and surprises that kept his men in the saddle all
the time. The loss of sleep is irritating to anybody
and, in his vexation at being struck by and striking
at an invisible foe, he sent me a message calling
me a horse thief. I did not deny it, but retorted
that all the horses I had stolen had riders, and
that the riders had sabres, carbines, and pistols.
There was a new regiment in his brigade that was
armed only with sabres and obsolete carbines.
When we attacked them with revolvers, they were
really defenceless. So I sent him word through

a citizen that the men of that regiment were not worth capturing, and he must give them six-shooters. We used neither carbines nor sabres, but all the men carried a pair of Colt pistols. We did not pay for them but the U. S. Government did.

Fauquier Co., Va.,[1]

Feb. 4, '63.

. . . I have been in this neighborhood over a week. Have had a gay time with the Yankees. Have captured twenty-eight Yankee cavalry, twenty-nine horses. . . . I have 15 men with me . . . Fount Beattie was captured by the Yankees, — his horse fell with him. There were over two hundred Yankees. The Yankees set what they thought was a sure trap to catch me a few nights ago. I went into it and brought the whole of them off, — killed and captured twelve.

During the first days as a partisan, there were more comic than tragic elements in the drama of war. About that time occurred an episode that would have furnished Goldsmith with all the elements of a comedy. It was a dark night with a deep snow on the ground, but the weather was warm and the snow soft. I received information that there was a pretty strong outpost on a cer-

---

[1] A letter to Mrs. Mosby.

tain road in Fairfax, and I was determined to capture it. Of course, the fine horses were a great attraction. Several citizens had joined my command and acted as guides. Near the post lived a man named Ben Hatton, who traded in the camps and was pretty familiar with them. So, around midnight, we stopped at his house about a mile from the picket post, and he told us that he had been there that evening — I suppose to get coffee and sugar. Ben was impressed as a guide to conduct us to the rear of the enemy. When we reached that point, I determined to dismount, leave our horses, and attack on foot. Ben had fully discharged his duty and, as he was a non-combatant, I did not want to expose him to unnecessary danger. The blazing fire by which the Yankees were sleeping and dreaming was sufficient for us. So the horses were tied to the trees, and two of my men — Jimmie, an Irishman, and another we called "Coonskin", from the cap he wore — stayed with Ben as a guard over the horses.

Walking on the soft snow, we made no noise and were soon upon the picket post. The surprise was complete, and they had no time to prepare for resistance. We were soon ready to start back with our prisoners and their horses, when a fire opened in our rear, where we had left the guard and horses. The best scheme seemed to be to mount the Yankee horses, dash back, and recapture our own. Some of the men were left to bring the prisoners on foot. A considerable fusillade had been going on where the guard had been left, but it ceased suddenly when we got near the place. To our surprise we found the horses all standing hitched to the trees, and Ben Hatton lying in a snowbank, shot through the thigh. But neither "Coonskin" nor Jimmie was there. Ben told us that the Yankees had come up and attacked them; that was all he knew, except that they had shot him. He did not know whether the Yankees had carried off Jimmie and "Coonskin", or whether they had carried off the Yankees, nor could he explain why the horses were there. That was a mystery nobody could solve. We mounted; Ben was lifted on a horse behind one of the men, and we started off with all the horses and prisoners. By that time the Yankees from the camp had been attracted by the firing. They came up and opened fire at us at long range, but let us leave without venturing to come near. Ben was bleeding profusely, but it was only a flesh wound. We left him at home, curled up in bed, with his wife to nurse him. He was too near the enemy's lines for me to give him surgical assistance, and he was afraid to ask any from the camps. The wound would have betrayed him to the Yankees had they known about it, and Ben would have been hung as a spy! He was certainly innocent, for he had no desire to serve any one but himself. His wound healed, but the only reward he got was the glory of shedding his blood for his country.

As soon as it was daylight, a strong body of cavalry was sent up the turnpike to catch us — they might as well have been chasing a herd of antelope. We had several hours' start of them, and they returned to camp in the evening, leading a lot of broken-down horses. The pursuit had done them more harm than our attack.

We brought off "Coonskin's" and Jimmie's horses, but we couldn't invent a theory to solve the mystery. Two days afterwards, "Coonskin" and Jimmie reappeared. They had trudged twenty-five miles through the snow, arriving within a few hours of each other, but from opposite directions, and each thought he was the only survivor. Neither knew that Ben Hatton had been shot, and each said that he had fought until they saw a body of Yankees riding down upon them. Then they ran off and left the horses in the belief that we were all prisoners.

By a comparison of their statements, I found out that the facts were about as follows. To keep themselves warm, the three had walked around among the trees and got separated. "Coonskin" saw Ben and Jimmie moving in the shadows and took them for Yankees. He opened on them and drew blood at the first fire. Ben yelled and fell. Jimmie took it for granted that "Coonskin" was a Yankee and returned his fire. So they were firing at each other and dodging among the trees when they saw us coming up at a gallop. As we had left them on foot, they could not understand how we could come back on horseback. So after wounding Ben Hatton and shooting at each other, they had run away from us.

A few days after this adventure, Fate compelled me to act a part in a comedy which appeared to be heroic, but for which I was really entitled to as little credit as Ben Hatton was for getting shot. From our rendezvous along the base of the Blue Ridge we continued to make night attacks on the outposts near Washington. So it was determined in Washington to put a stop to what were called our depredations, and an expedition was sent against us into Loudoun. Middleburg, a village, was supposed to be our headquarters, and it was thought that by surrounding it at night the marauders could be caught. The complaints against us did not recognize the fact that there are two parties of equal rights in a war. The error men make is in judging conduct in war by the standards of peace. I confess my theory of war was severely practical — one not acquired by reading the Waverley novels — but we observed the ethics of the code of war. Strategy is only another name for deception and can be practised by any commander. The enemy complained that we did not fight fair; the same complaint was made by the Austrians against Napoleon.

A Major Gilmer was sent with 200 men in expectation of extirpating my gang — as they called us. He might have done more if he had taken less whiskey along. But the weather was cold! Before daybreak he had invested the town and made his headquarters in the hotel where he had learned that I slept. I had never been in the village except to pass through. The orders were to arrest every man that could be found, and when his searching parties reported to him, they had a lot of old men whom they had pulled out of bed. Gilmer pretended to think these were the parties that had captured his pickets and patrols and stampeded his camps. If so, when he saw the old cripples on crutches, he ought to have been ashamed. He made free use of his bottle and ordered a soldier to drill the old men and make them mark time just to keep warm. As he had made a night march of twenty-five miles, he concluded to carry the prisoners to his camp as prizes of war. So each graybeard had to ride double with a trooper. There were also a number of colored women whom he invited, or who asked, to go with him. They had children, but the major was a good-natured man. So each woman was mounted behind a trooper — and the trooper took her baby in his arms. With such encumbrances, sabres and pistols would be of little use, if an attack was made. When they started, the column looked more like a procession of Canterbury Pilgrims than cavalry.

News came to me that the enemy were at Middleburg, so, with seventeen men, I started that way, hoping to catch some stragglers. But when we got to the village, we heard that they had gone, and we entered at a gallop. Women and children came out to greet us — the men had all been carried off as prisoners. The tears and lamentations of the scene aroused all our sentiments of chivalry, and we went in pursuit. With five or six men I rode in advance at a gallop and directed the others to follow more slowly. I had expected that

Major Gilmer might halt at Aldie, a village about five miles ahead, but when we got there a citizen told us that he passed on through. Just as we were ascending to the top of a hill on the outskirts of the village, two cavalrymen suddenly met us. We captured them and sent them to the rear, supposing they were videttes of Gilmer's command. Orders were sent to the men behind to hurry up. Just then I saw two cavalrymen in blue on the pike. No others were visible, so with my squad I started at a gallop to capture them. But when we got halfway down the hill we discovered a considerable body — it turned out to be a squadron — of cavalry that had dismounted. Their horses were hitched to a fence, and they were feeding at a mill. I tried to stop, but my horse was high-mettled and ran at full speed, entirely beyond my control. But the cavalry at the mill were taken absolutely by surprise by the irruption ; their videttes had not fired, and they were as much shocked as if we had dropped from the sky. They never waited to see how many of us there were. A panic seized them. Without stopping to bridle their horses or to fight on foot, they scattered in all directions. Some hid in the mill ; others ran to Bull Run Mountain near by.

Just as we got to the mill, I saw another body

of cavalry ahead of me on the pike, gazing in bewildered astonishment at the sight. To save myself, I jumped off my horse and my men stopped, but fortunately the mounted party in front of me saw those I had left behind coming to my relief, so they wheeled and started full speed down the pike. We then went back to the mill and went to work. Many had hidden like rats, and as the mill was running, they came near being ground up. The first man that was pulled out was covered with flour; we thought he was the miller. I still believed that the force was Major Gilmer's rearguard. All the prisoners were sent back, and with one man I rode down the pike to look for my horse. But I never got him — he chased the Yankees twenty-five miles to their camp.

I have said that in this affair I got the reputation of a hero; really I never claimed it, but gave my horse all the credit for the stampede. Now comes the funniest part of the story. Major Gilmer had left camp about midnight. The next morning a squadron of the First Vermont Cavalry, which was in camp a few miles away from him, was sent up the pike on Gilmer's track. Major Gilmer did not know they were coming. When he got a mile below Aldie, he saw in front a body of cavalry coming to meet him. He thought they were my men who had cut him off from his camp. He happened to be at the point where the historic Braddock road, along which young George Washington marched to the Monongahela, crossed the turnpike. As Major Gilmer was in search of us, it is hard to see why he was seized with a panic when he thought he saw us. He made no effort to find out whether the force in front was friend or foe, but wheeled and turned off at full speed from the pike. He seemed to think the chances were all against him. There had been a snow and a thaw, and his horses sank to their knees in mud at every jump. But the panic grew, the farther he went, and he soon saw that he had to leave some of his horses sticking in the road. He concluded now that he would do like the mariner in a storm — jettison his cargo. So the old men were dropped first; next the negro women, and the troopers were told to leave the babies in the arms of their mothers. The Braddock road had seen one such wreck and retreat a hundred years before.

I had not gone far before I met the old men coming back, and they told me of their ludicrous adventure and thanked me for their rescue. They did not know that the Vermont cavalry was entitled to all the glory for getting up the stampede, and that they owed me nothing. In the hurry to find my horse, I had asked the prisoners no questions and thought that we had caught a rear-guard. Among the prisoners were two captains. One was exchanged in time to be at Gettysburg, where he was killed. Major Gilmer was tried for cowardice and drunkenness and was dismissed from the army. Colonel Johnstone, who put him under arrest when he got back, said in his report, "The horses returned exhausted from being run at full speed for miles." They were running from the Vermont cavalry.

Among the accessions to my command was a young man named John Underwood, whom I found in the Fairfax forests. I was largely in-debted to his skill and intelligence for whatever success I had in the beginning of my partisan life. He was killed a few months afterward, and I never found his like again, for he was equally at home threading his way through the pines or leading a charge. Why he had stayed at home and let me discover him is a mystery to me. Soon after the affair in which Ben Hatton became an involuntary hero, Underwood reported another outpost in Fairfax which was in an exposed position. I could hardly believe it; the Yankees seemed to have learned nothing by experience. It looked much as though they had been put there just to be caught, or as a snare to catch me, so I resolved to give them another lesson in the art of war.

We had a suspicion that it was a trap set for us and that there was danger, but war is not an exact science, and it is necessary to take some chances. I determined to try my luck in the daytime — they would not be expecting us, as all our attacks had been at night. Underwood led us by paths through the woods to their rear until we arrived at a road leading from their camp to the picket. A vidette was there, but he was caught before he could fire and give the alarm. It was then plain that the surprise we had planned would be complete. A few hundred yards away the boys in blue were lounging around an old saw-mill, with their horses tied to a fence. It was past twelve o'clock, there was bright sunlight, and there was snow on the ground. They were Vermont cavalry, and they had no suspicion that an enemy was near. It was just the hour for their relief to come, and as we came from the direction of their camp, they thought, when they saw us, that we were friends.

When we got within a hundred yards of them, an order to charge was given. They were panic-stricken — they had no time to untie their horses and mount — and took refuge in the loft of the mill. I was afraid that if they had time to recover from their shock, they would try to hold the mill against us with their carbines until reinforcements came. There was a pile of dry timber and shavings on the floor, and the men were ordered, in a loud voice, to set the mill on fire. When we reached the head of the stairs, the Yankees surrendered. They were defenceless against the fire, and it was not their ambition to be cremated alive. Not a shot was fired. After all were mounted, we saw four finely-equipped horses tied in front of a near-by house. My men at once rushed to find the riders. They found a table spread with lunch. One of the men ran up-stairs where it was pitch dark; he called but got no answer. As a pistol shot could do no harm, he fired into the darkness. The flash of the pistol in his face caused one of the Yankees to move, and he descended through the ceiling. He had stepped on the lathing and caved it in. After he was brushed off, we saw that he was a major. The three other officers who were with him came out of their holes and surrendered. My men appropriated the lunch by right of war.

Just as the Yankee relief appeared, John Underwood was sent off with the prisoners. We kept a rear guard behind, but no attack was made on it, although one was threatened. Major Taggart, in his report of the affair, censured the officer in command, as he had a larger force than ours and made no attempt either to capture us or to recapture the prisoners. Major Wells, the major we captured, was exchanged in time to be at Gettysburg where he was promoted to be a brigadier-general.

There was more than one ludicrous affair that day. A man named Janney lived at the place and was permitted to conduct a store since he was inside the picket lines. He had just brought a barrel of molasses from Washington to retail to his neighbors, and he was in the act of filling a jug for a customer when he heard the yell of my men as they rushed at the picket post. As the place was occupied by the Unionists, he could not have been more surprised if a comet had struck it. Janney did not aspire to be a hero, so he ran away as fast as his heels could carry him, and, if possible, the molasses ran even faster. When he ventured to return to the store, he found the molasses spread all over the floor, and not a drop in the barrel.

After we were a safe distance away, the privates were paroled and allowed to go home, and the officers gave their paroles to report to Fitz Lee in Culpeper. Jake, a Hungarian, was sent with them as an escort. Now Jake had served under Kossuth and did not put much trust in paroles. They spent the night with a farmer and, when the officers went to bed, Jake volunteered to take their boots to the kitchen to be shined. As long as he had their boots, Jake had no fear of their going off in the snow. When he got back, Jake told me, with a chuckle, of the trick he had played on the Yankees.

War is not always grim-visaged, and incidents occur which provoke laughter in the midst of danger. In the Shenandoah Valley, a Yankee cavalry regiment went into camp one evening. One of the men rode off to a house to get something to eat and called a colored woman to the door. He wanted to feel safe, so he asked if anybody was there. "Nobody but Mosby," she replied.

"Is *Mosby* here?" he asked.

"Yes," she said.

He dashed off to the camp and reported that Mosby was in a house near by. Orders were given to saddle and mount quickly, and they marched to the house and surrounded it. The Colonel entered and asked the woman if Mosby was there.

"Yes," she answered.

"Where is he?" demanded the Colonel.

"There he is," she said, pointing to a negro baby in the cradle.

One night I was with one man near the enemy's camps in Fairfax. We were passing a house, when I heard a dog bark and somebody call, "Come here, Mosby." So I turned, rode up to the house, and asked the man if he had called me.

"No," he said, "I was calling *Mosby*. I wanted him to stop barking."

So I have had the distinction of having had negro babies and dogs named after me.

# CHAPTER XI

## The Raid on Fairfax

WHEN we captured prisoners, it was my custom to examine them apart, and in this way, together with information gained from citizens, I obtained a pretty accurate knowledge of conditions in the enemy's camps. After a few weeks of partisan life, I meditated a more daring enterprise than any I had attempted and fortunately received aid from an unexpected quarter. A deserter from the Fifth New York Cavalry, named Ames, came to me. He was a sergeant in his regiment and came in his full uniform. I never cared to inquire what his grievance was. The account he gave me of the distribution of troops and the gaps in the picket lines coincided with what I knew and tended to prepossess me in his favor. But my men were suspicious of his good faith and rather thought that he had been sent to decoy me with a plausible story. At first I did not give him my full confidence but accepted him on probation.

Ames stood all tests, and until he was killed I never had a more faithful follower.

Ames had come out from his camp on foot and proposed to me that he would go back into his camp and return on horseback, if I would accept him. A recruit, Walter Frankland, had just come to me, but he was not mounted. With my approval he agreed to go with Ames to get a horse. They trudged on foot through the snow — twenty-five miles — entered the camp of the Fifth New York Cavalry at night, unchallenged, and rode out on fine horses.

At the same time, with a number of men, I started on a raid in another direction and had rather a ludicrous adventure. We met an old country doctor, Doctor Drake, in a desolate condition, walking home through mud and snow. He told us he had been going the rounds, visiting his patients, when he had met a body of cavalry that was not far ahead of us. They had robbed him of his horse, saddlebags, and medicine. As the blockade had made medicine scarce, this was a severe loss to the community. We spurred on to overtake the raiders and intercepted a party that had stopped at a house. They exceeded us in numbers, but they were more intent on saving themselves and their plunder than on fighting.

They scampered away, with us close behind them. Soon they got to Horsepen Run, which was booming from the melting snows, and the foremost man plunged into the stream. He got a good ducking and was glad to get back a prisoner. His companions did not try to swim after him but preferred to surrender. They were loaded with silver spoons and valuables they had taken, but the chief prize was old Doctor Drake's saddlebags, which they had not opened. The silver was returned to the owners, and the prisoners were sent to Richmond.

When we got back to Middleburg, we found Ames and Frankland with their fine horses. I now determined to give Ames one more trial and so took him with me on a raid to Fairfax. But he went as a combatant without arms. I had found out that there was a picket post at a certain crossroads and went to attack it in a rain on a dark night, when there was snow on the ground. As only a raccoon could be supposed to travel on such a night, I knew the pickets would feel safe and would be sound asleep, so that a single shot would create a panic. We stopped to inquire of a farmer the location of the post. He had been there during the day and said that there were 100 men who slept in a schoolhouse. He asked me how many men I had, and I replied, "Seventeen, but they will think there are a hundred." They could not count in the dark. We made no attempt to flank the picket to prevent his giving the alarm, but we went straight down the road. One of the men, Joe Nelson, was sent ahead to catch the vidette. When the vidette saw Joe, he fired at him and started at full speed to the reserve; but we were on his heels and got there almost as soon as he did. The yells of my men resounded through the pines, and the Yankees all fled and left their horses hitched to the trees. As it was very dark, we could not catch many of the men, but we got all their horses. My attention was attracted to Ames, who struck a man with a carbine he got from him — I don't remember why. We were soon back on the pike and trotting towards the Blue Ridge with the prisoners and horses. When it was daylight, Wyndham mounted his squadrons and started full speed after us. After going twenty miles, he returned to camp with half of his men leading broken-down horses. Wyndham was soon afterwards relieved, but not before we had raided his headquarters and carried off his staff, his horses, and his uniform.

I now determined to execute my scheme to capture both General Stoughton and Wyndham at their headquarters. Ames, about whose fidelity there was no longer any question, knew where their headquarters were, and the place was familiar to me as I had been in camp there. I also knew, both from Ames and the prisoners, where the gaps in the lines were at night. The safety of the enterprise lay in its novelty; nothing of the kind had been done before.

On the evening of March 8, 1863, in obedience to orders, twenty-nine men met me at Dover, in Loudoun County. None knew my objective point, but I told Ames after we started. I remember that I got dinner that day with Colonel Chancellor, who lived near Dover. Just as I was about to mount my horse, as I was leaving, I said to him, "I shall mount the stars to-night or sink lower than plummet ever sounded." I did not rise as high as the stars, but I did not sink. I then had no reputation to lose, even if I failed, and I remembered the motto, "Adventures to the adventurous."

The weather conditions favored my success. There was a melting snow on the ground, a mist, and, about dark, a drizzling rain. Our starting point was about twenty-five miles from Fairfax Court House. It was pitch dark when we got near the cavalry pickets at Chantilly — five or six miles from the Court House. At Centreville, three miles away on the Warrenton pike and seven miles from the Court House, were several thousand troops. Our problem was to pass between them and Wyndham's cavalry without giving the alarm. Ames knew where there was a break in the picket lines between Chantilly and Centreville, and he led us through this without a vidette seeing us. After passing the outpost the chief point in the game was won. I think no man with me, except Ames, realized that we were inside the enemy's lines. But the enemy felt secure and was as ignorant as my men. The plan had been to reach the Court House by midnight so as to get out of the lines before daybreak, but the column got broken in the dark and the two parts travelled around in a circle for an hour looking for each other. After we closed up, we started off and struck the pike between Centreville and the Court House. But we turned off into the woods when we got within two or three miles of the village, as Wyndham's cavalry camps were on the pike. We entered the village from the direction of the railroad station. There were a few sentinels about the town, but it was so dark that they could not distinguish us from their own people. Squads were detailed to go around to the officers' quarters and to the stables for the horses. The court-house yard was the rendezvous where all were to report. As our great desire was to capture Wyndham, Ames was sent with a party to the house in which he knew Wyndham had his quarters. But fortune was in Wyndham's favor that time, for that evening he had gone to Washington by train. But Ames got his two staff officers, his horses, and his uniform. One of the officers, Captain Barker, had been Ames's captain. Ames brought him to me and seemed to take great pride in introducing him to me as his former captain.

When the squads were starting around to gather prisoners and horses, Joe Nelson brought me a soldier who said he was a guard at General Stoughton's headquarters. Joe had also pulled the telegraph operator out of his tent; the wires had been cut. With five or six men I rode to the house, now the Episcopal rectory, where the commanding general was. We dismounted and knocked loudly at the door. Soon a window above was opened, and some one asked who was there. I answered, "Fifth New York Cavalry with a dispatch for General Stoughton." The door was opened and a staff officer, Lieutenant Prentiss, was before me. I took hold of his nightshirt, whispered my name in his ear, and told him to take me to General Stoughton's room. Resistance was useless, and he obeyed. A light was quickly struck, and on the bed we saw the general sleeping as soundly as the Turk when Marco Bozzaris waked him up. There was no time for ceremony, so I drew up the bedclothes, pulled up the general's shirt, and gave him a spank on his bare back, and told him to get up. As his staff officer was standing by me, Stoughton did not realize the situation and thought that somebody was taking a rude familiarity with him. He asked in an indignant tone what all this meant. I told him that he was a prisoner, and that he must get up quickly and dress.

I then asked him if he had ever heard of "Mosby", and he said he had.

"I am Mosby," I said. "Stuart's cavalry has possession of the Court House; be quick and dress."

He then asked whether Fitz Lee was there. I said he was, and he asked me to take him to Fitz Lee — they had been together at West Point. Two days afterwards I did deliver him to Fitz Lee at Culpeper Court House. My motive in trying to deceive Stoughton was to deprive him of all hope of escape and to induce him to dress

quickly. We were in a critical situation, surrounded by the camps of several thousand troops
with several hundred in the town. If there had
been any concert between them, they could
easily have driven us out; but not a shot was
fired although we stayed there over an hour. As
soon as it was known that we were there, each
man hid and took care of himself. Stoughton had
the reputation of being a brave soldier, but a fop.
He dressed before a looking-glass as carefully as
Sardanapalus did when he went into battle. He
forgot his watch and left it on the bureau, but one
of my men, Frank Williams, took it and gave it
to him. Two men had been left to guard our
horses when we went into the house. There
were several tents for couriers in the yard, and
Stoughton's horses and couriers were ready to
go with us, when we came out with the general
and his staff.

When we reached the rendezvous at the court-
yard, I found all the squads waiting for us with
their prisoners and horses. There were three
times as many prisoners as my men, and each
was mounted and leading a horse. To deceive
the enemy and baffle pursuit, the cavalcade
started off in one direction and, soon after it got
out of town, turned in another. We flanked the

cavalry camps, and were soon on the pike between them and Centreville. As there were several thousand troops in that town, it was not thought possible that we would go that way to get out of the lines, so the cavalry, when it started in pursuit, went in an opposite direction. Lieutenant Prentiss and a good many prisoners who started with us escaped in the dark, and we lost a great many of the horses.

A ludicrous incident occurred when we were leaving Fairfax. A window was raised, and a voice inquired, in an authoritative tone, what that cavalry was doing in the street. He was answered by a loud laugh from my men, which was notice to him that we were not his friends. I ordered several men to dismount and capture him. They burst through the front door, but the man's wife met them in the hall and held her ground like a lioness to give her husband time to escape. He was Colonel Johnstone, who was in command of the cavalry brigade during Wyndham's absence. He got out through the back door in his night clothes and barefooted, and hid in the garden. He spent some time there, as he did not know when we left, and his wife could not find him.

Our safety depended on our getting out of the

Union lines before daybreak. We struck the pike about four miles from Centreville; the danger I then apprehended was pursuit by the cavalry, which was in camp behind us. When we got near the pike, I halted the column to close up. Some of my men were riding in the rear, and some on the flanks to prevent the prisoners from escaping. I left a sergeant, Hunter, in command and rode forward to reconnoitre. As no enemy was in front, I called to Hunter to come on and directed him to go forward at a trot and to hold Stoughton's bridle reins under all circumstances. Stoughton no doubt appreciated my interest in him.

With Joe Nelson I remained some distance behind. We stopped frequently to listen for the hoofbeats of cavalry in pursuit, but no sounds could be heard save the hooting of owls. My heart beat higher with hope every minute; it was the crisis of my fortunes.

Soon the camp fires on the heights around Centreville were in sight; my plan was to flank the position and pass between that place and the camps at Chantilly. But we soon saw that Hunter had halted, and I galloped forward to find out the cause. I saw a fire on the side of the road about a hundred yards ahead of us —

evidently a picket post. So I rode forward to reconnoitre, but nobody was by the fire, and the picket was gone. We were now half a mile from Centreville, and the dawn was just breaking. It had been the practice to place a picket on our road every evening and withdraw it early in the morning. The officer in charge concluded that, as it was near daylight, there was no danger in the air, and he had returned to camp and left the fire burning. That was the very thing I wanted him to do. I called Hunter to come on, and we passed the picket fire and then turned off to go around the forts at Centreville. I rode some distance ahead of the column. The camps were quiet; there was no sign of alarm; the telegraph wires had been cut, and no news had come about our exploit at the Court House. We could see the cannon bristling through the redoubts and hear the sentinel on the parapet call to us to halt. But no attention was paid to him, and he did not fire to give the alarm. No doubt he thought that we were a body of their own cavalry going out on a scout.

But soon there was a shot behind me and, turning around, I saw Captain Barker dashing towards a redoubt and Jake, the Hungarian, close behind him and about to give him another shot, when Barker's horse tumbled and fell on him in a ditch. We soon got them out and moved on. All this happened in sight of the sentinels and in gunshot of their camps.

After we had passed the forts and reached Cub Run, a new danger was before us. The stream was swift and booming from the melting snow, and our choice was to swim, or to turn back. In full view behind us were the white tents of the enemy and the forts, and we were within cannon range. Without halting a moment, I plunged into the stream, and my horse swam to the other bank. Stoughton followed and was next to me. As he came up the bank, shivering from his cold morning bath, he said, "Captain, this is the first rough treatment I have to complain of."

Fortunately not a man or a horse was lost. When all were over, I knew there was no danger behind us, and that we were as safe as Tam O'Shanter thought he would be if he crossed the bridge of Doon ahead of the witches. I now left Hunter in charge of the column, and with one of my men, George Slater, galloped on to see what was ahead of us. I thought a force might have been sent to intercept us on the pike we had left that runs through Centreville. I did not know that Colonel Johnstone, with his cavalry, had gone in the opposite direction.

We crossed Bull Run at Sudley Ford and were soon on the historic battlefield. From the heights of Groveton we could see that the road was clear to Centreville, and that there was no pursuit. Hunter soon appeared in sight. The sun had just risen, and in the rapture of the moment I said to Slater, "George, that is the sun of Austerlitz!" I knew that I had drawn a prize in the lottery of life, and my emotion was natural and should be pardoned.

I could not but feel deep pity for Stoughton when he looked back at Centreville and saw that there was no chance of his rescue. Without any fault of his own, Stoughton's career as a soldier was blasted.

There is an anecdote told of Mr. Lincoln that, when it was reported to him that Stoughton had been captured, he remarked, with characteristic humor, that he did not mind so much the loss of a general — for he could make another in five minutes — but he hated to lose the horses.

Slater and I remained for some time behind as a rear guard and overtook Hunter, who had gone on in command, at Warrenton. We found that the whole population had turned out and were giving my men an ovation. Stoughton and the officers had breakfast with a citizen named Beckham. The general had been a classmate at West Point with Beckham's son, now a Confederate artillery officer, and had spent a vacation with him at his home. Stoughton now renewed his acquaintance with his family.

We soon remounted and moved on south. After crossing the Rappahannock, the men and prisoners were put in charge of Dick Moran with orders to meet me near Culpeper Court House the next morning, while, with Hunter and the officers on parole, I went on in advance and spent the night near Brandy. As I had been in the saddle for thirty-six hours, I retired to rest as soon as we had eaten supper. The next morning there was a cold rain, but after breakfast we started for General Fitz Lee's headquarters.

When we arrived at our destination, we hitched our horses in the front yard and went into the house, where we found Fitz Lee writing at a table before a log fire. We were cold and wet. In the First Virginia Cavalry, Fitz Lee and I had been well acquainted. He was very polite to his old classmate and to the officers, when I introduced them, but he treated me with indifference, did not ask me to take a seat by the fire, nor seem impressed by what I had done.

As a matter of historical fact, it is well known

that this episode created a sensation in both armies, but the reception I received convinced me that I was not a welcome person at those headquarters. So, bidding the prisoners good-by and bowing to Fitz Lee, Hunter and I rode off in the rain to the telegraph office to send a report to Stuart, who had his headquarters at Fredericksburg. The operator told me that Stuart was on his way to Culpeper and would arrive on the train that evening, but he sent the dispatch and it was delivered to Stuart. I met him at the depot and can never forget the joy his generous heart showed when he met me. That was a sufficient reward. Major John Pelham was with Stuart. This was the last time I ever saw Pelham, for he was killed a week afterwards. As we walked off, Stuart handed me a commission as captain from Governor John Letcher. It gave me rank with the Virginia troops, but, as there were no such troops, it was a blank form, and I regarded it as a mockery. Stuart remarked that he thought the Confederate War Department would recognize it. I said, in rather an abrupt and indignant tone, "I want no recognition." I meant official recognition. I did not affect to be indifferent to public praise. Such a man is either too good or too bad to live in this world. Stuart published a general order announcing the capture of Stoughton and had it printed, giving me fifty copies. That satisfied me, and I soon returned to my field of operations and again began war on the Potomac.

Headquarters Cavalry Division,

March 12, 1863.

General Orders.

Captain John S. Mosby has for a long time attracted the attention of his generals by his boldness, skill, and success, so signally displayed in his numerous forays upon the invaders of his native soil.

None know his daring enterprise and dashing heroism better than those foul invaders, those strangers themselves to such noble traits.

His last brilliant exploit — the capture of Brigadier-General Stoughton, U. S. A., two captains, and thirty other prisoners, together with their arms, equipments, and fifty-eight horses — justifies this recognition in General Orders. This feat, unparalleled in the war, was performed in the midst of the enemy's troops, at Fairfax Court House, without loss or injury.

The gallant band of Captain Mosby shares his glory, as they did the danger of this enterprise, and are worthy of such a leader.

J. E. B. Stuart,
Major-General Commanding.

In a few days Fitz Lee wrote me that the detail of men I had from his brigade must return to their regiment. This attempt to deprive me of a command met with no favor from Stuart. I sent him Fitz Lee's letter, and he issued an order for them to stay until he recalled them. When the armies began to move in April, the men went back, but a considerable number of recruits had joined me, and what the enemy called my "depredations" continued. In the published records of the war is the following letter from General Robert E. Lee to President Davis, informing him of another success I had soon after the capture of Stoughton :

Headquarters, Army of Northern Virginia,

March 21, 1863.

You will, I know, be gratified to learn by the enclosed despatch that the appointment conferred a few days since on Captain John S. Mosby was not unworthily bestowed. The point where he struck the enemy is north of Fairfax Court-House, near the Potomac, and far within the lines of the enemy. I wish I could receive his appointment (as major) or some official notification of it, that I might announce it to him.

R. E. Lee, General.

A dispatch from Lieutenant O'Connor, Provost-Marshal at Fairfax Court House, sent to Washington an hour after we left the village, confirms the account I have given of our visit. He said :

Captain Mosby, with his command, entered this town this morning at 2 A.M. They captured my patrols, horses, etc. They took Brigadier-General Stoughton and horses, and all his men detached from his brigade. They took every horse that could be found, public or private; and the commanding officer of the post, Colonel Johnstone, of the Fifth New York Cavalry, made his escape from them in a nude state by accident. They searched for me in every direction, but being on the Vienna road visiting outposts, I made my escape.

And in a report the next day to Colonel Wyndham, O'Connor said:

On the night of the 8th instant, say about two or half past two A.M., Captain Mosby with his command entered the village by an easterly direction. They proceeded to Colonel Wyndham's headquarters and took all his horses and movable property with them. In the meantime another party of them entered the residence of Colonel Johnstone and searched the house for him. He had on their entering the town heard of their movements and believing them to be the patrol, went out to halt them, but soon found out his mistake. He then entered the house again — he being in a nude state — and got out backwards — they in hot pursuit of him. In the meantime others were dispatched to all quarters where officers were lodged, taking them out of their beds, together with the telegraph operator and assistant.

Stoughton was soon exchanged but did not return to the army. The circumstances of his capture wrecked him as a soldier. He was accused of negligence in allowing the gap in the picket line, through which we entered. The commander of the cavalry pickets, Colonel Wyndham, was responsible for that, and there is a letter in the War Records from Stoughton to Wyndham, calling his attention to it. I allowed Stoughton to write a letter, which I sent through a citizen, to Wyndham, in which he reproached him for the management of his outposts. But Wyndham ought not to be blamed, because he did not anticipate an event that had no precedent. He did exercise reasonable vigilance. In this life we can only prepare for what is probable, not for every contingency.

Colonel Johnstone lost his clothes and lay hidden for some time before he heard we were gone. O'Connor said he appeared in the state of Adam before the fall. But he could not survive the ridicule he incurred by it and disappeared.

Near Piedmont, Va., March 18, 1863.

General :

Yesterday I attacked a body of the enemy's cavalry at Herndon Station, in Fairfax County, completely routing them. I brought off twenty-five prisoners — a major, one captain, two lieutenants, and twenty-one men, all their arms, twenty-six horses, and equipments. One, severely wounded, was left on the ground. The enemy pursued me in force, but were checked by my rear-guard and gave up the pursuit. My loss was nothing.

The enemy have moved their cavalry from Germantown back of Fairfax Court House on the Alexandria pike.

In this affair my officers and men behaved splendidly.

(Signed)    Jno. S. Mosby.

(Indorsement)
Maj.-Gen. J. E. B. Stuart.


Headquarters of the Army of Northern Virginia,

March 21, 1863.

Respectfully forwarded for the information of the department and as evidence of the merit and continued success of Captain Mosby.

R. E. Lee,<br>General.


[This Dranesville affair led to the following interesting correspondence after the war. It is of special value in illustrating the feelings of his enemies — the men who actually fought with him — towards Mosby.

Washington, Vt., December 19, 1910.

Col. John S. Mosby,
   Washington, D. C.

Dear Colonel and Friend :

You will be surprised to receive a letter from me, one you know so little, but will remember. In noticing to-day the item of the enclosed clipping [Mosby's comment on President Taft's appointment of a Confederate soldier (White) to be Chief Justice of the Supreme Court] I could not resist the privilege of writing to you, as I believe now I am the only surviving one of the four officers — Major Wells, Capt. Schofield, Lieut. Watson, and myself — you captured at Herndon Station, near Dranesville, Va., St. Patrick's day, March 17, 1863, and with us the picket post of twenty-one men. Your treatment and [that of] your men to us on that occasion has always been gladly remembered by us all — in every respect courteous. And you kindly gave us our horses to ride from Upperville to Culpeper Court House, which was an act of the highest type of a man, and should bury deep forever the name of a "guerrilla" and substitute "to picket line a bad disturber." . . .

Most sincerely and cordially yours,
                    Lieut. P. C. J. Cheney.

Burlington, Vt., December 28, 1910.

Dear Col. Mosby :

The enclosed letter from Lieut. P. C. J. Cheney, of Washington, Vt., explains itself.

During the war for the Union he was a first lieutenant in the First Vermont Cavalry, and was captured by you at Herndon Station on the 17th of March,
1863. Lieut. Cheney was one of the bravest and
best officers in the regiment, and was dangerously
wounded in the charge made by the Company in front
of Round Top (Gettysburg) on the afternoon of July 3,
1863.

. . . I had the pleasure of meeting you at the
inauguration of President McKinley, at which time
I was adjutant of Vermont, and presented you to Hon.
Josiah Grout, then Governor of this state, who at the
Miskel Farm fight between the First Vermont Cavalry
and yourself was most dangerously wounded. . . .
You were kind enough to say that the First Vermont
Cavalry was one of the very best regiments you had
met in action. . . .

Yours very truly,

T. S. Peck.

General Stahel described the Miskel Farm affair in his report of April 2, 1863, as follows:

It appears that on the evening of the 31st ultimo,
Major Taggart, at Union Church two miles above
Peach Grove, received information that Mosby, with
about sixty-five men, was near Dranesville. He
immediately dispatched Capt. Flint, with 150 men of
the First Vermont, to rout or capture Mosby and his
force. . . . Turning to the right they followed up the
Broad Run to a place marked J. Meskel [sic]. Here

at a house, they came upon Mosby, who was completely surprised and wholly unprepared for an attack from our forces.  Had a proper disposition been made of our troops, Mosby could not, by any possible means, have escaped.  It seems that around this house was a high board fence and stone wall, between which and the road was also another fence and ordinary farm gate.  Capt. Flint took his men through the gate, and, at a distance from the house, fired a volley at Mosby and his men, who were assembled about the house, — doing but slight damage to them.  He then ordered a sabre charge, which was also ineffective, on account of the fence which intervened.  Mosby waited until the men were checked by the fence, and then opened the gate of the barnyard, where his men were collected, saddling and bridling their horses, and opened fire upon them, killing and wounding several.  The men became panic-stricken, and fled precipitately through this gate, through which to make their escape.  The opening was small; they got wedged together, and a fearful confusion followed; while Mosby's men followed them up, and poured into the crowd a severe fire.  Here, while endeavoring to rally his men, Capt. Flint was killed, and Lieut. Grout, of the same Company, mortally wounded (will probably die to-day).

Mosby, who had not had time to mount his horse, personally threw open the barnyard gate and ordered his men to charge through it, which they did with a terrific yell.]

Headquarters Army of Northern Virginia,

March 23, 1863.

Capt. J. S. Mosby,

Captain:

You will perceive from the copy of the order herewith enclosed that the President has appointed you captain of partisan rangers. The general commanding directs me to say that it is desired that you proceed at once to organize your company, with the understanding that it is to be placed on a footing with all the troops of the line, and to be mustered unconditionally in the Confederate service for and during the war. Though you are to be its captain, the men will have the privilege of electing the lieutenants so soon as its members reach the legal standard. You will report your progress from time to time, and when the requisite number of men are enrolled, an officer will be designated to muster the company into the service.

(Signed)   W. W. Taylor, A. A. G.

[Mosby's report to General Stuart]

Fauquier County, Va., April 7, 1863.

General:

I have the honor to submit the following report of the operations of the cavalry since rendering my last report. On Monday, March 16, I proceeded down the Little River pike to capture two outposts of the enemy, each numbering 60 or 70 men. I did not succeed in gaining their rear as I had expected, and only captured 4 or 5 videttes. It being late in the evening, and our horses very much jaded, I concluded to return. I had gone not over a mile back when we saw a large body of enemy's cavalry, which, according to their own reports, numbered 200 men, rapidly pursuing. I feigned a retreat, desiring to draw them off from their camps. At a point where the enemy had blockaded the road with fallen trees, I formed to receive them, for with my knowledge of the Yankee character I knew they would imagine themselves fallen into an ambuscade. When they had come within 100 yards of me I ordered a charge, to which my men responded with a vim that swept everything before them. The Yankees broke when we got in 75 yards of them; and it was more of a chase than a fight for 4 or 5 miles. We killed 5, wounded a considerable number, and brought off 1 lieutenant and 35 men prisoners. I did not have over 50 men with me, some having gone back with the prisoners and others having gone on ahead, when we started back, not anticipating any pursuit. On Monday, March 31, I went down in the direction of Dranesville to capture several strong outposts in the vicinity of that place. On reaching there I discovered that they had fallen back about 10 miles down the Alexandria pike. I then returned 6 or 8 miles back and stopped about 10 o'clock at night at a point about 2 miles from the pike. Early the next morning one of my men, whom I had left over on the Leesburg pike, came dashing in, and announced the rapid approach of the enemy. But he had scarcely given us the information when the enemy appeared a few hundred yards off, coming up at a gallop. At this time our horses were eating; all had their bridles off, and some even their saddles — they were all tied in a barnyard.

Throwing open the gate I ordered a counter-charge, to which my men promptly responded. The Yankees never dreaming of our assuming the offensive, terrified at the yells of the men as they dashed on, broke and fled in every direction. We drove them in confusion seven or eight miles down the pike. We left on the field nine of them killed — among them a captain and lieutenant — and about fifteen too badly wounded for removal; in this lot two lieutenants. We brought off 82 prisoners, many of these also wounded. I have since visited the scene of the fight. The enemy sent up a flag of truce for their dead and wounded, but many of them being severely wounded, they established a hospital on the ground. The surgeon who attended them informs me that a great number of those who escaped were wounded. The force of the enemy was six companies of the First Vermont Cavalry, one of their oldest and best regiments, and the prisoners inform me that they had every available man with them. There were certainly not less than 200; the prisoners say it was more than that. I had about 65 men in this affair. In addition to the prisoners, we took all their arms and about 100 horses and equipments. Privates Hart, Hurst, Keyes, and Davis were wounded. The latter has since died. Both on this and several other occasions they have borne themselves with conspicuous gallantry. In addition to those mentioned above I desire to place on record the names of several others, whose promptitude and boldness in closing in with the enemy contributed much to the success of the fight. They are Lieutenant Chapman (late of Dixie Artillery), Sergt. Hunter and Privates Wellington and Harry Hatcher, Turner, Wild, Sowers, Ames, and Sibert. There are many others, I have no doubt, deserving of honorable mention, but the above are only those who came under my personal observation. I confess that on this occasion I had not taken sufficient precautions to guard against surprise. It was 10 at night when I reached the place where the fight came off on the succeeding day. We had ridden through snow and mud upwards of 40 miles, and both men and horses were nearly broken down; besides, the enemy had fallen back a distance of about 18 miles.

(Signed)   John S. Mosby,
Captain Commanding.

Maj.-Gen. J. E. B. Stuart.

[Indorsements]

Headquarters Cavalry Division,

April 11, 1863.

Respectfully forwarded, as in perfect keeping with his other brilliant achievements. Recommended for promotion.

J. E. B. Stuart,
Major-General.

Headquarters Army Northern Virginia,

April 13, 1863.

Respectfully forwarded for the information of the Department. Telegraphic reports already sent in.

R. E. Lee,
General.

April 22, 1863.

Adjutant-General :

Nominate as major if it has not already been done.

J. A. S. (Seddon).

[Report of General Stahel]

Fairfax C. H., May 5, 1863.

. . . On the third of May, between 8 and 9 A.M., Mosby with his band of guerrillas, together with a portion of the Black Horse Cavalry and a portion of a North Carolina regiment, came suddenly through the woods upon 50 of our men of the First Virginia Cavalry, who were in camp feeding their horses, just having returned from a scout, the remainder of that regiment being out in a different direction to scout the country on the right of the Warrenton and Alexandria Railroad and toward the Rappahannock.

Our men being surprised and completely surrounded, rallied in a house close at hand and where a sharp fight ensued. Our men defended themselves as long as their ammunition lasted, notwithstanding the rebels built a large fire about the house, of hay and straw and brushwood. The flames reached the house and their ammunition being entirely expended they were obliged to surrender. At this juncture a portion of the Fifth Regiment New York Cavalry which was posted in the rear some distance from the First Virginia Cavalry came to their rescue, making a brilliant charge, which resulted in the complete annihilation of Mosby's command and recaptured our men and property. Our men pursued the rebels in every direction, killing and wounding a large number, and had our horses been in better condition and not tired out by the service of the last few days, Mosby nor a single one of his men would have escaped.

The rebel loss was very heavy, their killed being strewn along the road. . . . [One man was killed and about twenty wounded.]

[Telegram, Stahel to Heintzelman]

May 30, 1863.

We had a hard fight with Mosby this morning, who had artillery, — the same which was used to destroy the train of cars. We whipped him like the devil, and took his artillery. My forces are still pursuing him.

[Mosby's report to General Stuart]

June 6, 1863.

Last Saturday morning I captured a train of twelve cars on the Virginia and Alexandria Railroad loaded with supplies for the troops above. The cars were fired and entirely consumed. . . . Having destroyed the train, I proceeded some distance back, when I recognized the enemy in a strong force immediately in my front. One shell which exploded in their ranks sufficed to put them to flight. After going about a mile further, the enemy were reported pursuing. Their advance was again checked by a shot from the howitzer. In this way we skirmished for several miles, until seeing the approach of their overwhelming numbers and the impossibility of getting off the gun, I resolved to make them pay for it as dearly as possible. Taking a good position on a hill commanding the road we awaited their onset. They came up quite gallantly, not in dispersed order, but in columns of fours, crowded in a narrow lane. At eighty yards we opened on them with grape and following this up with a charge of cavalry, we drove them half a mile back in confusion. Twice again did they rally and as often were sent reeling back. At last our ammunition became exhausted, and we were forced to abandon the gun. We did not then abandon it without a struggle, and a fierce hand to hand combat ensued in which, though overpowered by numbers, many of the enemy were made to bite the dust. In this affair I had only 48 men — the forces of the enemy were five regiments of cavalry. My loss, one killed — Captain Hoskins, a British officer who fell when gallantly fighting, — four wounded. It is with pleasure I recommend to your attention the heroic conduct of Lieutenant Chapman and Privates Mountjoy and Beattie, who stood by their gun until surrounded by the enemy.

Middleburg, Va., June 10, 1863.

General:

I left our point of rendezvous yesterday for the purpose of making a night attack on two cavalry companies of the enemy on the Maryland shore. Had I succeeded in crossing the river at night, as I expected, I would have had no difficulty in capturing them; but unfortunately, my guide mistook the road and, instead of crossing by 11 o'clock at night, I did not get over until after daylight. The enemy (between 80 and 100 strong), being apprised of my movement, were formed to receive me. A charge was ordered, the shock of which the enemy could not resist; and they were driven several miles in confusion, with the loss of seven killed, and 17 prisoners; also 20 odd horses or more. We burned their tents, stores, camp equipage, etc. I regret the loss of two brave officers killed — Capt. Brawner and Lieut. Whitescarver. I also had one man wounded.

(Signed) John S. Mosby,
Major of Partisan Rangers.

Maj.-Gen. J. E. B. Stuart.
[Indorsement]

June 15, 1863.

Respectfully forwarded. In consideration of his brilliant services, I hope the President will promote Maj. Mosby.

J. E. B. Stuart,
Major General.

[Extracts from Stuart's Report of the Gettysburg
Campaign]

Maj. Mosby, with his usual daring, penetrated the
enemy's lines and caught a staff-officer of Gen. Hooker
— bearer of despatches to Gen. Pleasanton, commanding United States cavalry near Aldie. These despatches disclosed the fact that Hooker was looking to
Aldie with solicitude, and that Pleasanton, with infantry and cavalry, occupied the place; and that a
reconnaissance in force of cavalry was meditated toward
Warrenton and Culpeper. I immediately despatched
to Gen. Hampton, who was coming by way of Warrenton from the direction of Beverly Ford, this intelligence, and directed him to meet this advance at Warrenton. The captured despatches also gave the entire
number of divisions, from which we could estimate
the approximate strength of the enemy's army. I
therefore concluded in no event to attack with cavalry
alone the enemy at Aldie. . . . Hampton met the
enemy's advance toward Culpeper and Warrenton,
and drove him back without difficulty — a heavy
storm and night intervening to aid the enemy's retreat.

I resumed my own position now, at Rector's cross
roads, and being in constant communication with the
commanding general, had scouts busily employed
watching and reporting the enemy's movements, and
reporting the same to the commanding general. In
this difficult search the fearless and indefatigable
Maj. Mosby was particularly efficient. His information was always accurate and reliable.

# CHAPTER XII

## STUART AND THE GETTYSBURG CAMPAIGN

AFTER Chancellorsville, the armies resumed their positions on the Rappahannock. A brilliant but barren victory had been won, and the pickets on the opposite banks of the river again began to trade in coffee and tobacco. With the years of hardship and danger, war had not lost all of its romance, and the soldiers observed in their intercourse the courtesies of combatants as strictly as did the Crusaders.

General Lee now determined to cross the Potomac and make a strategic offensive. His main object was really to create a diversion and conduct a great foraging expedition into Pennsylvania for the relief of Virginia and his fasting army — the South was almost exhausted. The movement would temporarily draw the enemy from Virginia, but he did not hope to dictate a peace north of the Potomac, nor could he have expected to maintain his army there without a line of communication and base of supply.

When Lee crossed the Potomac, he had no objective point. His army was now organized with three corps, under Longstreet, Ewell, and A. P. Hill — Stonewall Jackson had crossed the Great River. Stuart was his Chief of Cavalry. Early in June the movement that terminated in the unexpected encounter at Gettysburg began from Fredericksburg up the river. Previously the cavalry corps had been sent in advance to Culpeper County to prevent the enemy's cavalry from crossing the Rappahannock and to get the benefit of the grazing ground. Lee followed with Longstreet and Ewell. A. P. Hill's corps was left behind to amuse Hooker. Lee wanted to conceal his march so that he could cross the Blue Ridge and surprise Milroy in the Shenandoah Valley. Hooker's man in the balloon discovered that some camp grounds had been abandoned, so a reconnaissance was ordered to find out what it meant. But the force met with such resistance that Hooker concluded that Lee's whole army was there.

To relieve the Administration of anxiety about invasion, Hooker telegraphed to Washington what the reconnoitring force reported — just what Lee wanted him to do. The impression was confirmed by pretended deserters, who said they belonged to reinforcements that had just come to Lee. Deception is the ethics of war.

On June 8, at Brandy Station in Culpeper County, there was a review of the cavalry. The spectators little imagined that the squadrons which appeared in the grand parade before the Commander-in-Chief would be in deadly combat on the same ground the next day —

"Rider and horse — friend, foe — in one red burial blent."

Hooker knew that the Confederate cavalry was there and thought it was assembled for a *raid* across the Potomac. So he sent his cavalry corps up the river to intercept it. On June 6 he wrote Halleck: "As the accumulation of the heavy rebel force of cavalry about Culpeper may mean mischief, I am determined, if practicable, to break it up in its incipiency. I shall send all my cavalry against them, stiffened by about 3000 infantry."

Buford's division had already reached the railroad. He was instructed: "On arriving at Bealeton, should you find yourself with sufficient force, you will drive the enemy out of his camps near Culpeper Court House across the Rapidan, destroying the bridges at that point." The Rapidan is a tributary of the Rappahannock.

Hooker's instructions to Pleasanton show that his object was not to get information, but to prevent a cavalry raid across the Potomac. But, to cover up his defeat, Pleasanton afterwards claimed that he was only making a *reconnaissance*. A reconnaissance is made to discover the position and strength of an enemy. A sufficient force is applied to compel him to display himself, and, when that is done, the object is accomplished and the attacking force retires. No matter whether Pleasanton was making a real attack, or a reconnaissance, his expedition was a failure. If he had discovered the presence of Lee, with Longstreet and Ewell, he would have reported it to Hooker. He had been instructed that he would be absent four or five days, and to take along five days' rations, with pack mules and tents for the officers. Such preparations do not indicate that he was expected to cross the Rappahannock in the morning and recross in the evening.

Stuart knew that the enemy's camps were over the river, and that their outposts were near. Confederate pickets lined the river with grand guards in support. On June 9, at daylight, the enemy began crossing at Beverly's and Kelly's fords — several miles apart, above and below the railroad bridge. The plan was for the two divisions to unite at Brandy — four miles away — and then move on six miles to the Court House where the camps of Stuart's cavalry corps were supposed to be. The Unionists did not expect to meet anything near the river except pickets. Their error was in thinking the Confederate camps were ten miles away, and that there would be no collision in force before the columns united. The fact was that Stuart's headquarters were between Brandy and the river and near the camps of two brigades. Another brigade, Jones's, was a mile and a half from Beverly's Ford, where Buford's division crossed. Each of Pleasanton's divisions was supported by a brigade of infantry.

Captain Grimsley's company was picketing at the bridge. Before daybreak a vidette informed him that he could hear troops crossing the railroad. The captain put his ear to the ground and, hearing the click of the artillery wheels passing over the iron rails, sent a courier with the information to Jones. Captain Gibson's company gallantly resisted the crossing at the ford. The leading regiment was the Eighth New York Cavalry under the command of a Mississippian, "Grimes" Davis. He had hardly reached the southern bank before he fell.

The camps were aroused by the firing at the

fords, and there was saddling and mounting in hot haste. The Seventh Virginia Cavalry was the grand guard, and it is said that many rode into the fight bareback and without their boots. For some unexplained reason Jones's artillery was between his camps and the pickets on the river. As a general rule, it was in the wrong place, but on this occasion it happened to be in the right place. On account of the scarcity of grain, the horses had been turned out to graze, and there would have been no time to harness and hitch them before the enemy reached the camp. The Yankees were driving a body of Confederate cavalry back and just emerging through the woods, when some of the men ran a gun into the road, by hand, and opened fire on the column. The troops halted; the delay was fatal, and the guns were saved.

As there was no precedent in war for an artillery camp so near an outpost Pleasanton naturally concluded that the Confederates knew he was coming and had prepared a masked battery to receive him; that he had run into an ambuscade. War is not a science, but an art. Pleasanton was surprised and halted — and lost. That he had miscalculated the resistance he would meet at the ford may be inferred from the dispatch he sent

Hooker at 7.40 A.M., "The enemy is in strong cavalry force here. We had a severe fight. They were aware of our movement and prepared."

To prepare Halleck for a surprise after he had promised so much, Hooker telegraphed him, "Pleasanton reports that after an encounter with the rebel cavalry over the Beverly ford he has not been able to make head against it."

At 2.30 P.M., as he had made no progress, Pleasanton telegraphed back, "I will recross this P.M." And so ended his expedition on which he had started to the Rapidan, on his so-called reconnaissance.

When the firing was first heard at the fords, Stuart sent Robertson's brigade below, towards Kelly's, to hold Gregg's division in check on that road, and with Hampton's brigade went at a gallop to meet the force at Beverly's ford. Buford's division would soon have been driven over the river, but the news came that Gregg's division was in his rear. At first Stuart would not believe this, but in some way Robertson had allowed Gregg to pass him unobserved on another road. So, leaving W. H. F. Lee's brigade, which had just come up, on Buford's flank to hold him in check, Stuart turned and went to meet Gregg with Hampton's and Jones's brigades.

On the field around Brandy there was now the greatest mounted combat of the war — probably of any war. Gregg was driven back over the river, leaving behind him three guns and six battle flags. Buford and Pleasanton followed him back to their camps. Pleasanton had repeated the Austrian manœuvre at Rivoli of having a double line of operations, and Stuart had done just what Bonaparte did there, when he was attacked in front and on his flanks and nearly surrounded — struck and defeated the columns in succession before they united.

Stuart's great credit is the manner in which he screened the movements of Lee and got information of the enemy. Referring to this operation in his work on Cavalry, General Bernhardi said:

> The American War of Secession showed in a surprising manner what could be done in this respect. Stuart's screening of the left wheel of the Confederate army, after the battle of Chancellorsville, for instance, was a masterpiece, and the reconnaissance carried out by Mosby's scouts during the same period was equally brilliant.

Early in the morning after Brandy, June 10, Ewell started to cross the Blue Ridge into the Shenandoah Valley. On June 13, Milroy, at Winchester, who had relied on Hooker to warn him of the approach of an enemy from that direction, found himself surrounded. Pleasanton had not discovered that Lee, with two army corps, was in Culpeper; and Hooker thought that the whole of Lee's army was still on his front on the lower Rappahannock. There was so little suspicion of the impending blow in the Valley that on June 12 Hooker invited President Lincoln to come down and witness some practice with an incendiary shell. Lincoln accepted, but afterwards, instead of going, sent Hooker this dispatch, "Do you think it possible that 15,000 of Ewell's men can be at Winchester?"

At first Hooker would not believe it, but he soon struck his tents and started to keep between Lee and Washington. To Schenck, at Baltimore, Lincoln, with characteristic humor, said, "Get Milroy from Winchester to Harper's Ferry, if possible. He will be gobbled up, if he is not already past salvation."

After capturing the most of Milroy's force, Ewell moved on and crossed the Potomac on June 15. Lee, with Longstreet and A. P. Hill, followed him to the Valley and halted a week, while Stuart's cavalry moved east of the ridge as a curtain to conceal the operation. The hostile armies marched in concentric circles, Lee having the initiative. When Lee moved, Hooker also moved so as always to cover Washington. Of course Lee must have expected that Hooker would maintain the same relative position and follow him after he had crossed the Potomac. The right of Hooker's army now rested on the river, where he had laid pontoons for crossing. Stuart was on his front to watch and report his movements to Lee. On June 15, Ewell, having crossed into Maryland, had sent his cavalry on to forage in Pennsylvania. At that time General Lee seems to have been undecided as to a plan of campaign, except to subsist on the enemy and draw him out of Virginia. On the nineteenth Lee wrote Ewell, who was about Hagerstown, that "should we be able to detain General Hooker's army from following you, you would be able to accomplish as much unmolested as the whole army could with General Hooker in its front. If your advance causes Hooker to cross the Potomac, or separate his army in any way, Longstreet can follow you."

So Lee's crossing the Potomac was contingent on Hooker's following Ewell. All that Ewell then had to do was to collect supplies, for he met no resistance. Lee said nothing about A. P. Hill crossing the river. This letter proves that he then had no objective, but a biographer, Long — his military secretary — asserted, in the face of the record, that Gettysburg was the objective when Lee started from Fredericksburg, and that he was surprised on hearing that Hooker had followed him over the Potomac. There was not a soldier or even a wagon-master in the army who was surprised to hear it. Lee seemed to be content to hold Hooker in Virginia, while Ewell was living on the Pennsylvania farmers, and his sending another corps across the Potomac depended on Hooker. So, when Lee concluded to follow Ewell, he must have been sure that Hooker was ready to cross.

On June 22, Lee ordered Ewell, at Hagerstown, to move into Pennsylvania, and told him that whether the rest of the army followed or not depended on the supplies he found in the country. Lee said :

I also directed General Stuart, should the enemy have so far retired from his front as to permit of the departure of a portion of the cavalry, to march with three brigades across the Potomac and place himself on your right and in communication with you, keep you advised of the movements of the enemy, and assist in collecting supplies for the army.

Lee told Ewell that his best course would be towards the Susquehanna, that he must be guided by circumstances, and, possibly, he might take Harrisburg. Lee had already written Stuart to leave two brigades to watch the enemy and take care of the flank and rear of the army and, with three brigades, to join Ewell, who was marching to the Susquehanna. Stuart was instructed to act as Ewell's Chief of Cavalry and to "collect all the supplies you can for the use of the army." As no enemy was following Ewell, and as there was none on his front, except militia, Stuart would really have had nothing but foraging to do, if he had joined Ewell, who, by this time, was sending back long trains loaded with provisions.

Longstreet was then in Virginia, near Ashby's Gap in the Blue Ridge, and this order was sent through him and was subject to his approval. Longstreet forwarded the order, and in a letter to Stuart said:

He speaks of your leaving *via* Hopewell Gap [in Bull Run Mountain] and passing by the rear of the enemy. I think that your passage of the Potomac by our rear [west of the Blue Ridge at Shepherdstown] at the present moment will, in a measure, disclose our plans. You had better not leave us, therefore, unless you take the proposed route in the rear of the enemy.

Longstreet wrote to General Lee, on the twenty-second:

Yours of 4 o'clock this afternoon is received. I have forwarded your letter to General Stuart with the suggestion that he pass by the enemy's rear, if he thinks that he may get through. We have nothing of the enemy to-day.

So it seems that General Lee suggested, and Longstreet urged, Stuart to pass by the enemy's rear. At that time Longstreet and A. P. Hill had not been ordered to follow Ewell. After the war Longstreet wrote an account of Gettysburg, in which he forgot his own orders to Stuart and charged him with disobeying his instructions. He said he ordered Stuart to march on his flank and to keep between him and the enemy; Lee's staff officers and biographers repeat the absurd story. They do not explain how Stuart could be with Ewell on the Susquehanna and, at the same time, on Longstreet's flank in Virginia. No precedent can be found for such a performance, except in the Arabian Nights.

When Lee was in the Shenandoah Valley, he wrote twice to President Davis that Hooker's army was drawing close to the Potomac and had a pontoon across it, and that he thought he could throw Hooker over the river. Lee also wrote to Imboden, who was moving farther west, thanked him for the cattle and sheep he had sent to him, and urged him to collect all he could. On June 23, 5 P.M., Lee wrote again to Stuart. He repeated the instructions about joining Ewell and authorized him to cross the Potomac west, at Shepherdstown, or east of the Blue Ridge, by the enemy's rear. "In either case," said General Lee, "after crossing the river you must move on and feel the right of Ewell's troops, collecting information, provisions, etc."

Lee seemed to be more intent about gathering rations than anything else. There is not a word in either of his dispatches to Stuart about reporting the enemy's movements to him. Lee's biographers say there was. He would neither order nor expect Stuart to do an impossible thing, but he told him what instructions to give the commanders of the two cavalry brigades he would leave behind. Stuart did give *each* of the commanders minute instructions to report the movements of the enemy directly to Lee, and to follow on the flank and rear of the army when the enemy left Virginia. There was no complaint against Jones and Robertson, the brigade commanders, for not having performed this duty — conclusive evidence that they did.

If Stuart had gone the western route by Shepherdstown, he would have had to cross and recross the Blue Ridge and to march in a zigzag circuit to join Ewell. Thus he would have been a long way from the enemy and out of communication with Lee. Lee's movements did not depend on the cavalry he had ordered to join Ewell. Stuart chose the most direct route to the Susquehanna by the rear of the enemy. It afforded an opportunity, as Lee had instructed him, "to do them all the damage you can" and to "collect provisions"; he would break the communications with Washington and destroy Hooker's transportation. Such a blow would compel the latter, instead of following Lee, to retreat to his base and wait for repairs.

The seven corps of Hooker's army were scattered through three counties in Virginia, with his right resting on the Potomac. The plan for Stuart to pass through Hooker's army was really a copy of the campaign of Marengo, when Bonaparte crossed the Alps and cut the Austrian communications in Italy. It was a bold enterprise — its safety lay in its audacity — the enemy would be caught unprepared, and at the same time it would protect Lee's communications by drawing off Hooker's cavalry in pursuit. It was known that the camps of the different corps were so far apart that a column of cavalry could easily pass between them.

I was at headquarters when Stuart wrote his last dispatch to Lee, informing him of the route he would go, and sat by him when he was writing it — in fact, I dictated a large part of it. I had just returned from a scout inside the enemy's lines and brought the intelligence that induced Stuart to undertake to pass through them. I remember that Fitz Lee and Hampton came into the room while we were writing.

I had arrived from this scout early on the morning of June 24, and found that Stuart had just received the orders to join Ewell with three brigades and had been given discretion to pass by the rear of the Union army. John Esten Cooke, the Ordnance Officer of the cavalry corps, was at headquarters. In his "Wearing of the Gray" (1867) he corroborated my statement about the effect on the campaign of the report I brought Stuart. He writes:

General Stuart came, finally, to repose unlimited confidence in his (Mosby's) resources and relied implicitly upon him. The writer recalls an instance of this in June, 1863. General Stuart was then near Middleburg, watching the United States Army — then about to move toward Pennsylvania — but could get no accurate information from his scouts. Silent, puzzled, and doubtful, the General walked up and down, knitting his brows and reflecting. When the lithe figure of Mosby appeared, Stuart uttered an exclamation of relief and satisfaction. They were speedily in private conversation, and Mosby came out again to mount his quick gray mare and set out in a heavy storm for the Federal camps. On the next day he returned with information which put the entire cavalry in motion. He had penetrated General Hooker's camps, ascertained everything, and safely returned. This he had done in his gray uniform with his pistols in his belt, and I believe that it was on this occasion that he gave a characteristic evidence of his coolness.

The adventure to which Cook refers occurred at the house of a citizen named Coleman, where I captured two cavalrymen who were sitting on their horses gathering cherries. This fact was confirmed by General Weld, of General Reynolds's staff, in his "War Diary." He said :

We found out to-day that our guide was captured at Coleman's house yesterday. Coleman lives about two miles from here, and he has a lot of forage; our guide and quarter-master went there for it and were caught by a "Secesh" there said to be Mosby.[1]

[1] Mosby rode along with his two prisoners and unexpectedly came upon a body of enemy cavalry. He thereupon threatened the two soldiers with certain death, and rode with the enemy a considerable distance, at length turning into a lane and getting safely away, with his prisoners.

Lee knew that while Stuart was passing between Hooker's army and Washington communication with him would be impossible. This was before the days of wireless! Lee must have relied for intelligence on the cavalry brigades he had with him, on his scouts, and his signal corps on the Blue Ridge. He had no other use for them. The cavalry commander said he frequently sent couriers to Lee with dispatches. I regret that Lee's report says that he expected Stuart to perform a miracle and keep in communication with him.

Three of Lee's staff officers, Marshall, Long, and Taylor, have given accounts of the Gettysburg campaign that misrepresent the orders Stuart received and claim that Lee relied on him for intelligence. Now the letters of Lee to Ewell, directing him to move to the Susquehanna and to Stuart to join Ewell with three brigades, are copied in Lee's dispatch book in the handwriting of Colonel Charles Marshall, who also wrote Lee's reports. The implications of disobedience against Stuart in the reports are contradicted by these letters. The dispatch book was in Marshall's possession when he delivered a philippic on Lee's birthday (1896) in which he imputed disobedience of orders to Stuart and asserted that Lee depended on him for information. He did not say what Lee expected the two cavalry brigades to do, nor did he say what they didn't do — he didn't mention them. The letter of 5 P.M., June 23, directing Stuart to go to Ewell on the Susquehanna and authorizing him to pass by the enemy's rear, is in the handwriting of Colonel Walter Taylor, Lee's Assistant Adjutant-General. He wrote an account of Gettysburg charging Stuart with disobedience in going to Ewell and not remaining with Lee and reporting the movements of the enemy to him, and blaming Stuart, as Marshall did, for the disaster at Gettysburg. Long falsified the record in the same way. Apparently they never dreamed that there would be a resurrection of Lee's dispatch book.

On the authority of the staff officers, a historian wrote that Stuart left Lee without orders and went off on a wild-goose chase. I wrote and asked him if he thought that Ewell was a wild goose. The truth is Lee was so anxious for Stuart to cross the river ahead of Hooker that he wrote him, "I fear he will steal a march on us and get across the Potomac before we are aware."

Yet his report says that he was astonished to hear, on June 28, at Chambersburg, that Hooker had crossed. The staff officers knew perfectly well how the battle was precipitated, but they concealed it. They intentionally misrepresented it. Their animus towards Stuart is manifest. Taylor, in his narrative of his service with General Lee, did not even mention the great cavalry combat at Brandy, which his chief rode on the field to witness. Marshall and Long, to disparage Stuart, referred to the battle and used the same phrase, "he was roughly handled." Long, to deprive Stuart of the glory of his victory, said that a division of infantry came to his support. The record shows that General Lee kept his infantry concealed that day.

Early on the morning of June 25, Stuart's column crossed the Bull Run, expecting to pass directly through Hooker's army and to reach the Potomac that evening. This could have been done easily on the day before. But on the morning of the twenty-fourth, A. P. Hill's corps, at Charles Town, moved to the Potomac in plain view of the Federal signal station on Maryland Heights. Longstreet, at Millwood, three times as far from the river as Hill, started at the same time, but he marched by Martinsburg and out of sight of the signal station, crossing at Williamsport. Hill had crossed the day before at Shepherdstown and waited for Longstreet. There was no emergency to require this movement. Hooker was waiting on Lee and had not sent a single regiment over the river, although Ewell was foraging in Pennsylvania. The news of Hill's and Longstreet's crossing the river was immediately telegraphed to Hooker, and the next morning he set his army in motion for the pontoons. As his corps crossed the Potomac, they marched west for South Mountain and occupied the Gaps. Longstreet and Hill united in Maryland and spent two days with General Lee within a few miles of Hooker's camps. Hooker's signal stations were in full view on peaks, flapping their flags. Each of Lee's corps had a signal corps, and Lee had a number of scouts to send on the mountain to see Hooker's army on the other side. The truth is that Lee and Stuart got their information of the enemy through individual scouts and not by using the cavalry in a body. Lee says that one of these scouts brought him the information at Chambersburg that Hooker had crossed the Potomac. I have no doubt that Lee used any means he could to get intelligence of the enemy, for the simplicity of the bucolic ages was not a characteristic of the Confederate commander.

The enemy crossed the Potomac in front of

the two cavalry brigades that were left to watch him. There is no doubt that the cavalry did their duty, and that Lee waited in Maryland for Hooker's army to get over the river. If A. P. Hill had only waited a day longer in his camps, Hooker would have stood still, and Stuart could easily have crossed the Potomac on the twenty-fifth. It would be a severe reflection on Lee and his generals to suppose that they spent two days so near an army of a hundred thousand men and didn't even suspect it. Hooker's army was crossing the river twenty-five miles below at the same time Lee was crossing. Stuart soon ran against Hooker's columns on the roads on which he had expected to march. But they had the right of way and kept on, while Stuart, after an artillery duel, had to make a detour around them and did not cross the river until the night of the twenty-seventh. Thus Stuart was delayed two days, but he sent a dispatch informing Lee that Hooker was moving to the Potomac. The appearance of a body of cavalry on the flank of Hooker's army created great anxiety for his rear, and Pleasanton's cavalry corps was kept as a rear guard and was the last to cross on the pontoons on the night of the twenty-seventh.

At the time Stuart was crossing the Potomac at

Seneca, Lee had reached Chambersburg. Ordinarily the Union cavalry should have been in front, harassing Lee's flank and rear, but up to the day of the battle Lee's communications were intact, and he had not lost a wagon or a straggler. The enemy's cavalry were in Hooker's rear, on the defensive, and they had no idea that Stuart was crossing the river between them and Washington.

Stuart spent the night (June 27) in Maryland, capturing a lot of boats carrying supplies to the army on the canal, and on the twenty-eighth moved north and marched all night to join Ewell. During the day Stuart caught a supply train going to headquarters from Washington, and, as his orders required, he took the supplies along to Ewell. The presence of the Confederate cavalry between the army and Washington created a panic, which was increased by the report that there was another body south of the river. For several days communication with the Union army was cut, Washington was isolated, and Stuart's column attracted more attention than Lee's army in the Cumberland Valley.

Meade took command of the Army of the Potomac on the afternoon of the twenty-eighth at Frederick City, and there was great commotion in his camps when the news came that Stuart had their mules and provisions. The quarter-master-general wired to Ingalls, "Your communications are now in the hands of General Fitzhugh Lee's brigade."

On June 27, the day that General Lee arrived at Chambersburg, the corps that Hooker had advanced to the Gaps in Maryland were withdrawn twenty miles to the east, and the Army of the Potomac was concentrated at Frederick City. As a result, Lee's communications were no longer even threatened. After crossing the river, Hooker had moved west, as he said, to strike Lee's rear, but the War Department interfered with the plan, and he asked to be relieved. Ewell was then marching to the Susquehanna, so Hooker's counter movement to Frederick was made to protect the Capital and Baltimore from any movement down the Susquehanna. Lee must have considered the probability of an operation against his rear, when he wrote President Davis, after he reached the Potomac, that he thought he could throw Hooker's army over the river, and that, as he did not have sufficient force to guard his communications, he would have to abandon them. But as he would live on the country, he did not have to guard a base of supply, and his communications were not vital.

Colonel Marshall, it seems to me in the light of the evidence, was unjust to his chief when he represented him to have been surprised and almost in a panic when he heard, at Chambersburg, on the night of the twenty-eighth, that Hooker had crossed the Potomac. He did not explain how Lee could have thought that the Northern army would remain in Virginia, while the Confederates were ravaging Pennsylvania, nor why he changed his plan of campaign to protect his communications.

The first news of the enemy that Meade received after he assumed command was the following discouraging dispatch from Halleck:

It is reported that your train of one hundred and fifty wagons has been captured by Fitzhugh Lee near Rockville. Unless cavalry is sent to guard your communications with Washington, they will be cut off. It is reported here that there is still a considerable rebel force south of the Potomac.

General Lee had passed near and left behind him at Harper's Ferry a force of 11,000 that did not seem to disturb him as a menace to his communications, but on the twenty-eighth Meade withdrew these troops to guard his rear and the line of the Potomac. General Lee was then to the west, in the Cumberland Valley, but Meade started off in the opposite direction on Stuart's trail. That did seem as hopeless as chasing a wild goose.

Meade said to Halleck, "I can now only say that it appears to me I must move towards the Susquehanna, keeping Washington and Baltimore well-covered, and, if the enemy is checked in his attempt, to cross the Susquehanna, or, if he turn towards Baltimore, to give him battle."

Meade spent a day at Frederick and on the thirtieth started on his campaign. Lee was still at Chambersburg. His staff officers say that at that time Gettysburg was the objective point on which both Lee and Meade were marching, and that there was a race between them to occupy it first. Lee could easily have occupied Gettysburg while Meade was still at Frederick. Meade's communications were now broken, and for several days he was drifting. He sent off to the east two of his cavalry divisions and three army corps to intercept Stuart, so after two days' marching a large part of Meade's army was as far from Lee as it was at Frederick. If General Lee had known how Ewell and Stuart would attract Meade to the east, he would not have recalled Ewell so soon.

On the night of the thirtieth Meade was still in a fog. He had not heard that Ewell had withdrawn from the Susquehanna, so he wrote to Halleck, by a courier, that he would push farther east the next day to the Harrisburg railroad, and open communication with Baltimore. But at 11.30 P.M., on the thirtieth, a telegram was sent from Harrisburg to be forwarded by a messenger to Meade, telling him that Lee was falling back. Meade received this news on the morning of July 1, and he at once recalled the orders he had issued to push on towards the Susquehanna and determined to take a defensive position. He wrote Halleck of the change and that he would not advance farther, but would retire to the line of Pipe Creek and await an attack — which would have satisfied Lee. If Ewell had remained a day longer at Carlisle and Early at York, Meade would have moved to the Susquehanna, and there would have been no battle at Gettysburg. Halleck must have been surprised by Meade's dispatch, for he had told him at Frederick that his object was to find and fight Lee.

After he got the news about Ewell, Meade issued a circular directing the corps commanders to hold the enemy in check, if attacked, and to retire to Pipe Creek. Reynolds, with the First Corps, was on his extreme left and had been directed to move early on July 1 on Gettysburg — merely in observation. Meade wrote Reynolds that he had been ordered to Gettysburg before the news came that Ewell had withdrawn from the Susquehanna. But Reynolds started early, never received Meade's letter or the circular of recall, and was killed.

On the night of the thirtieth Stuart arrived at Dover and learned that Early's division of Ewell's corps, which he expected to join at York, had marched west that morning. As he was ordered to report to Ewell, after a short rest Stuart moved on to Carlisle, where he knew Ewell had been. But he sent a staff officer on Early's track to report to General Lee, whom he found on the field of Gettysburg. Stuart reached Carlisle that night, but Ewell, with his cavalry and two divisions, had gone south. It was fortunate for Lee that Stuart did go to Carlisle.

Couch had collected a force of about 15,000 at Harrisburg and had been ordered to coöperate with Meade and attack Lee's communications. Stuart met his advance at Carlisle, an artillery duel ensued, and it was thought by the Federalists that Ewell had returned. So the troops on the march from Harrisburg turned back, and the trains that were bringing their supplies from different points in the country were stampeded by the firing. Stuart left that night for Gettysburg and arrived about noon the next day, in time to meet the two divisions of cavalry which had been away in pursuit of him. Couch's force started again from Harrisburg, but had to wait for rations. He did not get off until July 4, after the battle had been fought, and never overtook Lee's trains.

Stuart's march of a column of cavalry around the Union army will be regarded, in the light of the record, as one of the greatest achievements in war, viewed either as an independent operation or raid, or in its strategic relation to the campaign. But all the advantage gained by it was neutralized by the indiscretion of a corps commander and was obscured by the great disaster to our arms for which it was in no way responsible.

General Bernhardi wrote :

I hold therefore that such circumstances render a disturbance of the rear communications of an army an important matter. It will often do the opponent more damage, and contribute more to a favorable decision of arms than the intervention of a few cavalry divisions in the decisive battle itself. One does not, of course, exclude the possibility of the other. General Stuart, in the campaign of Gettysburg, rode all around the hostile army, broke up its communications, drew hostile troops away from the decisive point, and yet was in place on the wing of the army on the day of the battle. What this man performed with cavalry and the inestimable damage he inflicted on his opponent are worth studying. The fortune of war, which lay in might and in the nature of things, he could not turn.

Such was Stuart's ride around McClellan; the two armies stood still as spectators.

A *raid* is a predatory incursion, generally against the supplies and communications of an enemy. The object of a raid is to embarrass an enemy by striking a vulnerable point and destroying his subsistence. The operation should be in coöperation with, but independent of, an army. But Stuart's march was a combined movement with Ewell and not a raid. His objective was Ewell's flank on the Susquehanna. The spoil he captured was an *incident*, not the object, of the march. It was no more a *raid* than if he had crossed the Blue Ridge, as he was authorized by Lee, and travelled to join Ewell by a route on which he would have no opportunity for adventure. But General Lee's orders show that he was not indifferent either to the embarrassment of the enemy or to the spoil he might capture. Ewell already had an abundance of cavalry for ordinary outpost duty. It was the *personality* of Stuart that was needed — not cavalry.

During this campaign, the operations of the

cavalry were coördinate with the movements of the army as a unit. On the evening of June 27, Lee arrived at Chambersburg, while Hill turned east and went on seven miles. This shows that General Lee did not intend to move farther north, but to concentrate in that vicinity. Ewell had reached Carlisle — thirty miles distant. So Lee wrote him on the evening of the twenty-seventh to return to Chambersburg and informed him that Hooker had crossed the Potomac. This dispatch is not in the war records. But it seems that Lee changed his mind and, at 7.30 A.M. on the twenty-eighth, in a second letter repeated the substance of what he wrote Ewell "*last night*", and directed him that, if he had not already started, he move south with his trains, but east of South Mountain. It is clear that Ewell's destination was Cashtown — a village at the eastern base of the mountain — eight miles west of Gettysburg. Discretion was given to him as to the roads he should travel. Ewell's and Early's reports say that Cashtown was the appointed rendezvous; Lee's that it was Gettysburg. Cashtown was occupied on June 28 by a part of Heth's division. In the next two days Hill moved with two divisions to that point. Ewell had detached Early's division to make a demonstration towards the Susquehanna. On the way Gordon's brigade spent a night at Gettysburg, but it moved on and joined Early at York. If Gettysburg had been Lee's objective, he would have held it when he had it.

Lee's report says that on the night of June 28 a spy came in and informed him that Hooker was following him. The news, the report says, was a surprise; that he had thought Hooker's army was in Virginia, that he had expected Stuart to give him notice when Hooker crossed the Potomac; and that he abandoned a campaign he had planned against Harrisburg, recalled Ewell, and ordered his army to concentrate at Gettysburg. As he had uninterrupted communication with the Potomac, Lee knew that the Union army must be east of the mountain.

We accept as of poetical origin the legends of prehistoric Rome, which Livy transmitted; but it is as easy to believe the story of the rape of the Sabines, or that Horatius stood alone on the bridge over the Tiber against the army of the Gauls, as that Lee planned a campaign into Pennsylvania on the theory that his army could march to Harrisburg and Hooker's army would stay on the Potomac. If Lee had not known, when he was in Maryland, that Hooker was still on his front, he would have marched directly to Washington. If his statement be true that the news brought by a spy arrested a campaign he had planned to Harrisburg, such an anticlimax would make the campaign a subject for a comic opera.

If a spy had come from Frederick on June 28, he would have reported that Hooker's army was moving eastward toward Baltimore and was concentrated at Frederick. Colonel Marshall said :

On the night of the 28th of June I was directed by General Lee to order General Ewell to move directly upon Harrisburg, and to inform him that General Longstreet would move the next morning (the 29th) to his support. General A. P. Hill was directed to move eastward to the Susquehanna, and crossing the river below Harrisburg, seize the railroad between Harper's Ferry and Philadelphia; it being supposed that such a movement would divert all reinforcements that otherwise might be coming to General Hooker to the defense of that city; and that there would be such alarm created by their movement that the Federal Government would be obliged to withdraw its army from Virginia and abandon any plan it might have for attack upon Richmond. I sent the orders about 10 o'clock at night to General Ewell and General Hill and had just returned to my tent when I was sent for by the Commanding General. I went to his tent and found him sitting with a man in citizen's dress, who, General Lee informed me, was a scout of General Longstreet's who had just been brought to him. He told me that this scout had left the neighborhood of Frederick that morning and had brought information that the Federal army had crossed the Potomac, moving northward; and that the advance had reached Frederick and was moving westward towards the Mountains. The scout also informed General Lee that General Meade was then in command of the army; and also as to the movements of the enemy, which was the first information General Lee had received since he left Virginia. . . . While making this march the only information he possessed led him to believe that the army of the enemy was moving westward from Frederick to throw itself upon his line of communications with Virginia; and the object was, as I have stated, simply to arrest this supposed plan on the east side of the mountain. . . . By reason of the absence of the cavalry his own army, marching eastward from Chambersburg and southward from Carlisle, came unexpectedly on the Federal advance on the first day of July.

Marshall said that Lee countermanded his orders to Ewell and Hill to move to the Susquehanna and ordered them to Gettysburg, in order to counteract a movement against his communications. He did not mention Lee's letter of 7.30 A.M., June 28, which contradicts the story of the spy at Chambersburg on the night of June 28. That letter shows that when it was written, Lee thought that Hooker's army was still holding the Gaps in Maryland, and had not heard that it had been withdrawn to Frederick. Lee does not appear to have been uneasy about his communications. Instead of ordering Ewell to proceed to Harrisburg, he directed him to return to Cashtown. It is inconceivable that he could have ordered A. P. Hill to cross the Susquehanna and threaten Philadelphia, and at the same time should have ordered Early, at York, to come back to the Cumberland Valley. They would have passed each other marching in opposite directions. If the 7.30 A.M. letter should have been dated the twenty-ninth, as has been suggested, then neither of Lee's letters to Ewell could have reached him at Carlisle, as he would have left there before they arrived. Lee had written to Mr. Davis that he would have to abandon his communications; but if Hooker had moved west to intercept them, I am sure that General Lee would have imitated Napoleon at Austerlitz and marched to Washington.

Lee's report on the Gettysburg campaign was published immediately and made a deep and almost indelible impression. It is really a lawyer's brief and shows the skill of the advocate in the art of suppression and suggestion. Stuart's report, dated August 20, 1863, is a respectful answer, but it was buried in the Confederate archives. General Lee made a more elaborate report, in January, 1864, which repeated the implications of the first in regard to the cavalry, but contradicted what it said about his orders for the concentration at Gettysburg. Of course, he knew his own orders as well in July as in January.

Now the essence of the complaint against Stuart is that the cavalry — the eyes of an army — were improperly absent; that the Confederate army was ordered by Lee to Gettysburg, and, Colonel Marshall and Lee's Assistant Adjutant General, Colonel Walter Taylor, said, and the report implies, ran unexpectedly against the enemy. But the charge falls to the ground when Lee's second report admits that the army was not ordered to Gettysburg, and that the force that went there was only making a reconnaissance. However, the report does not say that there was any order for a reconnaissance, or any necessity for making one. Neither does it explain why Hill did not come back to Cashtown, nor why Lee followed him to Gettysburg. Hill's report says that on the thirtieth he sent a dispatch to General Lee, telling him that the enemy held Gettysburg. A collision, then, could not be un-

expected — *if he went there.* If, as Lee's report
says, the spy brought news on the twenty-eighth
that the Union army was at Frederick, it could not
have been expected to stand still; nor a surprise
to learn that it was moving north.

But there is even less color to the truth or justice in the complaint, when it is known that the
story that a spy diverted the army from Harrisburg is a fable, and that Hill and Heth went off
without orders and without Lee's knowledge on a
*raid* and precipitated a battle. There is a satisfactory explanation for Stuart's absence that day,
but a man who has to make an explanation is
always at a disadvantage.

Colonel Taylor does not seem to have known
where Lee's headquarters were on the morning of
July 1, for he said that A. P. Hill had a conference
at Cashtown with General Lee before he started.
If so, Lee was responsible for the blunder. Hill's
and Heth's reports say that they left Cashtown at
5 A.M., and soon ran against the enemy. Lee's
headquarters were then ten miles distant west of
the mountain at Greenwood. There was no long
distance 'phone over which he might talk with
Hill. That morning Lee wrote to Imboden, in
his rear, and said, "My headquarters for the
present will be at Cashtown, east of the moun-

tain." This letter is copied in his dispatch book in the handwriting of Colonel Marshall, who wrote Lee's report which states that Lee at Chambersburg, after the spy came in, ordered the army to Gettysburg and was unprepared for battle when the armies met, placing the blame on Stuart. Yet this dispatch shows that on the morning of July 1 the army had not been ordered to Gettysburg. Lee would not have had his headquarters at one place and his army eight miles off at another. Lee started during the day for Cashtown, as he told Imboden he would, and, when crossing the mountain, was surprised to hear the ominous sound of battle. He passed through Cashtown at full speed and never saw the place again. His surprise was not at the enemy being at Gettysburg, but that a part of his army was there. It is remarkable that Colonel Taylor, who was in close relations with General Lee, did not even mention a projected movement to Harrisburg that was arrested by a spy.

Lee's report omits all reference to Ewell's march in advance of the army to the Susquehanna and the order to Stuart to leave the army in Virginia and join him. As it complains that by the route he chose around the Union army communication with him was broken, it is natural to conclude from this statement that Stuart disobeyed orders to keep in communication with Lee. The report speaks of Ewell's entering Maryland and says that Longstreet and Hill followed and that the columns were reunited at Hagerstown. The inference is that the three corps united at that place and that Stuart was directed to join them in Maryland. The fact is that Ewell was then some days in advance in Pennsylvania and that the three corps united on the field of Gettysburg.

Stuart, says the report, was left to guard the passes, observe the movements of the enemy, and harass and impede him if he attempted to cross the Potomac. "In that event (Hooker's crossing) he was directed to move into Maryland, crossing the Potomac east or west of the Blue Ridge, as in his judgment should be best, and take position on the right of our column as it advanced."

Stuart's crossing the Potomac did not depend on Hooker's crossing, and he had no such instructions. Lee's orders to Stuart, which I repeat, were, "In either case after crossing the river (whether you go by the eastern or western route) you must move on and feel the right of Ewell's troops, collecting information, provisions, etc." The report states a part of the truth in saying that Stuart had the discretion to cross the Poto-

mac east or west of the Blue Ridge, but it omits
the *whole* truth and that he also had authority to
pass by the enemy's rear. That was the only
route he could go if he crossed east of the Ridge.
As the report complains of the Union army being
interposed and preventing communication with
him by the route he went, the inference is that
Stuart violated orders in passing by the enemy's
rear. Stuart had no orders, *as stated in the report*,
about guarding the Gaps, impeding the enemy,
and reporting his movements, nor to watch Hooker
in Virginia and forage for Ewell on the Susquehanna. Such an expectation implies a belief that
Stuart possessed a supernatural genius.

The report speaks of Stuart's efforts to impede
the progress of the Northern army. He made
no such efforts — he had no such orders — it
impeded him. The report makes no mention of
the use that Lee and Longstreet made of the two
cavalry brigades which Stuart left with them.
They must have done their duty, for there was no
complaint that they did not.

To return to Lee at Chambersburg. On the
night of the twenty-seventh he had written to
Ewell at Carlisle that Hooker had crossed the
Potomac and was in the Middletown Valley at
the east end of the Gaps, and directed him to

return to Chambersburg. It was time to concentrate the army. But Lee changed his mind, and, at 7.30 A.M. on the twenty-eighth he again wrote Ewell, repeating what he had told him in the "last night" letter about Hooker, but directed him to move south by the pike and east of the mountain. He did not mention Meade, who had not then been placed in command. The letter is indefinite as to the point of concentration — that was evidently a precaution in the event of its capture. Such an important dispatch would be sent by a staff officer so that he might explain it orally, and, as they were in the enemy's country, he would have a cavalry escort. Ewell sent a copy of this dispatch, by a staff officer, to Early, thirty-six miles away at York. It could not have been written after the night of the twenty-seventh. Early said that he received it on the evening of the twenty-ninth and started the next morning to unite with Ewell west of the mountain, but during the day he met a courier with a dispatch from Ewell, informing him of the change of destination. This statement proves that Ewell at Carlisle received two letters from Lee. Although he sent a copy of Lee's *first* order to Early, in his report Ewell only referred to the second order under which he marched with Rodes's division for Cashtown. Edward Johnson's division left Carlisle for Chambersburg on the morning of the twenty-ninth, before the second order arrived, and marched to Green Village — twenty miles — that day.

Lee's dispatch of the night of the twenty-seventh could not have reached Carlisle before the evening of the twenty-eighth. If it had been written on the night of the twenty-eighth, it could not have reached Ewell before he got to Harrisburg. The trains probably started back that night before Edward Johnson left, as they were passing Chambersburg at midnight on the twenty-ninth. They probably halted in the heat of the day as was the custom, to rest and feed the animals. Lee directed Ewell, if he received the second order in time, to move south with the trains by the eastern route. So it is clear that Early's and Johnson's divisions marched in accordance with the order of the twenty-seventh, which Ewell did not mention.

Early said he met Ewell that evening (June 30) with Rodes's division near Heidlersburg. Rodes told him that Cashtown was to be the point of concentration and that he was to march there the next morning. On July 1 Ewell had started, with Rodes's and Early's divisions, on the road to Cashtown, when he received a note from Hill that turned him off to Gettysburg. Ewell left Carlisle with Rodes's division on the thirtieth, after he had received Lee's *second* letter changing his destination. Ewell said, "I was starting on the twenty-ninth for that place (Harrisburg) when ordered by the General Commanding to join the main body at Cashtown, near Gettysburg." Although two of his divisions marched under the *first* order, Ewell's report speaks only of the *second* order. He is clearly inaccurate in saying that the *second* order to move south to Cashtown was the cause of his halting at Carlisle. He had already been halted by the *first* order. On this lapse of the pen is based the quibble that the date (June 27) of Lee's letter to Ewell is wrong, and Edward Johnson's division had started back to Chambersburg. The time of the marching of Ewell's three divisions accords with the dates of the two letters, and proves that before the spy is alleged to have appeared — the night of the twenty-eighth — Lee had sent orders to Ewell to return to Chambersburg, and that he afterwards directed him to Cashtown. In these letters he told Ewell where Hooker's, not Meade's, army was. Again, Lee's report says that as the spy had informed him on the *night* of the twenty-eighth that the head of

Hooker's column had reached the South Mountain, which was a menace to his communications, he resolved to concentrate at Gettysburg, east of the mountain, to prevent his further progress, and that he issued orders accordingly.

But Lee, on the night of the twenty-seventh and morning of the twenty-eighth, had directed the army to return. As he ordered Ewell back to Chambersburg on the night of the twenty-seventh and then to Cashtown on the morning of the twenty-eighth, the statement that he was preparing to move on to Harrisburg when the spy came in on the *night* of the twenty-eighth and brought news that Hooker was in pursuit cannot stand the test of reason. If the order to Ewell to return had been issued after the spy is alleged to have come in, it would not have overtaken Ewell before he got to Harrisburg. Nor could the order to concentrate at Cashtown have been the consequence of news brought by the alleged spy, as it had been issued before it is said that the spy came. If Gettysburg had been Lee's objective, he could easily have occupied it on the twenty-ninth, before Meade left Frederick. As Lee's Chambersburg letter contradicts his report, his biographers did not mention it.

Lee's second report speaks of two cavalry bri-

gades being in Virginia to guard the Gaps, and
says that as soon as it was known that the enemy
was in Maryland, orders were sent them to join
the army. They were not put there to guard the
Gaps, for the Gaps did not need a guard. Their
instructions were to watch and report the movements of the enemy to General Lee and to follow
on the flank of the army when the enemy moved
from their front. On the night of June 27
Hooker's rear guard crossed the river, and on the
twenty-ninth the two cavalry brigades crossed
the Blue Ridge and arrived at Chambersburg
on the night of July 2. If an order was sent for
them after the spy came in, as the report says, it
could not have reached them on the twenty-ninth
in Loudoun County, Virginia, before they started.
They marched in accordance with Stuart's orders.

The allegation is that the Confederate army
was surprised at Gettysburg on account of the
absence of the cavalry. The gist of the complaint
is that Gettysburg was Lee's objective, as his
first report says; that the leading divisions of
Hill's corps ran unexpectedly against the enemy
there; and that he had to fight a battle under
duress to save his trains. The trains were then
in the Cashtown Pass, and Longstreet's corps
and Imboden's command were at the western

end of it, while Lee, with two corps, was at the
other end.   Now the party surprised is, as a rule,
the party attacked.   But in the three days'
fighting around Gettysburg, Lee's army was the
assailant all the time and got the better of it on
the first and second days.   If Lee had selected
Gettysburg as a battleground, it is strange that he
should apologize for fighting there.   General Lee
was surprised by A. P. Hill — not by the enemy.
It is a curious thing that Lee's report should have
shielded A. P. Hill and Heth, who broke up his
plan of campaign.   It is not claimed that Lee
needed cavalry *in* the battle, but *before* the battle,
to bring him intelligence.   How he suffered in
this respect his report does not indicate, but it
says that the spy told him where the enemy were
on the night of the twenty-eighth when Meade's
army was fifty miles away at Frederick.   If this
was the case, Lee had ample time to concentrate
at Gettysburg.   If he had this information, it is
immaterial how he got it.   *Nobody can show that
Lee did anything or left anything undone for want
of information that cavalry could have given him.*

Stuart was absent from the battlefield on the
first day because he was away doing his duty
under orders, and two divisions of Meade's cavalry
were in pursuit of him.   Lee and Longstreet were

absent from the field on that day because they did not expect a battle at Gettysburg, and did not have foreknowledge of what Hill and Heth were going to do. While the spy that is alleged to have appeared on the stage at night and to have changed the program of invasion is an invention for dramatic effect, *a* spy did appear in a commonplace way two days afterwards, when the army was on the march to Cashtown. He brought interesting but unimportant news.

Colonel Freemantle, an English officer and a guest at Longstreet's headquarters, said in his diary:

June 30th, Tuesday. . . . We marched from Chambersburg six miles on the road toward Gettysburg. In the evening General Longstreet told me that he had just received intelligence that Hooker had been disrated and Meade was appointed in his place.

In another item Freemantle alluded to a spy. So it was on the thirtieth, after Lee had left Chambersburg, and not on the twenty-eighth of June, that a spy reported. Longstreet had a picture of the spy in his book, and under it was inscribed that he brought the first news that Meade was in command. The report makes news brought by a spy the cause of what had occurred before it was brought.

Marshall said that the spy appeared at head-quarters on the night of the twenty-eighth and told of the change of commanders, and he also said how much surprised Lee was to hear that Hooker had crossed the Potomac, and that he spoke of returning to Virginia. Now it is be-tween fifty and sixty miles from Frederick City, where Meade took command of the army on the afternoon of that day (June 28), to Chambers-burg. The order for the change was kept a secret until it was published that evening. Every road, path, and gap was closely picketed. The spirit in "Manfred" that rode on the wind and left the hurricane behind might have made the trip in that time, but no mortal could have done it. In this use of a spy, the author of the report imitated a Greek dramatist who brought down a god from the clouds to assist in the catastrophe of his tragedies.

Lee's report says that the spy informed him that the Union army had reached South Mountain. It was there when Lee was in Maryland. But if the spy had just come out of Hooker's lines, as Marshall said, and told of the change in com-manders, he would also have told that the army had been withdrawn from the mountain on the twenty-seventh and had marched east to Frederick City. Lee's letter to Ewell speaks of *Hooker's* army, which shows that he had not heard of any change of commanders when it was written — and there had not been — and he does not mention Meade. The tale of the spy must take its place with Banquo's ghost and other theatrical fictions.

On June 30, Heth, with his division, was at Cashtown and sent Pettigrew, with his brigade, to Gettysburg to get a lot of shoes that were said to be there. When Pettigrew got in sight of the place, he saw a body of cavalry coming in ; so he returned and reported to Heth — who proposed to go there the next morning. The cavalry was Buford's division, which kept close to Meade's left flank. At 5 A.M. on July 1, Hill, with Heth's and Pender's divisions and artillery, left camp for Gettysburg in the same spirit of adventure that took Earl Percy to hunt the deer at Chevy Chase. They evidently intended a *raid* and to return to camp and meet Lee that evening. All of the *impedimenta were left behind.* General Lee would be at Cashtown that day, and the army would be concentrated by evening. Lee said that he had no idea of taking the offensive. Heth's leading brigade, Archer's, soon ran against Buford's pickets ; the latter fought his cavalry dismounted and checked Heth until Reynolds arrived. Reynolds had left his camp early that morning for Gettysburg before Meade's order had come to retire to Pipe Creek. Heth's report reads:

It may not be improper to remark that at this time — nine o'clock on the morning of July 1st — I was ignorant what force was at or near Gettysburg, and supposed it consisted of cavalry, most probably supported by a brigade or two of infantry. . . . Archer and Davis were now directed to advance, the object being to feel the enemy, to make a forced reconnaissance and determine in what force they were — whether or not he was massing his forces on Gettysburg. Heavy columns of the enemy were soon encountered. . . . General Davis was unable to hold his position.

Archer's brigade was soon shattered, and he and a large portion of his brigade were captured. If Heth had any curiosity about the enemy being there in force, he and Hill ought now to have been satisfied and should have retired — that is, if they were only seeking information. But Pender's division was now put in to support Heth's and was faring no better. Hill would have been driven back to Cashtown, but Ewell, without orders, came to his relief and won the day. Early's division gave the final stroke as he did at Bull

Run. Hill said that his division was so exhausted that it could not join in pursuit of the enemy. Yet he called the affair, which had lasted nearly a whole day, a reconnaissance just to conceal his blunder.

After the war, Heth published an article in which he said nothing about their making a reconnaissance, but that they went for shoes. He claimed that he and Hill were surprised and said it was on account of the want of cavalry, yet both said they knew the enemy was there. The want of cavalry might have been a good reason for *not* going there — it was a poor one for going. Heth did not pretend that he and Hill had orders to go to Gettysburg, nor was there any necessity for their going. All that the army had to do was to live on the country and wait for the enemy at Cashtown Pass — as Lee intended to do.

The truth is that General Lee was so compromised by his corps commanders that he stayed on the field and fought the battle on a point of honor. To withdraw would have had the appearance of defeat and have given the moral effect of a victory to the enemy. A shallow criticism has objected that Lee repeated Hooker's operation with his cavalry at Chancellorsville. Both Lee and Hooker did right; both retained sufficient cavalry with the main body for observation and outpost duty. The difference in the conditions was that Lee sent Stuart to join Ewell, and the damage he would do on the way would be simply incidental to the march. Hooker's object in detaching his cavalry, on the other hand, was to destroy Lee's supplies and communications. With his superior numbers Hooker had a right to calculate on defeating Lee, and, in that event, his cavalry would bar Lee's retreat as Grant's did at Appomattox.

That the inventions of the staff officers have been accepted by historians as true is the most remarkable thing in literary history since the Chatterton forgeries. But the history of the world is a record of judgments reversed.

I have told in brief the story of Gettysburg, of the way in which defeat befell the great Confederate commander, and have criticised the report which has his signature, but which it is well known was written by another. It does as great injustice to Lee as to Stuart. Lee may have had so much confidence in the writer that he signed it without reading it, or, if it was read to him, he was in the mental condition of the dying gladiator in the Coliseum — his mind

"Was with his heart, and that was far away."

Stuart was the protagonist in the great drama, and no other actor performed his part so well. In a late work by Colonel Furse, of the English army, we read:

Stuart was a genial man of gay spirits and energetic habits, popular with his men and trusted by his superiors as no other officer in the Confederate army. His authority was exercised mildly but firmly; no man in the South was better qualified to mould the wild element he controlled into soldiers. His raids made him a lasting name and his daring exploits will ever find a record alongside the deeds of the most famous cavalry leaders. He was mortally wounded in an encounter with Sheridan's cavalry at Yellow Tavern, May, 1864, and died a few days afterward.

I will add that after General Lee lost Stuart he had no cavalry corps and no Chief of Cavalry. No one was there who could bend the bow of Ulysses.

"And these are deeds which should not pass away
And names that must not wither, though the earth
Forgets her empire with a just decay."

[The defence of Stuart's conduct in the Gettysburg campaign occupied Mosby's study and thought over a considerable period of years. His championship of his beloved chief resulted in various controversies, to some of which acrimonious may be truthfully applied, as well as in considerable writing and publication on the subject. The account given in these pages was his final work and seems to answer all criticisms which have been aimed at his conclusions. The following letter to Mrs. Stuart explains, in a measure, some of his work on the Gettysburg campaign and the discussions which followed.]

Washington, D.C.,
June 9, 1915.

Mrs. General J. E. B. Stuart:
Dear Mrs. Stuart:

I have received your letter in reply to mine inquiring if you had any unpublished correspondence left by General Stuart which I might use in my Memoirs of the war which I am preparing. I return McClellan's letter which is dated March 22nd, 1899.[1] He claims credit for having first published, in reply to Colonel Marshall, General Lee's and Longstreet's orders to General Stuart which authorized him to go the route in rear of Hooker's army in the Gettysburg campaign. Governor Stuart and you know that this is not true. . . . In the winter of 1886–87 I was in Washington settling my accounts as Consul at Hong Kong. Longstreet about that time had an article in the *Century* charging General Stuart with disobedience of orders; and Long's "Memoirs of Lee" also appeared about the

[1] Major H. B. McClellan, author of "The Life and Campaigns of General Stuart", Boston and Richmond, 1885.

same time with a similar charge. As I knew the inside history of the transaction and that the charge was false, I went to the office where the Confederate archives were kept and got permission to examine them. The three volumes of the Gettysburg records had not then been published. Colonel Scott gave me a large envelope that had the reports and correspondence of the campaign on printed slips. Very soon I discovered Lee's and Longstreet's instructions to Stuart to do the very thing that he did. I was delighted and so expressed myself to Colonel Scott. He was surprised that McClellan had made no use of them and told me that McClellan had spent several days in his office and that he had given him the same envelope and papers that he had given me. I told Mr. Henry Stuart, whom I met at the National Hotel, all about my discovery and that I should reply to Longstreet and publish this evidence to contradict him and Long. I also wrote to Mr. Wm. A. Stuart and to McClellan of my discovery and told them that I should reply to Longstreet. Mr. Stuart advised me to publish what I had discovered. These documents with a communication from me appeared in the *Century* about May or June, 1887. See "Battles and Leaders." . . . In 1896 Colonel Charles Marshall delivered a violent philippic on General Lee's birthday against General Stuart. He imputed to Stuart's disobedience all the blame for the Gettysburg disaster. I replied to Marshall's attack in a syndicated article which was published in Richmond and Boston and again published Lee's and Longstreet's instructions to Stuart. With this article

I also published for the first time Lee's letter to Ewell, written from Chambersburg on June 28th, 1863, which exploded the mythical story of the spy on which Marshall had built his fabric of fiction. Some time after my article appeared, in reply to Marshall, Mc-Clellan also published a reply to him with the documents which I had published *nine* years before in the *Century.* . . . But McClellan, like Lee's biographers, was silent about the Chambersburg letter. That it contradicts Lee's report, which Marshall wrote, is admitted by Stuart's critics; but to avoid the effect of it they say the date in the records is wrong. The only evidence they produce is that the report written a month afterward is not consistent with the letter. That was the reason I published the letter. But I have demonstrated that the time that a copy of it was received by Early from Ewell and the marching of Ewell's divisions in accordance with it confirm the correctness of the date. McClellan says that Marshall had not dared to answer him; and I can say that although I was the first to attack him he never dared to answer me. He also speaks of John C. Ropes, of Boston, having written him that his answer was conclusive. But Mr. Ropes had read my article in the *Boston Herald* and had written me the same thing a month before McClellan's appeared. Some years before I had read a review by Ropes of McClellan's "Life of Stuart", in which he seemed to be very friendly to Stuart, but he said that McClellan had made a very unsatisfactory defense of him on the Gettysburg campaign. I then wrote to Ropes and sent him *Belford's*

*Magazine* (October–November, 1891) with an article of mine that had Stuart's orders from Lee and Longstreet. Ropes wrote me that my article had changed his opinion, and that in the next volume of his history his views would conform to mine. Unfortunately he died before the volume was finished. So you see how unfounded McClellan's claim of precedence is. His book, as I told Mr. Henry Stuart nearly thirty years ago, does General Stuart great injustice. It deprives him of the credit of the ride around McClellan — I heard Fitz Lee urge General Stuart not to go on — it defends Fitz Lee against the just criticism of Stuart's report for his disobedience of orders that saved Pope's army from ruin and came near getting Stuart and myself captured; and it represents the great cavalry combat and victory at Brandy as "a successful reconnaissance" by Pleasanton, which means that he *voluntarily* recrossed the Rappahannock after he had accomplished his object and not because he was defeated. . . .

Very truly yours,<br>(Signed) Jno. S. Mosby.

# CHAPTER XIII

## The Year after Gettysburg

[The period between the battle of Gettysburg and the arrival of Sheridan in Shenandoah Valley, in August, 1864, was one of incessant activity on the part of Mosby's command. Scouts, raids, and pitched battles followed each other in rapid succession. Mosby destroyed supply trains, broke up the means of conveying intelligence, thus isolating troops from their base, and confused plans by capturing dispatches, while at the same time compelling the use of large numbers of the enemy's troops to protect Washington and the Potomac. Attracted by the chance of booty and desire for adventure, without the irksome duties of camp life, brave and dashing spirits were drawn to Mosby's battalion until the fifteen men with whom he had started his partisan warfare became five companies, regularly mustered into the Confederate service. The main events of these months are told in the following reports which Colonel Mosby made to his superiors.

Unlike the usual formal report of the War Records, these records are permeated by the zeal and enthusiasm for his partisan warfare to which was due, in large measure, Mosby's striking success. The spirit of the man, his boundless energy, and the unbridled zest with which he made war on his country's foes are reflected in every line of his official story.]

[Report, Mosby to Stuart]

July, 1863.

I sent you in charge of Sergeant Beattie, one hundred and forty-one prisoners that we captured from the enemy during their march through this county. I also sent off forty-five several days ago. Included in the number, one Major, one Captain and two lieutenants. I also captured one hundred and twenty-five horses and mules, twelve wagons (only three of which I was able to destroy), fifty sets of fine harness, arms, etc., etc.

[Report, Mosby to Stuart]

Fauquier Co., Va., Aug. 4, 1863.

I send over in charge of Sergeant Beattie about 30 prisoners captured on an expedition into Fairfax, from which I have just returned. Most of them were taken at Padgett's, near Alexandria. I also captured about 30 wagons, brought off about 70 horses and mules, having only ten men with me. We lost a good many on the way back, as we were compelled to travel narrow, unfrequented paths. Among the captures were three sutlers' wagons.

At Fairfax Court House a few nights ago I captured 29 loaded sutlers' wagons, about 100 prisoners and 140 horses. I had brought all off safely near Aldie, where I fell in with a large force of the enemy's cavalry, who recaptured them. The enemy had several hundred. I had only 27 men. We killed and captured several. My loss: one wounded and captured.

[Report, Mosby to Stuart]

Culpeper, August 20, 1863.

On Tuesday, August 11, I captured a train of 19 wagons near Annandale, in Fairfax County. We secured the teams and a considerable portion of the most valuable stores, consisting of saddles, bridles, harness, etc. We took about 25 prisoners.

[Report, Mosby to Stuart]

Sept. 30, 1863.

. . . On the morning of August 24, with about 30 men, I reached a point (Annandale) immediately on the enemy's line of communication. Leaving the whole command, except three men who accompanied me, in the woods, concealed, I proceeded on a reconnaissance along the railroad to ascertain if there were any bridges unguarded. I discovered there were three.

I returned to the command just as a drove of horses with a cavalry escort of about 50 men were passing. These I determined to attack and to wait until night to burn the bridges. I ordered Lieutenant Turner to take half of the men and charge them in front, while with the remainder I attacked their rear.

In the meantime the enemy had been joined by another party, making their number about 63. When I overtook them they had dismounted at Gooding's Tavern to water their horses. My men went at them with a yell that terrified the Yankees and scattered them in all directions. A few taking shelter under cover of the houses, opened fire upon us. They were soon silenced, however. At the very moment when I had succeeded in routing them, I was compelled to retire from the fight, having been shot through the side and thigh. My men, not understanding it, followed me, which gave time to the Yankees to escape to the woods. But for this accident, the whole party would have been captured. As soon as I perceived this, I ordered the men to go back, which a portion of them did, just as Lieutenant Turner, who had met and routed another force above, came gallantly charging up.

Over 100 horses fell into our possession, though a good many were lost in bringing them out at night; also 12 prisoners, arms, etc. I learn that 6 of the enemy were killed. . . . In this affair my loss was 2 killed and 3 wounded. . . .

I afterwards directed Lieutenant Turner to burn the bridges. He succeeded in burning one.

During my absence from the command, Lieutenant Turner attacked an outpost of the enemy near Waterloo, killing 2 and capturing 4 men and 27 horses.

About September 15 he captured 3 wagons, 20 horses, 7 prisoners and a large amount of sutlers' goods near Warrenton Junction.

On the 20th and 21st instant, I conducted an expedition along the enemy's line of communication, in which important information obtained was forwarded to the army headquarters, and I succeeded in capturing 9 prisoners and 21 fine horses and mules.

On the 27th and 28th instant, I made a reconnaissance in the vicinity of Alexandria, capturing Colonel Dulaney, aide to the bogus Governor Pierpont, several horses, and burning the railroad bridge across Cameron's Run, which was immediately under cover of the guns of two forts.

The military value of the species of warfare I have waged is not measured by the number of prisoners and material of war captured from the enemy, but by the heavy detail it has already compelled him to make, and which I hope to make him increase, in order to guard his communications and to that extent diminishing his aggressive strength.

[Indorsements]

Headquarters Cavalry Corps, October 5, 1863.

Respectfully forwarded, and recommend that Major Mosby be promoted another grade in recognition of his valuable services. The capture of these prominent Union officials, as well as the destruction of bridges, trains, etc., was the subject of special instructions which he is faithfully carrying out.

J. E. B. Stuart, Major-General.

Headquarters, November 17, 1863.

Respectfully forwarded.

Major Mosby is entitled to great credit for his boldness and skill in his operations against the enemy. He keeps them in constant apprehension and inflicts repeated injuries. I have hoped that he would have been able to raise his command sufficiently for the command of a Lieutenant-Colonel, and to have it regularly mustered into the service. I am not aware that it numbers over 4 companies.

R. E. Lee, General.

[Letter to Mrs. Mosby]

Fauquier Co.,<br>Oct. 1, '63.

My dearest Pauline :

Just returned from a raid. I went down in the suburbs of Alexandria and burned a railroad bridge in a quarter of a mile of two forts and directly in range of their batteries, also captured Colonel Dulaney, aide to (Governor) Pierpont. Dulaney lives in Alexandria, — has a son in my command, who was with me at the time. . . . It was quite an amusing scene,

the interview between Colonel Dulaney and his son.
Just as we were about leaving the Colonel sarcasti-
cally remarked to his son that he had an old pair of
shoes he had better take, as he reckoned they were
darned scarce in the Confederacy, whereupon the son,
holding up his leg, which was encased in a fine pair of
cavalry boots just captured from a sutler, asked the
old man what he thought of that. I am now fixing
my triggers for several good things which, if they
succeed, will make a noise. Old Mrs. Shacklett is
going to Baltimore next week and I shall send for some
things for you all. . . . In Richmond I got some
torpedoes, which have just arrived, and my next trip
I shall try to blow up a railroad train. Went to see
the Secretary of War, — he spoke in the highest terms
of the services of my command, — said he read all my
official reports. Also saw old General Lee, — he was
very kind to me and expressed the greatest satisfaction
at the conduct of my command.

### [Report, Mosby to Stuart]

October 19, 1863.

. . . On Thursday, 15th, came down into Fairfax, where I have been operating ever since in the
enemy's rear.

I have captured over 100 horses and mules, several
wagons loaded with valuable stores, and between 75
and 100 prisoners, arms, equipments, etc. Among the
prisoners were 3 captains and 1 lieutenant.

I had a sharp skirmish yesterday with double my

number of cavalry near Annandale in which I routed them, capturing the captain commanding and 6 or 7 men and horses. I have so far sustained no loss. It has been my object to detain the troops that are occupying Fairfax, by annoying their communications and preventing them from operating in front. . . . I contemplate attacking a cavalry camp at Falls Church to-morrow night.

[Report, Mosby to Stuart]

Nov. 6, 1863.

I returned yesterday from a scout in the neighborhood of Catlett's. I was accompanied by Captain Smith and 2 men of my command. We killed Kilpatrick's division commissary and captured an adjutant, 4 men, 6 horses, etc. Kilpatrick's Division (now reported unfit for duty) lies around Weaverville. . . . I sent you 4 cavalrymen on Wednesday captured by my scouts.

[Report, Mosby to Stuart]

Nov. 22, 1863.

Since rendering my report of the 5th [sic] inst. we have captured about 75 of the enemy's cavalry, over 100 horses and mules, 6 wagons, a considerable number of arms, equipments, etc.

It would be too tedious to mention in detail the various affairs in which these captures have been made, but I would omit the performance of a pleasant duty if I failed to bring to your notice the bold onset of Capt. Smith, when, with only about 40 men, he dashed into the enemy's camp of 150 cavalry near Warrenton, killed some 8 or 10, wounded a number and brought off 9 prisoners, 27 horses, arms, equipments, etc. In various other affairs several of the enemy have been killed and wounded. I have sustained no loss. . . .

[Report, Mosby to Stuart]

January 4, 1864.

I have the honor to report that during the month of December there were captured by this command over 100 horses and mules and about 100 prisoners. A considerable number of the enemy have also been killed and wounded. It would be too tedious to mention the various occasions on which we have met the enemy, but there is one which justice to a brave officer demands to be noticed. On the morning of January 1, I received information that a body of the enemy's cavalry were in Upperville. It being the day on which my command was to assemble, I directed Capt. William R. Smith to take command of the men while I went directly toward Upperville to ascertain the movements of the enemy. In the meantime the enemy had gone on toward Rectortown, and I pursued, but came up just as Capt. Smith with about 35 men had attacked and routed them (75 strong), killing, wounding, and capturing 57.

[Indorsements]

Headquarters Cavalry Corps, February 13, 1864.

Respectfully forwarded.

A subsequent report of subsequent operations has been already sent in, this having been mislaid. Major Mosby continues his distinguished services in the enemy's rear, relieving our people of the depredations of the enemy in a great measure.

J. E. B. Stuart,
Major-General.

February 15, 1864.

A characteristic report from Colonel Mosby, who has become so familiar with brave deeds as to consider them too tedious to treat unless when necessary to reflect glory on his gallant comrades. Captain Smith's was a brilliant and most successful affair.

J. A. Seddon, Secretary of War.

[Report, Mosby to Stuart]

February 1, 1864.

On Wednesday, January 6, having previously reconnoitered in person the position of the enemy, I directed Lieutenant Turner, with a detachment of about 30 men, to attack an outpost of the enemy in the vicinity of Warrenton, which he did successfully, routing a superior force of the enemy, killing and wounding several, and capturing 18 prisoners and 42 horses, with arms, equipments, etc.

On Saturday, January 9, having learned through Frank Stringfellow (Stuart's scout), that Cole's (Maryland) Cavalry was encamping on Loudon Heights, with no supports but infantry, which was about one-half mile off, I left Upperville with about 100 men, in hopes of being able to completely surprise his camp by a night attack. By marching my command by file, along a narrow path, I succeeded in gaining a position in the rear of the enemy, between their camp and the Ferry. On reaching this point, without creating any alarm, I deemed that the crisis had passed, and the capture of the enemy a certainty. I had exact information up to dark of that evening of the number of the enemy (which was between 175 and 200), the position of their headquarters, etc. When within 200 yards of the camp, I sent Stringfellow on ahead with about 10 men to capture Major Cole and staff, whose headquarters were in a house about 100 yards from their camp, while I halted to close up my command. The camp was buried in a profound sleep; there was not a sentinel awake. All my plans were on the eve of consummation, when suddenly the party sent with Stringfellow came dashing over the hill toward the camp, yelling and shooting. They had made no attempt to secure Cole. Mistaking them for the enemy, I ordered my men to charge.

In the meantime the enemy had taken the alarm, and received us with a volley from their carbines. A severe fight ensued, in which they were driven from their camp, but, taking refuge in the surrounding houses, kept up a desultory firing. Confusion and delay having ensued from the derangement of my plans, consequent on the alarm given to the enemy, rendered it hazardous to continue in my position, as reinforcements were near the enemy. Accordingly, I ordered the men to retire, which was done in good order, bringing off 6 prisoners, and between 50 and 60 horses.

My loss was severe; more so in the worth than the number of the slain. It was 4 killed, 7 wounded (of whom 4 have since died), and 1 captured. A published list of the enemy's loss gives it at 5 killed and 13 wounded. Among those who fell on this occasion were Capt. William R. Smith and Lieutenant Turner, two of the noblest and bravest officers of this army, who thus sealed a life of devotion and of sacrifice to the cause they loved.

In numerous other affairs with the enemy, between 75 and 100 horses and mules have been captured, about 40 men killed, wounded, and captured. A party of this command also threw one of the enemy's trains off the track, causing a great smash up.

[Indorsement]

Headquarters Cavalry Corps,

Respectfully forwarded.          February 9, 1864.

The conduct of Major Mosby is warmly commended to the notice of the commanding general. His sleepless vigilance and unceasing activity have done the enemy great damage. He keeps a large force of the enemy's cavalry continually employed in Fairfax in the vain effort to suppress his inroads. His exploits are not surpassed in daring and enterprise by those of *petite guerre* in any age. Unswerving devotion to duty, self-abnegation, and unflinching courage, with a quick perception and appreciation of the opportunity, are the characteristics of this officer. Since I first knew him, in 1861, he has never once alluded to his own rank or promotion; thus far it has come by the force of his own merit. While self-consciousness of having done his duty well is the patriot soldier's best reward, yet the evidence of the appreciation of his country is a powerful incentive to renewed effort, which should not be undervalued by those who have risen to the highest point of military and civic eminence. That evidence is promotion. If Major Mosby has not won it, no more can daring deeds essay to do it. . . .

J. E. B. Stuart, Major-General.

[One of those wounded in a fight at Dranesville, February 22, was Baron von Massow, who later became the Chief of Cavalry in the Imperial German Army. Von Massow was the son of the chamberlain to the King of Prussia and came to America to see some fighting. He offered his services to General Stuart who sent him to Mosby. In the Dranesville fight Mosby's command charged a California regiment from two directions and routed it. The Baron was fight-

ing with the rest when he espied Captain Reid
of the Californians. Von Massow made a rush
at Reid, as if he were about to chop his head off
with his sword — the Prussian clung to the sword
in a fight instead of using a revolver, as did the
rest of Mosby's men. Captain Reid was caught
so that he could not defend himself and made a
motion which the Baron interpreted as a sign of
surrender. The latter signed for Reid to go to
the rear and rode on into the *mêlée*. As he turned
his back Reid drew a revolver and shot him. At
almost the same instant Captain Chapman, who
had seen the incident and divined the Californian's
intention to shoot, drew his revolver and shot
Captain Reid. Reid was instantly killed, and Von
Massow was so seriously injured that he was never
able to rejoin Mosby's command.]

[Report, Mosby to Lieutenant-Colonel Taylor,
Assistant Adjutant-General]

September 11, 1864.

On March 10th with a detachment of about 40
men, I defeated a superior force of the enemy's cavalry
near Greenwich, severely wounding 3, and capturing
9 prisoners, 10 horses, arms, etc. On the same day
Lieut. A. E. Richards, with another detachment of
about 30 men, surprised an outpost of the enemy

near Charles Town, killed the major commanding and a lieutenant, several privates, and brought off 21 prisoners with their horses, arms, etc. In neither engagement did my command sustain any loss.

During the months of March and April but few opportunities were offered for making any successful attacks on the enemy, the continual annoyances to which they had been subjected during the winter causing them to exert great vigilance in guarding against surprises and interruptions of their communications. During most of these months I was myself engaged in scouting in the enemy's rear for Major-General Stuart and collecting information which was regularly transmitted to his headquarters, concerning the movements, numbers, and distribution of the enemy's forces both east and west of the Blue Ridge. During this time my men were mostly employed in collecting forage from the country bordering on the Potomac.

About April 15, Captain Richards routed a marauding party of the enemy's cavalry at Waterford, killing and wounding 5 or 6 and bringing off 6 or 8 prisoners, 15 horses, arms, etc.

About April 25 I attacked an outpost near Hunter's Mills, in Fairfax, capturing 5 prisoners and 18 horses. The prisoners and horses were sent back under charge of Lieutenant Hunter, while I went off on a scout in another direction. The enemy pursued and captured the lieutenant and 6 of the horses.

About May 1st, with a party of 10 men, I captured 8 of Sigel's wagons near Bunker Hill, in the Valley, but was only able to bring off the horses attached (34 in number) and about 20 prisoners. The horses and prisoners were sent back, while with another detachment of 20 men who had joined me I proceeded to Martinsburg, which place we entered that night, while occupied by several hundred Federal troops, and brought off 15 horses and several prisoners.

Returning to my command, I learned that General Grant had crossed the Rapidan. With about 40 men I moved down the north bank of the Rappahannock to assail his communications wherever opened, and sent two other detachments, under Captains Richards and Chapman, to embarrass Sigel as much as possible. Captain Richards had a skirmish near Winchester in which several of them were killed and wounded. Captain Chapman attacked a wagon train, which was heavily guarded, near Strassburg, capturing about 30 prisoners with an equal number of horses, etc. Near Belle Plain, in King George, I captured an ambulance train and brought off about 75 horses and mules, and 40 prisoners, etc.

A few days after I made a second attempt near the same place, but discovered that my late attack had caused them to detach such a heavy force to guard their trains and line of communication that another successful attack on them was impracticable.

About May 10 I attacked a cavalry outpost in the vicinity of Front Royal, capturing 1 captain and 15 men and 75 horses and sustained no loss.

About May 20, with about 150 men, I moved to the vicinity of Strassburg with the view of capturing the wagon trains of General Hunter, who had then moved up the Valley. When the train appeared I discovered that it was guarded by about 600 infantry and 100 cavalry. A slight skirmish ensued between their cavalry and a part of my command, in which their cavalry was routed with a loss of 8 prisoners and horses, besides several killed, but falling back on their infantry, my men in turn fell back, with a loss of 1 killed. While we did not capture the train, one great object had been accomplished — the detachment of a heavy force to guard their communications. After the above affair, only one wagon train ever went up to Hunter, which was still more heavily guarded. He then gave up his line of communication.

After the withdrawal of the enemy's forces from Northern Virginia, for several weeks but few opportunities were offered for any successful incursions upon them. Many enterprises on a small scale were, however, undertaken by detachments of the command, of which no note has been taken.

About June 20 I moved into Fairfax and routed a body of cavalry near Centreville, killing and wounding 6 or 8, and capturing 31 prisoners, securing their horses, etc.

A few days afterwards we took Duffield's Depot, on the Baltimore and Ohio Railroad; secured about 50 prisoners, including 2 lieutenants and a large number of stores. The train had passed a few minutes before we reached the place. On my way there I had left Lieutenant Nelson, commanding Company A, at Charles Town, for the purpose of intercepting and notifying me of any approach in my rear from Harper's

Ferry.  As I had anticipated, a body of cavalry, largely superior in numbers to his force, moved out from that point.  Lieutenant Nelson gallantly charged and routed them, killing and wounding several and taking 19 prisoners and 27 horses.  We sustained no loss on this expedition.

On July 4, hearing of General Early's movement down the Valley, I moved with my command east of the Blue Ridge for the purpose of coöperating with him and crossed the Potomac at Point of Rocks, driving out the garrison (250 men, strongly fortified) and securing several prisoners and horses.  As I supposed it to be General Early's intention to invest Maryland Heights, I thought the best service I could render would be to sever all communication both by railroad and telegraph between that point and Washington, which I did, keeping it suspended for two days.

As this was the first occasion on which I had used artillery [sic] the magnitude of the invasion was greatly exaggerated by the fears of the enemy, and panic and alarm spread through their territory.  I desire especially to bring to the notice of the commanding general the unsurpassed gallantry displayed by Captain Richards, commanding First Squadron.  Our crossing was opposed by a body of infantry stationed on the Maryland shore.  Dismounting a number of sharpshooters, whom I directed to wade the river above the point held by the enemy, I superintended in person the placing of my piece of artillery in position, at the same time directing Captain Richards whenever the enemy had been dislodged by the sharpshooters and artillery, to charge across the river in order to effect their capture. The enemy were soon routed and Captain Richards charged over, but before he could overtake them they had retreated across the canal, pulling up the bridge in their rear. My order had not, of course, contemplated their pursuit into their fortifications, but the destruction of the bridge was no obstacle to his impetuous valor, and hastily dismounting and throwing down a few planks on the sills, he charged across, under a heavy fire from a redoubt. The enemy fled panic stricken, leaving in our possession their camp equipage, etc. . . .

On the morning of July 6, while still encamped near the Potomac, information was received that a considerable force of cavalry was at Leesburg. I immediately hastened to meet them. At Leesburg I learned that they had gone toward Aldie, and I accordingly moved on the road to Ball's Mill in order to intercept them returning to their camp in Fairfax, which I succeeded in doing, meeting them at Mount Zion Church, and completely routing them, with a loss of about 80 of their officers and men left dead and severely wounded on the field, besides 57 prisoners. Their loss includes a captain and lieutenant killed and 1 lieutenant severely wounded; the major commanding and 2 lieutenants prisoners. We also secured all their horses, arms, etc.

My loss was 1 killed and 6 wounded — none dangerously.

After this affair the enemy never ventured, in two months after, the experiment of another raid through that portion of our district.

A few days afterward I again crossed the Potomac in coöperation with General Early, and moved through Poolesville, Md., for the purpose of capturing a body of cavalry encamped near Seneca. They retreated, however, before we reached there, leaving all their camp equipage and a considerable amount of stores. We also captured 30 head of beef cattle.

When General Early fell back from before Washington I recrossed the Potomac, near Seneca, moving thence to the Little River Pike in order to protect him from any movement up the south side of the river. The enemy moved through Leesburg in pursuit of General Early and occupied Ashby's and Snicker's Gaps. I distributed my command so as to most effectually protect the country. These detachments — under Captains Richards and Chapman and Lieutenants Glasscock, Nelson, and Hatcher — while they kept the enemy confined to the main thoroughfares and restrained their ravages, killed and captured about 300, securing their horses, etc. My own attention was principally directed to ascertaining the numbers and movements of the enemy and forwarding the information to General Early, who was then in the Valley.

At the time of the second invasion of Maryland by General Early, I moved my command to the Potomac, crossed over 3 companies at Cheek's and Noland's Fords, while the remaining portion was kept in reserve on this side with the artillery, which was posted on the south bank to keep open the fords, keeping one company, under Lieutenant Williams, near the ford, on the north bank. Two were sent under Lieutenant

Nelson, to Adamstown, on the Baltimore and Ohio Railroad, for the purpose of intercepting the trains from Baltimore, destroying their communications, etc. Apprehending a movement up the river from a considerable body of cavalry which I knew to be stationed below, I remained with a portion of the command guarding the fords.

Lieutenant Nelson reached the road a few minutes too late to capture the train, but destroyed two telegraph lines. On his return he met a force of the enemy's cavalry, near Monocacy, which was charged and routed by the gallant Lieutenant Hatcher, who took about 15 men and horses, besides killing and wounding several.

We recrossed the river in the evening, bringing about 75 horses and between 20 and 30 prisoners.

Our loss, 2 missing.

[The battle at Mount Zion attracted great attention at the time — especially in the North, and made the already redoubtable figure of Mosby an altogether awe-inspiring one. The capture of Major Forbes, "Colonel Lowell's fighting Major", was also an important incident in Mosby's life, as here began the lifelong friendship between the two families.

The story of the battle was well told in the official report of Colonel Charles R. Lowell, Jr., Second Massachusetts Cavalry. The report reads :]

Near Falls Church, Va., July 8, 1864.

I have the honor to report Major Forbes' scout as completely as is yet possible.   I have not talked with Lieutenant Kuhls or Captain Stone, who is badly wounded, but send what I learned on the ground.

Major Forbes left here with 150 men (100 Second Massachusetts Cavalry, 50 Thirteenth New York Cavalry) Monday, P.M.   Tuesday, A.M., went through Aldie, and found all quiet toward the Gaps.   Tuesday, P.M., went by Ball's Mill to Leesburg.   Heard of Mosby's raid at Point of Rocks, and learned that he had sent four or five wagons of plunder through Leesburg, under a guard of about 60 men, the afternoon before.   Heard nothing of any other force this side of the ridge.   He returned that night to the south of Goose Creek, as directed, and, on Wednesday, A.M., went again by Ball's Mill to Leesburg.   Still heard nothing of Mosby or any force.   From what I learned from citizens, I think Mosby passed between Leesburg and the Potomac some time on Tuesday, crossed Goose Creek, and moved westward toward Aldie on Wednesday; learned of Major Forbes' second visit to Leesburg, and laid in ambush for him at Ball's Mill.   Major Forbes returned from Leesburg by Centre's Mill (4 miles above), came down by Aldie, and halted for two or three hours about one and a half miles east, on the Little River Pike; when Mosby learned this he moved south and struck the pike about one and a quarter miles east of the Major's position, being hidden till he had reached about half a mile west on the pike.

Major Forbes was duly notified by his advance guard, mounted his men, and moved them from the north to the south of the pike. As the rear was crossing, Mosby fired one shell from his 12-pounder, which burst entirely too high. As Major Forbes formed on the south, his advance guard, which had dismounted and fired as Mosby came up, fell back, still keeping a little north of the pike, and took an excellent position somewhat on the flank. Up to this time, I think, all the dispositions were admirable. Major Forbes' two squadrons were formed, his third squadron and rear guard not formed but nearly so, and no confusion. Mosby's men, who were not in any order, but were down the road in a "nick," had just reached the fence corner some 225 yards off, and a few had dismounted, under a fire from the advanced guard, to take down the fence. When two panels of the fence were down the men trotted through for about 75 yards, and came gradually down to a walk, and almost halted. Major Forbes' first platoon was ordered to fire with carbines. Here was the first mistake. It created confusion among the horses, and the squadron in the rear added to it by firing a few pistol shots. Had the order been given to draw sabres and charge, the rebels would never have got their gun off, but I think Major Forbes, seeing how uneasy his horses were at the firing, must have intended to dismount some of his men. At any rate, he attempted to move the first squadron by the right flank. The rebels saw their chance, gave a yell, and our men, in the confusion of the moment, broke. The two rear squadrons went off in confusion. Attempts were made, with some success, to rally parts of the first squadron in the next field, and again near Little River Church, one mile off.

Captain Stone was wounded here, and I believe all the non-commissioned officers of A and L Companies present were wounded or killed. There was little gained. I have only to report a perfect rout and a chase for five to seven miles. We lost Major Forbes, Lieutenant Amory, and Mr. Humphreys (Chaplain), from Second Massachusetts, and Lieutenant Burns, Thirteenth New York Cavalry, prisoners, all unhurt. Captain Stone, Second Massachusetts, and Lieutenant Schuyler, Thirteenth New York, very badly wounded. Lieutenant Kuhls alone came safely to camp. Of men, we lost, killed outright, 7, Second Massachusetts; 5, Thirteenth New York: wounded, we brought in 27 and left 10 too bad to move. I fear of the wounded at least 12 will die. About 40 others have come to camp half mounted, and Mosby reported to have 44 prisoners; quite a number, you will see, still unaccounted for. Some of them are probably wounded, and some still on their way to camp, and others will be made prisoners.

Mosby went up toward Upperville with his prisoners and his dead and wounded about midnight Wednesday. I reached the ground about 11.30 A.M. and remained in plain sight for about three hours; then searched through all the woods and moved to Centreville, where I again waited an hour in hopes some stragglers would join us. We only picked up half a dozen, however.

The soldiers and citizens all speak in high terms of

the gallantry of the officers; Major Forbes especially remained in the first field till every man had left it, emptied his revolver, and, in the second field, where Company A tried to stand, he disabled one man with his sabre, and lunged through Colonel Mosby's coat. His horse was then killed and fell on his leg, pinning him till he was compelled to surrender.

More than 100 horses were taken. Accoutrements, arms, etc., will also be missing. I cannot yet give the precise number.

Mosby's force is variously estimated at from 175 to 200, Mrs. Davis and her daughter putting it at 250 to 300 men. I think he had probably about 200. What his loss is I cannot say, as he picked up all his dead and wounded and took them off in the night. The Union people in Aldie report that he took them in five wagons. A wounded sergeant reports hearing the names of 3 or 4 spoken of as killed; one mortally wounded man was left on the ground. [Mosby actually lost seven men wounded. His force was about 175 men.] I think the chance was an excellent one to whip Mosby and take his gun. I have no doubt Major Forbes thought so, too, as the wounded men say there was not enough difference in numbers to talk about. The chance was lost.

# CHAPTER XIV

## The Campaign against Sheridan

According to Grant's design, Sheridan left his base at Harper's Ferry on August 10, 1864, and started up the Shenandoah Valley. Grant's main object was to cut Lee's line of communication with the southwest, for, if this were accomplished, the inevitable result would be the fall of Richmond and the end of the war. It was immaterial whether Sheridan secured this result by defeating Early — who was defending the Valley — in battle or by pushing him south by flank movements.

During this campaign of 1864, my battalion of six companies was the only force operating in the rear of Sheridan's army in the Shenandoah Valley. Our rendezvous was along the eastern base of the Blue Ridge, in what is known as the Piedmont region of Virginia. Fire and sword could not drive the people of that neighborhood from their allegiance to what they thought was right, and in the gloom of disaster and defeat they never wavered in their support of the Confederate cause. The main object of my campaign was to vex and embarrass Sheridan and, if possible, to prevent his advance into the interior of the State. But my exclusive attention was not given to Sheridan, for alarm was kept up continuously by threatening Washington and occasionally crossing the Potomac. We lived on the country where we operated and drew nothing from Richmond except the gray jackets my men wore. We were mounted, armed, and equipped entirely off the enemy, but, as we captured a great deal more than we could use, the surplus was sent to supply Lee's army. The mules we sent him furnished a large part of his transportation, and the captured sabres and carbines were turned over to his cavalry — we had no use for them.

I believe I was the first cavalry commander who discarded the sabre as useless and consigned it to museums for the preservation of antiquities. My men were as little impressed by a body of cavalry charging them with sabres as though they had been armed with cornstalks. In the Napoleonic wars cavalry might sometimes ride down infantry armed with muzzle-loaders and flintlocks, because the infantry would be broken by the momentum of the charge before more than one effective fire could be delivered. At Eylau the French cavalry rode over the Russians in a snowstorm because the powder of the infantry was wet and they were defenceless. Fixed ammunition had not been invented. I think that my command reached the highest point of efficiency as cavalry because they were well armed with two six-shooters and their charges combined the effect of fire and shock. We were called bushwhackers, as a term of reproach, simply because our attacks were generally surprises, and we had to make up by celerity for lack of numbers. Now I never resented the epithet of "bushwhacker" — although there was no soldier to whom it applied less — because bushwhacking is a legitimate form of war, and it is just as fair and equally heroic to fire at an enemy from behind a bush as a breastwork or from the casemate of a fort.

The Union cavalry who met us in combat knew that we always fought on the offensive in a mounted charge and with a pair of Colt's revolvers. I think we did more than any other body of men to give the Colt pistol its great reputation. A writer on the history of cavalry cites as an example of the superiority of the revolver a fight that a squadron of my command, under Captain Dolly[1] Richards, had in the Shenandoah Valley, in which more of the enemy were killed than the entire total by sabre in the Franco-Prussian War. But, to be effective, the pistol must, of course, be used at close quarters.

As I have said, during this campaign our operations were not confined to this valley. The troops belonging to the defences of Washington and guarding the line of the Potomac were a portion of Sheridan's command. To prevent his being reinforced from this source, I made frequent attacks on the outposts in Fairfax and demonstrations along the Potomac. The Eighth Illinois Cavalry, the largest and regarded as the finest regiment in the Army of the Potomac, had been brought back to Washington, largely recruited, and stationed at Seneca (or Muddy Branch) on the river above Washington. There were a number of other detachments of cavalry on the Maryland side, and two regiments of cavalry in Fairfax. General Augur commanded at Washington. Stevenson, at Harper's Ferry, had nine thousand men, who were expected

[1] Adolphus E. Richards.

to keep employed in watching the canal and railroad.

Sheridan wanted to take the Eighth Illinois to the Valley, but Augur objected, on the ground that they could not be spared from Washington.

[Sheridan to Augur]

Harper's Ferry, August 8, 1864. [The day after Sheridan took formal command of the Army of the Shenandoah.]

What force have you at Edwards's and Noland's ferries? (On the Potomac.) Where is Colonel Lazelle posted? Mosby has about 200 cavalry at, or near, Point of Rocks.

[Augur to Sheridan]

Washington, D.C., August 3.

Colonel Lazelle is posted at Falls Church (Fairfax County) and pickets from the Potomac near Difficult Creek to Orange and Alexandria Railroad. Major Waite (Eighth Illinois) has near 600 cavalry along the Potomac from Great Falls to the mouth of the Monocacy watching the different fords.

[Sheridan to Augur]

August 8th.

Can the Eighth Illinois Cavalry be spared? I find that the cavalry has been so scattered up here that it is no wonder that it has not done so well.

[Augur to Sheridan]

August 8th.

The Eighth Illinois is scattered worse than anything you have. The headquarters of six companies are in General Wallace's department. Major Waite, with four companies, is guarding the Potomac between Great Falls and the Monocacy; another company is near Port Tobacco, and another is with the Army of the Potomac. I do not see how Major Waite's command can be spared, as I have no cavalry to replace it.

[Sheridan to Augur]

August 8th.

Your dispatch in reference to the Eighth Illinois received. Colonel Lowell left about 600 men of Gregg's cavalry division in support of Major Waite. They moved this morning towards the mouth of the Monocacy, and will remain in that vicinity. I will not change the Eighth Illinois Cavalry for the present.

[Augur to Waite]

Upper Potomac, August 8th.

General Sheridan reports that Mosby, with about 300 men, is at or near the Point of Rocks. Look out well for him.

[Taylor to Augur]

August 10th.

General Sheridan has ordered concentration of the Eighth Illinois Cavalry at Muddy Branch to picket the river from Monocacy to Washington. The river is well guarded from mouth of Monocacy to Harper's Ferry.

### [Sheridan to Augur]

Charles Town, August 18th.

Keep scouts out in Loudon County. I have ordered the Eighth Illinois Cavalry to rendezvous at Muddy Branch Station. The line of the Potomac should be watched carefully, and information be sent to me should any raiding parties attempt to cross.

### [Augur to Waite]

August 18th.

Mosby is reported to have within reach and control from 400 to 500 men and two pieces of artillery. It will be necessary for you to move with the utmost caution.

General Lee apprehended a raid by the cavalry from Washington on the Central Railroad, and instructed me, if possible, to prevent it. The only way that I could do so was to excite continual alarm in their camps. Their outposts were often attacked all along their lines on the same night. This was the only way we could keep them at home. On the same day three or four different detachments would go out; some to operate on Sheridan west of the ridge, some to keep Augur in remembrance of his duty to guard the Capital.

Sheridan was obviously greatly solicitous about preserving his communications, for he knew that they were weak and a vital necessity for his army. He evidently had some information which increased his anxiety about his rear. One night, when his headquarters were at Berryville, I sent my best scout, John Russell, with two or three men, to reconnoitre, intending to deliver a blow at Sheridan's rear and thus cripple him by cutting off his supplies. John reported long trains passing down along the valley pike. I started for the vicinity with some 250 men and two howitzers, one of which became an encumbrance by breaking down. Through Snicker's Gap we crossed the Blue Ridge Mountains after sundown and passed over the Shenandoah River not far from Berryville. I halted at a barn for a good rest and sent Russell to see what was going on upon the pike. I was asleep when he returned with the news that a very large train was just passing along. The men sprang to their saddles. With Russell and some others I went on in advance to choose the best place for attack, directing Captain William Chapman to bring on the command. About sunrise we were on a knoll from

which we could get a good view of a great train
of wagons moving along the road and a large
drove of cattle with the train. The train was
within a hundred yards of us, strongly guarded,
but with flankers out. We were obscured by
the mist, and, if noticed at all, were doubtless
thought to be friends. I sent Russell to hurry
up Chapman, who soon arrived. The howitzer
was made ready. Richards, with his squadron,
was sent to attack the front; William Chapman
and Glasscock were to attack them in the rear,
while Sam Chapman was kept near me and the
howitzer.

My scheme was nearly ruined by a ludicrous
incident, the fun of which is more apparent now
than it was then. The howitzer was unlimbered
over a yellow-jacket's nest. When one of the
men had rescued the howitzer, a shell was sent
screaming among the wagons, beheading a mule.
The shot was like thunder from a clear sky, and
the mist added to the enemy's perplexity. This
shot was our signal to charge, and we met little
resistance. Panic reigned along their line, and
I only lost two men killed and three wounded.
Before the fighting ended, as I knew that the
guard would soon recover from the panic, I had
men unhitching mules, burning wagons, and hurry-

ing prisoners and spoils to the rear. There were 325 wagons, guarded by Kenly's brigade and a large force of cavalry. They had not stopped to find out our numbers. We set a paymaster's wagon on fire, which contained — this we did not know at the time — $125,000. I deployed skirmishers as a mask, until my command, the prisoners, and booty were well across the Shenandoah River. We took between 500 and 600 horses, 200 beeves, and many useful stores; destroyed seventy-five loaded wagons, and carried off 200 prisoners, including seven officers.

The following dispatches illustrate the character and effect of my partisan operations in Sheridan's rear.

### [Stevenson to Sheridan]

#### Harper's Ferry, Aug. 17th.

Finding all trains threatened by guerillas, and that they are in force, largely increased by a concentration of several organizations under Mosby [there had been no such concentration], making the vicinity of Charles Town their theater of operations, I am of opinion that the only safety of our trains and couriers is the posting of a force at Charles Town, with General Duffie, at Berryville, and one thousand of Averell's force at Charles Town, with orders by constant scouting to keep the country clear. I think we can send forward everything without loss. As matters now stand no small party of trains with small guard is safe.

[Stevenson to Averell]

August 17th.

Rebels occupy Charles Town (in Sheridan's rear) with small force this evening. Attacked party of couriers coming in about five o'clock, capturing two of them; heard nothing of your command. A large supply train will start from here in the morning, so as to reach Charles Town by 6 A.M. Have but a small guard. If you could have a force at that point before the train to join escort and move with it to Berryville, it would secure the safety of train. Mosby, with his command, is waiting to attack train, and will capture it, if possible. The supplies are needed at the front, and will be put through by all means.

[Lazelle to Augur]

Fairfax County, August 9th.

I have the honor to report that two parties sent out from this command, consisting of thirty men each, met yesterday afternoon at Fairfax Station, and that while united and acting together were attacked by a force of rebels, variously estimated at from forty to fifty men, and were completely dispersed and routed. Citizens report that Mosby himself was in command of the rebels. So far as known, our loss is as follows: Captain J. H. Fleming, Sixteenth New York Cavalry, missing; thirty-three men missing. Thirty-nine horses missing. The number of the killed and wounded is not yet known. Captain Fleming, who at the time of the attack had command of the party, is reported killed.

[Captain Harrison to Kelly]

Martinsburg, August 14th.

Several of our scouts here say they cannot get through to Sheridan, Mosby having driven them back.

[Lazelle to De Russy]

Fairfax County, August 24th.

The attack at Annandale has ceased, and the rebels withdrew, perhaps with the intention of attacking some other part of my picket line. The attacking party is said to have consisted of from less than 200 to 300, even to 500 men, with two pieces of artillery, all under Mosby.

[Augur to Sheridan]

Washington, September 1st.

Major Waite has returned from Upperville, in the vicinity of Snicker's Gap; reports no rebel forces in that vicinity, except Mosby's.

[Lazelle to Augur]

September 1st.

Last night at about 10.30 o'clock one of our pickets was attacked near this camp; the attacking party was driven off, with a loss to the rebels of one horse, and it is believed one man wounded. About the same hour the picket posts on the Braddock Road and on the road to Falls Church and Annandale, were attacked simultaneously and driven in. This morning at about 6 A.M., one of our pickets, about half a mile west of the village of Falls Church, was attacked and one vi-dette captured. Late to-day two of our picket posts between here and Annandale were attacked at about the same time by a force of between twenty and thirty men. Five men were captured and seven horses, while four men escaped. At about the same hour the picket post on the Little River pike, towards Fair-fax Court House, from Annandale, was attacked, and one sergeant and a horse were wounded; two men and three horses captured.

### [Augur to Lazelle]

September 1st.

I have reliable information that Mosby is still lying in the woods in front of your lines, and expects to make an attack to-night somewhere upon it. Please have all your men on duty notified of this, that they may be on their guard and take proper precautions. If not successful to-night, he proposes to remain until he strikes some important blow.

### [Gansevoort to Augur]

Fairfax, September 19th.

Information considered very reliable has reached here to-day that in the skirmish with the Thirteenth

New York Cavalry, on the last scout of that regiment, Colonel Mosby was seriously wounded, a pistol bullet striking the handle of the pistol in his belt and glancing off in his groin. He was able, however, to ride off, but soon fainted, and was carried in a wagon to a place of safety.

[Lazelle to Augur]

September 29th.

Private Henry Smith, of Company H, Thirteenth New York Cavalry, is the man who wounded him (Mosby). It was a bold deed, and Smith deserves credit for it.

[Sheridan to Augur]

Strassburg, September 21st.

I wish you to send to Winchester all the available troops possible to the number of between four thousand to five thousand, without delay, to relieve the troops left there to guard my communication. If necessity should require, they can be returned at short notice.

[Stevenson to Stanton]

Harper's Ferry, Sept. 26th.

Both of my last courier parties were attacked by Rebel cavalry; dispersed part of them, capturing the first party at Strassburg, the second at a point between Charles Town and Bunker Hill. Message No. 31 was sent by both parties, and both have failed. I shall try another duplicate to-night. The country between this and Sheridan yesterday and to-day seemed to be alive with parties of Rebel guerillas and cavalry. Last night they attacked ambulances with scout of seventeen men between this and Charles Town; severely wounded Sergeant of Sixteenth Pennsylvania Cavalry. I doubt if we should be able to get any dispatches through without sending much larger body of cavalry than I can get hold of. I have but small force for such duty, and it is badly worn down.

[Edwards to Neil]

Martinsburg–Winchester, Oct. 2d.

The train that left Martinsburg arrived here last night. I have no forces here to escort it to the front, except 400 cavalry (and 100 of these cannot be relied on); also, some straggling infantry, without organization, numbering 300 men. I have detained the train here on account of insufficiency in men to properly guard it. A train of its size to go through the country where it has to should have an escort of at least 2000 men with it. Captain Blazer, of the Independent Scouts, comes in this morning and reports Mosby's command hovering in the neighborhood of Newtown, etc. No escort with dispatches can get through with less than 500 cavalry.

[Stevenson to Stanton]

Harper's Ferry, Oct. 1st.

There are no organized troops of enemy in Valley this side of Staunton, except Mosby's guerillas.

[Neil to Stanton]

Martinsburg, September 30th.

About 300 or 400 guerillas are operating between Winchester and Bunker Hill. I do not consider my post safe unless I have stronger force to protect the large amount of Government property rapidly collecting here.

As the Federal dispatches said, I was wounded on September 14, four days before the battle of Winchester. But it was hardly the bold deed Lazelle described. Two of my men, Tom Love and Guy Broadwater, and myself met five of the enemy's cavalry in Fairfax. As we were within a few yards of each other, we all fired at the same time. Two of the enemy's horses fell dead, and I was seriously wounded. The other three cavalry then fled full speed with Love and Broadwater after them until I called them back to my assistance. We then left the other men under the dead horses, and I was carried, for safety, to my father's home near Lynchburg. Captain William Chapman commanded my battalion during my absence.

On the day after I was wounded, 400 of Sheridan's cavalry came over the Blue Ridge at night, expecting, by aid of a spy, to capture a good many of my men. The expedition was commanded by General George H. Chapman of Indianapolis. He caught several of my men and started back, with Captain Chapman in pursuit of the General. Captain Chapman did not go on his trail, but took a road running along the top of the Blue Ridge in order to intercept the Union troops before they got to the Shenandoah River. It was an excessively hot day and the Union troops had ridden all night. The General had heard of my being wounded and may have calculated that my command was disorganized or would be less active. So when the troops reached Snicker's Gap, all lay down in the shade and went to sleep. Captain Chapman soon came plunging down the mountainside like an avalanche and was firing among the men before they were awake. They had not expected an enemy to come like a bolt from the sky, and the attack caused a general stampede. All the prisoners were recaptured, and many of the enemy were killed, wounded, and captured.

General Chapman returned to camp and wrote in his report:

About an hour had elapsed and the men had mostly fallen asleep, when they were suddenly charged upon by a force of from fifty to eighty of the enemy, and, being stampeded by the surprise, a number were killed, wounded, and captured before I reached the scene of the encounter with the main body. They had approached the Gap across the mountains and charged down an easy slope, and they retired the same way, pursued for two miles by my men. It was near sundown, and in the exhausted state of men and horses, I did not deem further pursuit expedient.

Captain Tompson had captured twelve of the enemy but they were recaptured. From citizens I ascertained that Mosby was wounded some time ago and had gone to Richmond. Judging from indications, I should estimate the force operating under Mosby and his colleague at from 200 to 250. If they have any encampment it must be in the neighborhood and beyond Upperville.

It will be observed that General Chapman did not say that he was bushwhacked.

But these constant raids aroused the Federal officers to such an extent that on September 22 they attempted to take revenge by hanging some of my men.

An eye witness described the scene in a Confederate newspaper as follows:

The Yankee Cavalry, under General Torbert, entered the town (Front Royal), and drove out the four Confederates on picket, who fell back to Milford. At this latter point General Wickham met the Yankee force and repulsed it. A part of Mosby's men, under

Captain Chapman, annoyed the enemy very much on their return to Front Royal, which, with the mortification of their defeat by Wickham, excited them to such savage doings as to prompt them to murder six of our men who fell into their hands. Anderson, Overby, Love, and Rhodes were shot and Carter and one other, whose name our informant did not recollect, were hung to the limb of a tree at the entrance of the village. . . . Henry Rhodes was quite a youth, living with his widowed mother and supporting her by his labor. He did not belong to Mosby's command. His mother entreated them to spare the life of her son and treat him as a prisoner of war, but the demons answered by whetting their sabres on some stones and declaring they would cut his head off and hers too, if she came near. They ended by shooting him in her presence. The murders were committed on the 22nd day of September, Generals Torbert, Merritt, and Custer being present. It is said that Torbert and Merritt turned the prisoners over to Custer for the purpose of their execution.

An account in the *Richmond Examiner* was as follows:

On Friday last Mosby's men attacked a wagon train, which was protected by a whole brigade, so that their charge was repelled with the loss of six prisoners. Two of their prisoners the Yankees immediately hung to a neighboring tree, placing around their necks placards bearing the inscription, 'Hung in retaliation

for the Union officer killed after he had surrendered
— the fate of Mosby's men.' The other four of our
prisoners were tied to stakes and mercilessly shot
through the skull, each one individually. One of
those hung was a famous soldier named Overby, from
Georgia. When the rope was placed around his neck
by his inhuman captors, he told them that he was
one of Mosby's men, and that he was proud to die as a
Confederate soldier, and that his death was sweetened
with the assurance that Colonel Mosby would swing in
the wind ten Yankees for every man they murdered.

This action on the part of the enemy led to
my writing the following letter:

November 11, 1864.

Major General P. H. Sheridan,
    Commanding U. S. Forces in the Valley.

General:

Some time in the month of September, during my
absence from my command, six of my men who had
been captured by your forces, were hung and shot in
the streets of Front Royal, by order and in the immediate presence of Brigadier-General Custer. Since
then another (captured by a Colonel Powell on a
plundering expedition into Rappahannock) shared a
similar fate. A label affixed to the coat of one of the
murdered men declared "that this would be the fate
of Mosby and all his men."

Since the murder of my men, not less than seven

hundred prisoners, including many officers of high rank, captured from your army by this command have been forwarded to Richmond; but the execution of my purpose of retaliation was deferred, in order, as far as possible, to confine its operation to the men of Custer and Powell. Accordingly, on the 6th instant, seven of your men were, by my order, executed on the Valley Pike — your highway of travel.

Hereafter, any prisoners falling into my hands will be treated with the kindness due to their condition, unless some new act of barbarity shall compel me, reluctantly, to adopt a line of policy repugnant to humanity.

Very respectfully,
your obedient servant,
John S. Mosby,
Lieut. Colonel.

No further "acts of barbarity" were committed on my men.

Although Sheridan defeated Early in the battle at Winchester, on September 19, 1864, and was urged by Grant to move on south, press Early, and end the war, he really made no farther progress and spent the winter, with an overwhelming force, where he had won a victory in September. On September 23, after Fisher's Hill, Grant had telegraphed him, "Keep on and you will cause the fall of Richmond."

On the twenty-ninth Sheridan wrote to Grant from Harrisonburg:

My impression is that most of the troops which Early had left passed through these mountains to Charlottesville. Kershaw's division came to his assistance and, I think, passed along the west base of the mountain to Waynesboro. The advance of my infantry is at Mount Crawford, eight miles south of Harrisonburg. From the most reliable accounts Early's army was completely broken up and dispirited. It will be exceedingly difficult for me to carry the infantry over the mountains and strike at the Central road. I cannot accumulate stores to do so, and think it best to take some position near Front Royal and operate with cavalry and infantry.

In reply to Grant's dispatch a few days before he had said, "I am now about eighty miles from Martinsburg, and find it exceedingly difficult to supply this army."

Grant rejoined:

Your victories have caused the greatest consternation. If you can possibly subsist your army to the front for a few days more, do it, and make a great effort to destroy the roads about Charlottesville, and the canal wherever your cavalry can reach.

If this advice had been acted on, Sheridan's army would have been thrown into the rear of General Lee. Grant did not, of course, mean that Sheridan should stop at Charlottesville. He wanted him first to gain a foothold there, accumulate supplies by the Orange Railroad, and make it a new starting point for further operations.

The Orange and Alexandria Railroad runs south by Gordonsville and Charlottesville to Lynchburg. From Manassas Junction — twenty-five miles from Washington — a branch road runs west through the Blue Ridge to Front Royal and Strassburg. It was assumed that if the Northern army held the Manassas Gap line, my command would retire south of the Rappahannock. In this way a double purpose would be effected; a more convenient line of supplies would be secured, as well as the annexation of more territory to the United States. The sequel shows that I had not been consulted.

Without securing the fruits of his victory, on October 6 Sheridan began his retrograde movement, no doubt much to Grant's chagrin.

On October 3 Grant telegraphed Sheridan:

You may take up such position in the Valley as you think can and ought to be held, and send all the force not required for this immediately here. I will direct the Railroad to be pushed towards Front Royal, so that you may send our troops back that way.

[Halleck to Sheridan]

October 3rd.

The Orange and Alexandria road was repaired to the Rappahannock, in the expectation that you would pursue the enemy through the mountains and receive your supplies from Culpeper. By General Grant's order, the workmen have been changed to the Manassas Gap road, which will be opened to Front Royal.

On October 4 Halleck said to Grant, with reference to the opening and holding the railroad from Alexandria to Front Royal:

In order to keep up my communication on this line to Manassas Gap and Shenandoah Valley, it will be necessary to send south all rebel inhabitants between that line and the Potomac, and also to clean out Mosby's gang of robbers, who have so long infested that district of country; and I respectfully suggest that Sheridan's cavalry should be required to accomplish this object before it is sent elsewhere. The two small regiments (Thirteenth and Sixteenth New York, stationed in Fairfax) under General Augur, have been so often cut up by Mosby's band that they are cowed and useless for that purpose. If these dispositions are approved and carried out, it will not be necessary to keep so large a force at Harper's Ferry and guarding the canal and Baltimore and Ohio Railroad.

By sending some of Sheridan's troops to Grant, it was calculated that through the sudden augmentation of Grant's strength, he could make a successful assault on Lee at Petersburg before Early's troops could reach him, or to extend his lines so as to seize the Southside Railroad. This combination was defeated.

The following dispatch (October 4) from Stevenson at Harper's Ferry, to Edwards at Winchester, is significant as showing the dangers that beset Sheridan's line of supply.

Escorts with dispatches have to cut their way and generally lose half their men. I think a train of 200 wagons should have an escort of one thousand infantry and 500 cavalry going to the front. The train going out this morning will have nearly 1500 escort. I do not think I overestimate the danger between here and there.

Although I was still on crutches, I had now resumed command of my men. On October 4 a body of infantry, with construction force, came up on the Manassas road; they could not have anticipated any resistance, as they had only a single company of cavalry for couriers, and General Augur did not accompany them. The next day I attacked this force, and General Lee reported the results to the Secretary of War:

Chaffin's Bluff, October 9, 1864.

Hon. James A. Seddon, Secretary of War:

Colonel Mosby reports that a body of about a thousand of the enemy advanced up the Manassas road on the 4th, with trains of cars loaded with railroad material, and occupied Salem and Rectortown. He attacked them at Salem, defeating them, capturing fifty prisoners, all their baggage, camp equipage, stores, etc., and killed and wounded a considerable number. His loss, two wounded. The enemy is now entrenched at Rectortown, with two long trains of cars. The railroad is torn up and bridges burned in their rear, and all communications cut.

All work repairing the railroad was stopped, and both the soldiers and workmen went to building stockades for their own safety. A courier was sent immediately to Gordonsville with a telegram to General Lee informing him of the movement on the railroad. In reply General Lee said, "Your success at Salem gives great satisfaction. Do all in your power to prevent reconstruction of the road."

[The following undated fragment of letter to Mrs. Mosby probably refers to this action, — see page 331.]

. . . at Salem, and completely routed them. Captured fifty prisoners, and all their baggage, tents, rations, etc. Yesterday in a fight near the Plains my horse (or rather yours) ran entirely through the Yankees in a charge. He was badly shot and tumbled over me, but we whipped them. They are camped all along the railroad. Bowie, Ames, have both been killed. I don't think the Yankees will be here long. I will bring you all over as soon [as they leave the Manassas railroad].

The intentions cf the enemy were now plainly developed, and it was my duty to do all I could to defeat them. To do so with my slender means looked a good deal like going to sea in a saucer. The troops at Salem fled to Rectortown, where the railroad runs through a gorge. Here they took shelter. On the sixth and seventh we shelled them to keep them on the defensive. My guns could not be depressed sufficiently to do them much damage, but the enemy kept under cover.

On the seventh of October, from Woodstock, Sheridan sent the following dispatch to General Grant:

I commenced moving back yesterday morning. I would have preferred sending troops to you by the Baltimore and Ohio Road. It would have been the quickest and most concealed way of sending them. The keeping open of the road to Front Royal will require large guards to protect it against a very small number of partisan troops.

At the same time Sheridan requested Halleck not to send railroad transportation to Front Royal, as he might be delayed. It will be remembered that in his dispatch to General Grant on September 29, he had suggested falling back to Front Royal and operating from there as a base. Unless he used the railroad, his supplies would have to be brought by wagons from Harper's Ferry. On the same day he said to Halleck:

I have been unable to communicate more frequently on account of the operations of guerillas in my rear. They have attacked every party, and I have sent my dispatches with a view of economizing as much as possible.

Sheridan went to Front Royal to see to the embarkation of 10,000 troops for Grant, but he found nothing but a roadbed without iron. The troops remained there for three days waiting for Augur to build the road, but he could not do it; his troops had all they could do to take care of themselves, for my men were rather active those days.

In the following dispatch to Halleck, Sheridan admitted that he did not use the railroad because Augur could not repair it:

October 12th.

I have ordered the Sixth Corps (except one brigade now at Winchester) to march to Alexandria to-morrow morning. I have ordered General Augur to concentrate all his forces at Manassas Junction or Bull Run until he hears from me. He could not complete the railroad to Front Royal without additional forces from me, and to give him that force to do the work and transport the troops by rail to Alexandria would require more time.

# CHAPTER XV

## THE GREENBACK RAID

THROUGHOUT the fall and winter of 1864 I kept up an incessant warfare on Sheridan and his communications. On October 12 I wrote to my wife:

Near Middleburg.

My dearest Pauline:

I have been engaged in a perpetual strife with the Yankees ever since my arrival. They are now engaged in repairing the railroad (Manassas). I attacked a camp of 800. . . .

As we operated in Sheridan's rear, the railroad that brought his supplies was his weak point and consequently our favorite object of attack. For security it had to be closely guarded by detachments of troops, which materially reduced his offensive strength. We kept watch for unguarded points, and the opportunity they offered was never lost.

Early in October one of my best men, Jim Wiltshire, afterwards a prominent physician in

Baltimore, discovered and reported to me a gap
through which we might penetrate between the
guards and reach that railroad without exciting
an alarm. It was a hazardous enterprise, as
there were camps along the line and frequent communication between them, but I knew it would
injure Sheridan to destroy a train and compel
him to place stronger guards on the road. So I
resolved to take the risk. Jim Wiltshire had a
time-table and we knew the minute when the
train was due and so timed our arrival that we
would not have to wait long.

There was great danger of our being discovered
by the patrols on the road and our presence reported to the camps that were near. The situation was critical, but we were so buoyant with
hope that we did not realize it. The western-
bound passenger train was selected from the
schedule as I knew it would create a greater sensation to burn it than any other; it was due about
two o'clock in the morning. Wiltshire conducted
us to a long, deep cut on the railroad. No patrol
or picket was in sight. I preferred derailing the
train in a cut to running it off an embankment,
because there would be less danger of the passengers being hurt. People who travel on a railroad in a country where military operations are

going on take the risk of all these accidents of war. I was not conducting an insurance business on life or property.

It was a lovely night, bright and clear, with a big Jack Frost on the ground. I believe that I was the only member of my command who went through the war without a watch, but all of my men had watches, and we knew it would not be long before the train would be due. Videttes were sent out, and the men were ordered to lie down on the bank of the railroad and keep quiet. We had ridden all day and were tired and sleepy, so we were soon peacefully dreaming. I laid my head in the lap of one of my men, Curg Hutchinson, and fell asleep. For some reason — I suppose it was because we were sleeping so soundly — we did not hear the train coming until it got up in the cut, and I was aroused and astounded by an explosion and a crash. As we had displaced a rail, the engine had run off the track, the boiler burst, and the air was filled with red-hot cinders and escaping steam. A good description of the scene can be found in Dante's "Inferno." Above all could be heard the screams of the passengers — especially women. The catastrophe came so suddenly that my men at first seemed to be stunned and bewildered. Knowing that the railroad guards would soon hear of it and that no time was to be lost, I ran along the line and pushed my men down the bank, ordering them to go to work pulling out the passengers and setting fire to the cars.

By this time Curg Hutchinson had recovered from the shock and had jumped on the train. When the train came up, he was snoring and dreaming that he was in Hell; and when he was awakened by the crash, he found himself breathing steam and in a sparkling shower. He had no doubt then that his dream was not all a dream. But he recovered his senses when I gave him a push, and he slid down a bank.

It did not take long to pull out the passengers. While all of this was going on, I stood on the bank giving directions to the men. One of them reported to me that a car was filled with Germans, and that they would not get out. I told him, "Set fire to the car and burn the Dutch, if they won't come out." They were immigrants going west to locate homesteads and did not understand a word of English, or what all this meant. They had through tickets and thought they had a right to keep their seats. There was a lot of *New York Heralds* on the train for Sheridan's army. So my men circulated the papers through the train and applied matches. Suddenly there was a grand illumination. The Germans now took in the situation and came tumbling, all in a pile, out of the flames. I hope they all lived to be naturalized and get homes. They ought not to blame me, but Sheridan; it was his business, not mine, to protect them.

While we were helping the passengers to climb the steep bank, one of my men, Cab Maddux, who had been sent off as a vidette to watch the road, came dashing up and cried out that the Yankees were coming. I immediately gave orders to mount quickly and form, and one was sent to find out if the report was true. He soon came back and said it was not. The men then dismounted and went to work again. I was very mad with Cab for almost creating a stampede and told him that I had a good mind to have him shot. Cab was quick-witted, but, seeing how angry I was, said nothing then. But he often related the circumstance after the war. His well-varnished account of it was that I ordered him to be shot at sunrise, that he said he hoped it would be a foggy morning, and that I was so much amused by his reply that I relented and pardoned him. Years afterwards Cab confessed why he gave the false alarm. He said he heard the noise the train made when it ran off the track and knew the men were gathering the spoils and did not think it was fair for him to be away picketing for their benefit. He also said that after he got to the burning cars he made up for lost time.

A great many ludicrous incidents occurred. One lady ran up to me and exclaimed, "Oh, my father is a Mason!" I had no time to say anything but, "I can't help it." One passenger claimed immunity for himself on the ground that he was a member of an aristocratic church in Baltimore.

Just as Cab dashed up, two of my men, Charlie Dear and West Aldridge, came to me and reported that they had two U. S. Paymasters with their satchels of greenbacks. Knowing it would be safer to send them out by a small party, which could easily elude the enemy, one of my lieutenants, Charlie Grogan, was detailed with two or three men to take them over the ridge to our rendezvous.

Whether my men got anything in the shape of pocketbooks, watches, or other valuable articles, I never inquired, and I was too busy attending to the destroying of the train to see whether they did. We left all the civilians, including the ladies, to keep warm by the burning cars, and the sol-

diers were taken with us as prisoners. Among
the latter was a young German lieutenant who
had just received a commission and was on his
way to join his regiment in Sheridan's army. I
was attracted by his personal appearance, struck
up a conversation with him, and rode by him for
several miles. He was dressed in a fine beaver-
cloth overcoat; high boots, and a new hat with
gilt cord and tassel. After we were pretty well
acquainted, I said to him, "We have done you no
harm. Why did you come over here to fight
us?" "Oh," he said, "I only come to learn de
art of war." I then left him and rode to the head
of the column, as the enemy were about, and
there was a prospect of a fight. It was not long
before the German came trotting up to join me.
There had been such a metamorphosis that I
scarcely recognized him. One of my men had
exchanged his old clothes with him for his new
ones, and he complained about it. I asked him
if he had not told me that he came to Virginia
to learn the art of war.

"Yes," he replied.

"Very well," I said, "this is your first lesson."

Now it must not be thought that the habit of
appropriating the enemy's goods was peculiar to
my men — through all ages it has been the

custom of war. Not long after this incident I had to suffer from the same operation — was shot at night and stripped of my clothes. Forty years afterwards a lady returned to me the hat which I was wearing. She said that her uncle, Lieutenant-Colonel Coles of the regiment that captured it, had given it to her as a relic of the war. That is war. I am willing to admit, however, that in a statement of mutual accounts at that time my men were largely in debt to Sheridan's men.

Before we reached the Shenandoah River, a citizen told us that a Captain Blazer was roving around the neighborhood looking for us. He commanded a picked corps, armed with Spencer carbines — seven-shooters — that had been assigned by Sheridan to the special duty of looking for me. My men had had an easy time capturing the train, and, although they were not indifferent to greenbacks, their mettle was up when they heard that "Old Blaze", as they called him, was about. They were eager for a fight in which they could win more laurels. It was not long before we struck Blazer's trail and saw his camp fires where he had spent the night. I could no longer restrain the men — they rushed into the camp "as reapers descend to the harvests of death." But

Blazer was gone! He was a bold but cautious commander and had left before daybreak. But this only postponed his fate for a few weeks, when Captain Dolly Richards met him near the same spot and wiped him out forever.

We crossed the Shenandoah and Blue Ridge before noon and found Grogan's party with the greenbacks waiting for us at the appointed place in Loudoun County. The men were ordered to dismount and fall in line, and three were appointed — Charlie Hall, Mountjoy, and Fount Beattie — to open the satchels and count the money in their presence. I ordered it to be divided equally among them and no distinction to be made between officers and men. My command was organized under an act of the Confederate Congress to raise partisan corps; it applied the principle of maritime prize law to land war. Of course, the motive of the act was to stimulate enterprise.

The burning of this train in the midst of Sheridan's troops and the capture of his paymasters created a great sensation. Of course, the railroad people thought that Sheridan had not given adequate protection to their road. The following dispatch shows what General Lee thought of the importance of the blow I struck.

Chaffin's Bluff,
October 16th, 1864.

On the 14th instant Colonel Mosby struck the Baltimore and Ohio Railroad at Duffield's, destroyed U. S. military train consisting of locomotive and ten cars, securing twenty prisoners and fifteen horses. Amongst the prisoners are two paymasters with $168,000 in Government funds.

(Signed)   R. E. Lee, General.
Hon. James A. Seddon, Secretary of War.

The paymasters and other prisoners were sent south to prison, and one of them, Major Ruggles, died there. They were unjustly charged with being in collusion with me, but their capture was simply an ordinary incident of war. As the Government held them responsible for the loss of the funds, they had to apply to Congress for relief. After the war, Major Moore came to see me to get a certificate of the fact that I had captured the money. The certificate stated that my report to General Lee of $168,000 captured was based upon erroneous information and was sent off before I had received the report of the commissioners appointed to count and distribute the money. The sum captured was $173,000.

The attack was made on the train on the night of October 13 between Martinsburg and Harper's Ferry. During the day, as the following dispatch shows, we had operated on the Valley Pike and moved at night to the railroad.

[Seward, at Martinsburg, to Stevenson, at Harper's Ferry]

Four scouts have just arrived and reported that they were attacked about eight miles this side of Winchester by a party of fifty guerrillas this afternoon. They all seem to be positive that they were attacked by Mosby's men and that Mosby with one foot bound up was with them.

It is true that I was there and with one foot bound up. In fact I had on only one boot. I suppose the scouts heard this from some citizen who saw me. A few days before my horse had been shot in a fight, and a Yankee cavalryman rode over me. His horse trod on my foot and bruised it so that for some time I could wear only a sock and had to use a cane when I walked. I was in this condition when we captured the train.

[Stanton, Secretary of War, to Stevenson, Harper's Ferry]

Washington, October 14, 1864.

It is reported from Martinsburg that the railroad has been torn up and a paymaster and his funds captured.

When and where did this occur and have any measures
been taken for recapture? Immediate answer.

### [Stevenson to Stanton]

Just heard from captured train. The attacking
party was part of Mosby's command. They removed
a rail, causing train to be thrown off track, then robbed
the passengers and burned train. The point of
attack was about two miles east of Kearneysville,
about 2.30 A.M. Paymasters Moore and Ruggles
with their funds were captured and carried off. . . .
General Seward telegraphs that his courier parties
were attacked last night twice by Mosby's command
between Bunker Hill and Winchester and dispersed.

### [Stevenson to Stanton]

The cavalry sent out in pursuit of Mosby's guerrillas, who burned the train, have returned. Report
they failed to overtake them. They learned that they
moved off in the direction of the Shenandoah and
having several hours' start, succeeded in getting away
with their prisoners and plunder.

At that time there were a number of paymasters
at Martinsburg on their way to pay off Sheridan's
soldiers, and they were now in a state of blockade.
One of them who was shut up there said in a
dispatch:

I have my funds in the parlor of the United States
Hotel here, guarded by a regiment. The express train

was burned eight miles west of Harper's Ferry between 2 and 3 o'clock this A.M. Major Ruggles' clerk escaped and is now with me. . . . General Seward, who is in command here, says he will use all his efforts to protect us and our money. I shall make no move till I can do so with safety.

The following telegram from Stevenson to Sheridan shows his anxiety about the safety of the trains and that Sheridan had as much cause to give his attention to his rear as to his front:

Mosby has now concentrated his guerrillas in your rear and commenced operations; burning railroad trains, robbing passengers, which without cavalry I am powerless to prevent. He at the same time threatens all your supply trains.

### [Stevenson to Halleck]

At least 1000 good cavalry should be attached to this command to protect us against the sudden dashes of the guerrilla organizations infesting this part of the country. [My battalion was the only Confederate force in that region.] If I had this cavalry I could safely say Mosby could not reach the railroad.

But our operations that day were not confined to the Shenandoah Valley, but extended east of the Blue Ridge to the vicinity of Washington, where preparations were made to keep us south of the Potomac. Later in the same day we captured the train ten miles west of Harper's Ferry. Captain William Chapman, with two companies of my battalion, crossed the Potomac a few miles east of it and struck the canal and railroad in Maryland. The alarm caused by the burning of the train in the morning had not subsided before news came of a fresh attack on the road at another point, and troops were hurried from Baltimore and other places to meet it. But, of course, when the troops got there, the damage had been done and my men had gone.

[Stevenson to French]

Move with all your available cavalry at once to Point of Rocks, Md.; unite your force with the forces in that vicinity and attack a body of rebel cavalry near Adamstown.

[Lawrence, A. A. G., to Halleck]

Bal't., Oct. 14th, 1864.

The enemy was at Buckeyestown, four miles from the Monocacy, at 4 P.M. this evening.

Another dispatch said:

All lost. Even citizens were passing through here from Poolsville with horses to get away from the rebels. They report 2000 rebels between there and Monocacy.

[Prescott Smith to President Garrett of the Baltimore and Ohio Railroad]

October 15.

We have no fresh alarms but the two affairs badly
damaged the working of the road and will involve an
immense loss to the company in every way.

This meant that the railroad must be more
strongly guarded if communication was to be
kept up between the Shenandoah Valley, Washington, and Baltimore. Troops were rushed from
many points to guard the railroad and the canal.
My object had then been accomplished.

# CHAPTER XVI

## LAST DAYS IN THE VALLEY

AFTER returning from the so-called "Greenback Raid", two of my companies, under Richards and Mountjoy, made a demonstration on Washington to keep reinforcements from Sheridan.

[Taylor, A. A. G., to De Russy]

Washington, October 17th, 1864.

I have telegraphed General Slough to send at once 500 infantry to Annandale. A small infantry force at either place, Annandale or Buffalo, will be sufficient to drive off Mosby, who cannot have 100 men.

[Taylor to Slough]

October 17th, 1864, — 5 P.M.

Notify Lazelle at Fall's Church that he may not be surprised. Your infantry certainly is strong enough to hold any force of Mosby's in check.

[Slough to Taylor]

October 17th, 1864. 8 P.M.

Mosby has driven in Lazelle's pickets. Send Wells' cavalry, if any is in Alexandria, to Lazelle and let the Fifth Wisconsin move rapidly to Annandale.

[Winship to Taylor]

Alexandria, October 17th, 1864.

It is reported that Mosby with about 300 men is in the vicinity of Burke's station this afternoon.

[Augur to Taylor]

Rectortown, October 18th, 1864.

I have sent the Eighth Illinois down through Centreville to find Mosby's force.

The panic in Washington was very great, as is shown by many similar dispatches in the war records. When the Eighth Illinois got to Fairfax, they found that we had gone back towards the Blue Ridge. They did what I was manœuvring to make them do — spend their time and waste their strength in pursuit of a Jack-o'-lantern.

About this time I heard that a force was moving to repair the Manassas Railroad to make a new base for Sheridan, and I determined to move against it and, if possible, defeat it. My success in accomplishing this was of greater military value than anything I did in the war, for it saved Richmond for several months. I sent Tom Ogg, one of my scouts, to reconnoitre and report to me at Haymarket, a little village on the road, which the enemy had not occupied. When we got near Haymarket about eleven o'clock that night, we saw a large number of camp fires. The Yankees were ahead of us!

After Tom got the information he was sent for, he came to meet me according to our appointment. He saw the camp fires and naturally thought they were mine. When he got near them, a picket halted him and called out, "Who comes there?" Ogg had no suspicion that the demand came from an enemy, so he replied, "Ogg, Tom Ogg. Don't you know Ogg?"

The picket had never heard of Ogg. He did not know whether he was friend or foe, so, according to military rule, he ordered Tom to dismount and advance. Tom protested and again told the picket that he was Tom Ogg, that he had been sent by "the Colonel" on a scout, and asked the picket to what company he belonged.

The picket replied, "Company E", and swore he had never heard of Ogg. Tom then said, indignantly, "I thought you were one of that d—d green Company E." [E was a new company I had just organized.]

At last Ogg was compelled to dismount and advance on foot leading his horse. It was pitch dark, and Tom did not discover, until he got right up against the sentinel, that the latter had a musket and a bayonet was pointed at his breast.

But Tom never lost his presence of mind. So he said, "I am lame, and you must let me ride to see the Colonel."

The poor picket did not suspect Tom's stratagem and consented. He really thought that he was only doing his duty and was talking to a brother in arms. Tom mounted and, as soon as he was in the saddle, drove his spurs into his horse, and darted off in the darkness, shouting to his men, "Break, boys!"

A volley was fired on his track, but it never overtook Ogg. It was a coincidence that this occurred just after we approached the camp from the opposite direction. When I heard the firing, I laughed and told the men that I would bet it was Tom Ogg and that he had ridden into the Yankees by mistake. But all is well that ends well. Tom lived many years after the war, and we often laughed about his surprise that the Yankees had never heard of "Ogg, Tom Ogg!"

Near Upperville,
Oct. 22, '64.

My dearest Pauline:

I have just returned from a successful trip to the valley, — captured a brigadier general (Duffie), capturing ambulance horses, etc. Sent them out, then returning by another route, captured seven wagons, fifty-five prisoners, and forty-one horses. As soon as the Yankees leave the Manassas road I will send for you all.

[Fragment of a letter to Mrs. Mosby, probably November, 1864]

We killed and captured about 600 from the time of their occupying to their abandonment of the railroad (Manassas road). Since my return to my command, I have been in the saddle the whole time.

[From a Confederate newspaper, 1864]

The following is a clear admission of the injuries Mosby has been inflicting on the enemy of late. When they begin war on unoffending persons in this way it is evidence of the desperation to which they are driven.

" Working parties are now engaged in felling timber on each side of the Manassas Gap Railroad, to prevent its use by guerrillas as a place of concealment. Orders have been issued that if another attack should be made on a Government train, similar to the last one, in which so many lives were lost, every house of a rebel within five miles of the road, on either side, shall be immediately destroyed, meanwhile every train bears a party of rebel sympathizers, selected from the abundant number in Alexandria, to receive such bullets as their friends the guerrillas may choose to fire at them. Three physicians and one clergyman were among the first party thus sent."

[Another Confederate paper quoted "the Yankee newspaper" published at Alexandria as follows:]

General Slough, acting under special orders from the War Department, yesterday arrested a number of well-known rebel sympathizers in this city, for the purpose of sending them out on trains of the Orange and Alexandria and Manassas Gap Railroad, in order to secure their property against guerrilla attacks. . . . When once the guerrillas hear that the trains are run for the special accommodation of their friends, they will not disturb the road. . . . P.S. Since the above was in type, we learn that all those arrested in this city yesterday were sent out on the railroad train to-day.[1]

By December, 1864, the war had practically ceased between the contending armies in the Shenandoah Valley. The greater portion of Early's forces had been transferred to the lines about Petersburg, while Sheridan had taken up his winter quarters at Winchester. My own command, which had been operating against his communications, never went into winter quarters, but kept up a desultory warfare on outposts, supply trains, and detachments. And, although

---

[1] Word was sent to Mosby that a number of women and children would be sent on certain trains. His answer was that he did not understand that it hurts women and children to be killed any more than it hurts men.

the Southern army had disappeared from his
front, these few hundred rangers kept Sheridan's
soldiers as busily employed to guard against surprises as when that army confronted them.  Unable to exterminate the hostile bands by arms,
Sheridan had applied the torch and attempted
to drive us from the district in which we operated
by destroying everything that could support man
or horse.  But so far from quelling, his efforts
only stimulated the fury of my men.  In snow,
sleet, and howling storms, through the long
watches of the winter nights, his men had to
wait for a sleepless enemy to capture or kill them.

[Telegram — Sheridan to Halleck]

Kernstown, Va.; Nov. 26, 1864.

I will soon commence work on Mosby.  Heretofore
I have made no attempt to break him up, as I would
have employed ten men to his one, and for the reason
that I have made a scapegoat of him for the destruction
of private rights.  Now there is going to be an intense
hatred of him in that portion of the valley which is
nearly a desert.  I will soon commence on Loudoun
County, and let them know there is a God in Israel.
Mosby has annoyed me considerably; but the people
are beginning to see that he does not injure me a great
deal, but causes a loss to them of all that they have
spent their lives in accumulating.  Those people who

live in the vicinity of Harper's Ferry are the most villainous in this valley, and have not yet been hurt much. If the railroad is interfered with, I will make some of them poor. Those who live at home in peace and plenty want the duello part of this war to go on; but when they have to bear the burden by loss of property and comforts, they will cry for peace.

As I wanted to have a conference with General Robert E. Lee about my plans for future operations, I turned my command over to the next in rank, William Chapman, and, taking one of my men, Boyd Smith, went on a visit to the army headquarters near Petersburg. When I got off the train there, I recognized in the crowd the face of Doctor Monteiro, an old college mate whom I had not seen for thirteen years. I had changed so much that he did not recognize me until I told him my name. He was then a surgeon with Wise's brigade, and I told him he was the very man I wanted, for the surgeon I had, Doctor Will Dunn, was too fond of fighting. I wanted a surgeon that took more pride in curing than killing. I had Monteiro transferred to my command before I returned.

After spending a few hours with General Lee and getting his recommendation for the promotion of two of my officers, Chapman and Richards,

I returned to Richmond, and in a few days was back with my men. On the day after my return, December 21, I had gone to the house of Joe Blackwell, a farmer in upper Fauquier, to attend the wedding of my ordnance sergeant, Jake Lavender. A report came that a body of the enemy's cavalry was advancing on the road to Salem, a few miles away. Not caring to interrupt the wedding festivities, with one man — Tom Love — I rode off to reconnoitre. We were riding across the field of the Glen Welby farm, as it was safer than going by the main road, where there was danger of running against the enemy's column, when we saw two cavalrymen approaching. Soon a number of others appeared and began firing at us. I knew then that these were the flankers of the main body of the enemy out of sight over the hill. So Love and I galloped away a few hundred yards and then halted on an eminence. They did not pursue, and we soon saw the whole column in blue moving on the road to Rectortown. After reaching there, they kindled fires and seemed to be preparing to bivouac for the night.

It was about dusk; a cold, drizzling rain was falling and freezing, the road was covered with sleet, and icicles hung in clusters from the trees.

After reconnoitring the encampment and satis-
fying myself that they had prepared to spend
the night there, I dispatched a man to inform
Chapman and Richards that I wanted them to
attack the Northern camp about daybreak the
next morning, and to get their men ready. Love
and I then started off in another direction for the
purpose of notifying some of the other officers and
collecting the men. (When we stayed inside the
enemy's lines we were obliged to disperse for
safety.) As we were passing the house of a
citizen, Ludwell Lake, who was famous for always setting a good table, the lights shining
through the windows tempted me, as I was cold
and hungry, to stop where I knew we would be
welcome. So, when we got to the front gate,
I proposed to dismount and to go in to get warm
and something to eat. Love said he would
stay out at the gate and keep watch while I was
eating my supper.

"No, Tom," I said; "it wouldn't do me any
good if you were out here in the cold. There is
no danger; get down."

We tied our horses and went in. The family
was at supper, and we were soon seated at the
table enjoying some good coffee, hot rolls, and
spareribs. Among those there was a Mrs. Skin-

ner, whose husband was then a prisoner at Point Lookout. She had managed to get a pass through the lines to visit him and had seen a number of my men who were also prisoners there. We were enjoying our supper and her account of the trip and the various devices to which the prisoners resorted for amusement, when suddenly we heard the tramp of horses around the house. One door of the dining room opened toward the back yard, and on opening it, I discovered several cavalrymen. Hastily shutting the door, I turned to the other one, but just then a number of Northern officers and soldiers walked into the room.

I was better dressed that evening than I ever was during the war. Just before starting to Richmond I got through the blockade across the Potomac a complete suit from head to foot. I had a drab hat with an ostrich plume, with gold cord and star; a heavy, black beaver-cloth overcoat and cape lined with English scarlet cloth, and, as it was a stormy evening, over this I wore a gray cloak, also lined with scarlet. My hat, overcoat, and cape were lying in the corner. I wore a gray sack coat with two stars on the collar to indicate my rank as lieutenant-colonel, gray trousers with a yellow cord down the seam, and long cavalry boots. As the Northerners entered the room, I placed my hands on my coat collar to conceal my stars, and a few words passed between us. The situation seemed desperate, but I had made up my mind to take all the chances for getting away. I knew that if they discovered my rank, to say nothing of my name, they would guard me more carefully than if I were simply a private or a lieutenant.

But a few seconds elapsed before firing began in the back yard. One of the bullets passed through the window, making a round hole in the glass and striking me in the stomach. Old man Lake, who weighed about three hundred pounds and was as broad as he was long, and his daughter, Mrs. Skinner, were standing between me and the window. It was a miracle how the shot could have missed them and hit me — but it did. I have always thought that Yankee had a circular gun. My self-possession in concealing the stars on my collar saved me from being carried off a prisoner, dead or alive. The officers had not detected the stratagem, when I exclaimed, "I am shot!" The fact was that the bullet created only a stinging sensation, and I was not in the least shocked. My exclamation was not because I felt hurt, but to get up a panic in order that I might escape. It had the desired effect. Old man Lake and his daughter waltzed around the room, the cavalrymen on the outside kept up their fire, and this created a stampede of the officers in the room with me. In the confusion to get out of the way there was a sort of hurdle race, in which the supper table was knocked over, and the tallow lights put out. In a few seconds I was left in the room with no one but Love, Lake, and his daughter.

I saw that this was my opportunity. There were nine hundred and ninety-nine chances out of a thousand against me. I took the single chance and won. There were at least three hundred cavalry surrounding the house, and, if I had not been wounded, I should have tried to get off in the dark. But by this time the terrible wound was having its effect; I was bleeding profusely and getting faint. There was a door which opened from the dining room into an adjoining bedroom, and I determined to play the part of a dying man. I walked into the room, pulled off my coat, on which were the insignia of my rank, tucked it away under the bureau so that no one could see it, and then lay down with my head towards the bureau. After several minutes the panic subsided, and the Northerners returned to the scene from which the shots of their own men had frightened them. They found my old friend Lake dancing a hornpipe. He missed a button from his waistcoat and swore that the bullet which had killed me had carried it off. Having heard me fall on the floor, he thought I was dead — the truth was he was almost as near dead as I was. The daughter was screaming, the room in which I lay was dark, and it was some minutes before the soldiers collected their senses sufficiently to strike a light.

During all this time I lay on the floor with the blood gushing from my wound. In those few minutes it seemed to me that I lived my whole life over again; my mind traveled away from the scenes of death and carnage, in which I had been an actor for four years, to the peaceful home and the wife and children I had left behind.

I overheard the soldiers ask Mrs. Skinner who I was — I was well acquainted with her, and her brother was in my command — and I listened with fear and trembling for her answer. She declared that I was a stranger — that she had never seen me before — that I was not one of Mosby's men, and she did not know my name. I am sure that in the eternal records there is nothing registered against that good woman who denied my name and saved my life.

At last, after a candle had been lighted, my enemies came into the room, and the first thing they asked me was my name. I gave a fictitious one. They wanted to know to what command I belonged. I did not tell them the right one. My reason for doing so was that I wanted to conceal my identity. As I knew the feeling at the North against me and the great anxiety to either kill or capture me, I was sure I would be dragged away as a trophy, if they knew who their prisoner was. I had on a flannel shirt which was now soaked with my blood. The soldiers opened my clothes and looked at my wound, while I apparently gasped for breath. A doctor examined the wound and said that it was mortal — that I was shot through the heart. He located the heart rather low down, and even in that supreme moment I felt tempted to laugh at his ignorance of human anatomy. I only gasped a few words and affected to be dying. They left the room hurriedly, after stripping me of my boots and trousers, evidently supposing that a dead man would have no use for them. The only sensible man among them was an Irishman, who said, as he took a last look at me, "He is worth several dead men yet."

There was a good deal of whiskey in the crowd, but they had sense enough left to take away my clothes. Fortunately they never saw my coat.

I listened to hear them getting away — they passed out and left my fat friend and his daughter under the impression that I was ready for the grave. I lay perfectly still for some five or ten minutes — it seemed to me that many hours — but at last, as I felt assured that the enemy had gone, I rose from the pool of blood in which I was lying and walked into the room where Lake and his daughter were sitting by the fire. They were as much astonished to see me as if I had risen from the tomb; they had thought me dead and were now sure the general resurrection had come. There was a big log fire blazing, and the room was warm. We examined the wound, but we could not tell whether the bullet had passed straight into the body, or, after penetrating, had passed around it. Shortly I became sick and faint. My own belief was that the wound was mortal; that the bullet was in me; that the intestines had been cut. Mrs. Skinner gave me some coffee, but I was too sick to drink it. My fear was that I had some documents in my pockets which would disclose my name. Although Providence had not protected me from the bullet, it had saved me from getting caught. That day I had been at Glen Welby, the home of the Carters, and for some unaccountable reason, just as I was leaving to go to the wedding, I took from my pocket several official documents and gave them to one of the young ladies to keep for me. If I had not done this, I would never have lived to write an account of this adventure, for if I had been taken off as a prisoner that night, I could not have survived it.

The force of cavalry that I had seen go into camp at Rectortown was the Thirteenth and Sixteenth New York, under command of Major Frazar. They had only built fires to warm themselves, and, after staying there a short time, they started on to Middleburg to join Colonel Clendenin, with the Eighth Illinois Cavalry, from which they had separated a few hours before. That night they encamped at Middleburg. Several of my men, including Love, were prisoners, and they were shown my hat and overcoat and asked if they knew the person who had worn them. All denied any knowledge of him. The next day the Unionists returned to camp, little dreaming who it was that had been a prisoner in their hands. My own belief is that I was in-debted to whiskey for my escape, and I have always thought since then that there is a deal of good in whiskey.

As soon as Lake recovered from the shock at seeing me alive, he went out and got a couple of negro boys to yoke up a pair of young, half-broken oxen to haul me away to a place of safety, for we feared that the enemy would find out who I was and return. After a while the ox-cart was announced, and I was rolled up in quilts and blankets and put into it. It was an awful night — a howling storm of snow, rain, and sleet. I was lying on my back in the cart — we had to go two miles to the house of a neighbor, over a frozen road cut into deep ruts. When we reached there, I was almost perfectly stiff with cold, and my hair was a clotted mass of ice. The family had not gone to bed, and one of my men, George Slater, was at the house. A courier was sent to the wedding party to carry the news to my brother and my other men, and before daybreak a great many of the men and two surgeons were with me. Slater had been present when Stuart had been shot a few months before. After I had been laid by the fire, I called him to me and said,

"George, look at my wound, I think I am shot just like General Stuart was."

Slater pulled up my shirt — I was bleeding pro-fusely — and told me that he thought the bullet had run around my body. This turned out to be the case, for it had lodged in my right side. Early in the morning chloroform was admin-istered, and the ball extracted.

Another of the good effects of the whiskey on my captors was that they went off leaving my horse standing at the front gate, with the pistols in the holsters. If I had had them with me in the house, I am very confident I could have cleared the way through the back yard and es-caped in the dark. Neither Love nor I had a chance to fire a shot, and there is no truth in the reports that shots were fired from the house. I had nothing to shoot with. As I said, a Northern officer was standing near, talking to me when I was shot. Although I was a prisoner at the time, I have never complained of it, for it proved to be a lucky shot for me. It was the means of my es-cape from imprisonment. A few days afterwards tidings came to the camp down in Fairfax that I was the man who was wounded at Lake's. A force of cavalry was sent to search for me, but although I was still in the neighborhood, they did not find me. At the same time General Torbert, returning from an unsuccessful expedition to Gordonsville, passed within a few miles of where I was lying, but also failed to discover me.

About a week after all this occurred I was taken to my father's house near Lynchburg. Richmond papers had already announced my death. Doctor Monteiro had not reached my command before I was brought away, so he came to my father's house to see me. Monteiro was a great wit and had been with me only a few minutes when he got me to laughing. This produced a hemorrhage from my wound, and it took all his surgical skill to repair the damage his talk had done.

Major Frazar reported my capture and escape as follows:

Fairfax Court House,
December 31, 1864.

Colonel William Gamble, Commanding Cavalry
   Brigade,
Colonel:

In obedience to your command, I have the honor to report concerning the wounding of Colonel Mosby. He was shot by a man of my advance guard, under Captain Brown, in Mr. Lake's house, near the Rector's Cross-roads, on the evening of the 21st instant.; about 9 P.M.; at which time I was in command of the 13th and 16th New York regiments. Several shots were fired, and I was informed that a rebel lieutenant was wounded. I immediately dismounted and entered the house, and found a man lying on the floor, apparently in great agony. I asked him his name — he answered, "Lieutenant Johnson, Sixteenth Virginia Cavalry." He was in his shirtsleeves — a light blue cotton shirt — no hat — no boots — no insignia of rank; nothing to denote in the slightest degree that he was not what he pretended to be. I told him I must see his wounds to see whether to bring him or not. I opened, myself, his pants and found that a pistol bullet had entered the abdomen about two inches below and to the left of the navel; a wound that I felt assured was mortal. I therefore ordered all from the room, remarking, "He will die in twenty-four hours." Being behind time on account of skirmishing all the afternoon with the enemy, I hurried on to meet Lieutenant-Colonel Clendenin at Middleburg, according to orders received. Nearly every officer in my command, if not all, saw this wounded man, and no one had the slightest idea that it was Mosby. Captain Brown and Major Birdsall were both in the room with me when this occurred. After arrival at Middleburg I reported the fact of having wounded a rebel lieutenant to Lieutenant-Colonel Clendenin. As soon as the camp fires were lit so that things could be seen, an orderly brought me Mosby's hat dressed with gold cord and star. I took the hat and went immediately among the prisoners, eight in number, of Mosby's men that I had captured, and told them the man who wore that cap was shot dead, and asked them if it was Mosby or not; it was no use to conceal it if it was, as he was shot dead. They all said "No," that it was not Mosby, that he never had such a hat, etc., etc. Some of them said it was Major Johnson, Sixth Virginia Cavalry, home on leave. In the morning I reported the facts and showed the cap to Colonel Clendenin and Mr. Davis, the guide; all this, while I considered, as did all my other officers, that the wound was mortal. From Middleburg I came to camp. On this scout, from which I have just returned to-day, I have the honor to state that the man shot in Lake's house was Colonel Mosby. He was moved half an hour after he was shot to Quilly Glasscock's, about a mile and a half distant, where he remained three days and had the ball extracted, it having passed around or through the bowels, coming out behind the right side. I conversed with several persons who saw him. He was very low the first two days, the third much better. I tracked him to Piedmont, thence to Salem, and out of Salem towards the Warrenton Pike. I met pickets in various parts of the country, and understood that until within the last night or two they had extended as far down as Aldie. Various signalling was carried on by means of white flags above Piedmont. Several persons who saw him in the ambulance report him spitting blood, and it seems to be the general impression that he cannot live. There is no doubt in my mind but what he is yet in the country, concealed; seriously, if not mortally wounded. In both expeditions I lost neither men nor horses and captured nine prisoners.

(Signed)   Douglas Frazar,<br>
Major Commanding.

[Indorsement]

Headquarters First Separate Brigade,
Fairfax C. H., Va., Jan. 1, 1865.

Respectfully forwarded to department headquarters.
I exceedingly regret that such a blunder was made.
I have given direction that all wounded officers and
men of the enemy be hereafter brought in, although
any officer ought to have brains and common sense
enough to do so without an order.

(Signed) W. Gamble,
Colonel Commanding Brigade.

[Gamble to Augur]

I am also informed that Major Frazar was too much
under the influence of liquor to perform his duty at
the time in a proper manner. Under the circumstances I have deemed it best to send Major Frazar
with 300 men to scour the neighborhood and ascertain,
if possible, something definite about it, he being the
officer present at the time the rebel officer was shot in
the house where it is supposed Mosby was wounded.

Sheridan seemed as much delighted to hear of
my death as the troops in Fairfax. No doubt he
expected no more annoyances that winter. A
short time afterward he sent a body of cavalry
under a Major Gibson to that neighborhood one
night, but Dolly Richards got after him and sent
most of his men prisoners to Richmond. The

last heard of Major Gibson was that he had been unhorsed and was getting back to his camp full speed over the snow in a sleigh.

### [Stevenson to Sheridan]

December 29, 1864.

Mosby was shot by a party from General Augur's command at Rector's Crossroads.  There were two or three men in the party;  they fired at Mosby and some of his men through the windows, wounding Mosby in the abdomen.  He was then moved to the house of widow Glasscock.  Torbert tried to catch him there, but he had been taken away in an ambulance.  Torbert searched the house of Rogers at Middleburg, but he was not there.  Mosby's wound is mortal.  He and his party were eating supper when the attack was made on the house by General Augur's men.

### [Augur to Sheridan]

December 30, 1864.

Richmond papers of the 27th report Mosby's death as having occurred at Charlottesville.

### [Sheridan to Emory]

December 31, 1864.

How are you getting along?  The storm is unfortunate.  I have no news to-day except the death of Mosby.  He died from his wound at Charlottesville.

The following account of the wounding of Mosby was written by a "Yankee Major General" for the *New York Herald* of December 31, 1864, and was copied by the Confederate newspapers:

On Tuesday, December 17, an expedition comprising the Thirteenth and Sixteenth New York and Eighth Illinois Cavalry, under the command of Lieutenant-Colonel Clendenin, started to scout the country this side of the Blue Ridge, in search of Mosby. On arriving at White Plains on Wednesday the command separated. . . . The first named (13th New York) proceeded toward Salem, and when a short distance from Middleburg came upon the house at which Mosby was then dining. Captain Taylor's Company of the 13th New York were in the advance, and manœuvered to surround the house, near which two horses, with cavalry equipment were fastened. Corporal Cane or Kane, of Company F, rode near the house and was about to secure the horses, when Mosby opened the door and fired at the Corporal. Kane raised his carbine to fire in return ; when Mosby closed the door and ran into another part of the house. The Corporal, seeing him pass a window, instantly fired, shooting Mosby through the bowels. Captain Taylor and others hastily entered the house. Some of the men proposed finishing the rebel ; but Captain Taylor, having examined his wound, pronounced it mortal. Major Frazar, 13th New York Cavalry, also examined the wound and declared that the man would die. The rank and name of the wounded man were not known at this time. He had on a magnificent cloak of gray, trimmed with English scarlet and gold clasps. This cloak had often been talked about by inhabitants of the valley as belonging to Mosby, and was described by citizens as the richest article of the kind in either army. The boots of the wounded man were carried off and found to agree exactly, in make and maker's name, with a pair taken from Mosby's house when burned last summer. The rebel accounts show that their conclusions were correct; but, if we are to believe the rebel stories, Mosby is not yet dead. He may possibly recover: "The devil takes care of his own."

# CHAPTER XVII

## FINAL SCENES [1]

THE war drama was now drawing to a close. According to General John B. Gordon, Lee's troops were subsisting on parched corn, and one day a private accosted him with the request, "I say, General, can't you give us a little fodder?" Gordon also said that Lee's surgeons reported to him that the men were in such bad condition that, if wounded, they would become gangrened. Grant's remorseless policy had caused the Confederates "to rob the cradle and the grave." And the blockade had all the time been aiding the Federal armies, silently but effectively.

Colonel Mosby was wounded on December 21, 1864, and, naturally, it was some time before he could get to work again.

[1] This chapter was prepared from material collected by Colonel Mosby.

[Extracts from the diary of Mosby's mother]

Sunday, Jan. 1, 1865.

Hear by the papers to-day that dear John is recovering. We feel intense anxiety about John. No tidings from John.

Tuesday, 3rd.

This evening . . . John arrived safely and doing well.

Feb. 24th.

John sent Mrs. J. S. Mosby his photograph and a piece dedicated to Mosby and his men — "They Will Never Win Us Back." We feel so sad at the thought of our dear John leaving us to-morrow.

Feb. 25th.

The day has come and the hour has passed that saw our dearest one leave once more the household group to go back to battle for his country and all that is dear to man and woman. It is one of the saddest events of my life, when I have to part from my dear boys, to go to the Army, yet I know God is there as well as around the peaceful and secure fireside. . . . A crisis is upon us. We are beset on all sides by a powerful enemy.

But while Colonel Mosby was recovering his men were by no means idle.

[Extract from a Confederate newspaper]

The part attributed to Captain Taylor's Company, in a notice copied into yesterday's paper, was in reality an exploit of Major Richards, of Mosby's command, as accurate accounts have since established. On Thursday last, Major Richards, with a force of sixty men, struck the Baltimore and Ohio Railroad between Duffield and Martinsburg, and captured a train of fifteen cars propelled by two engines and loaded with supplies for Sheridan's army. The engines were blown up and the cars consumed by fire. Our adventurous soldiers loaded their horses with such articles as they could carry; many of them possessing themselves in this manner of sacks of coffee, besides other desirable supplies. Major Richards has already established his fame as one of the most active and successful of Mosby's indefatigables.

When Mosby went to Richmond early in December, 1864, he presented the following letter to the Confederate War Department:

December 6, 1864.

Hon. James A. Seddon,
    Secretary of War.

Sir:

I beg leave to recommend, in order to secure greater efficiency in my command, that it be divided into two battalions, each to be commanded by a Major. The scope of duties devolving upon me being of a much wider extent than on officers of the same rank in the regular service, but small time is allowed me to attend to the duties of organization, discipline, etc. I am confident that the arrangement I propose would give me much more time both for planning and executing enterprises against the enemy. I would recommend Capt. Wm. H. Chapman (Commanding Co. C. 43d Va. P. R. Battalion) and Captain Adolphus E. Richards (Commanding Co. B. same battalion) for the command of the two . . . [letter mutilated] have both on many occasions . . . valor and skill to which my reports . . . so in engagements with the . . . Aldie, Charles Town, and . . .

> Very respectfully,
> Your obedient servant,
> (Signed) John S. Mosby,
> Lieutenant Colonel.

On January 9, 1865, Mosby's commission as a colonel was issued. William Chapman, whose brother Sam, a Baptist preacher, whom Colonel Mosby described as the only man he ever saw who really enjoyed fighting, and who generally went into the fray with his hat in one hand and banging away with his revolver with the other, became a lieutenant-colonel.

On March 27, 1865, Colonel Mosby was put in command of all northern Virginia. And then on April 9th came the surrender of Lee at Appomattox.

The Colonel often said that if his small mother had been in command of the Southern armies, the war would have been going on yet.

[Extracts from the diary of Mosby's mother]

Saturday, March 6.

To-day will be a day never to be forgotten. We heard the Yankees occupied Charlottesville last evening and are advancing up here. All is consternation and confusion. We are trying to get our things out of the way. Rumor after rumor arrives, and we know not how to proceed. We expect to be driven from our homes. Oh! may we be spared, and our house, and the vile Yankees driven back.

Saturday, April 3.

Captain Kennon left and Mr. Moore to go to Col. Mosby's command. . . . There is a craven spirit abroad with our people. If overpowered we will have to submit to the powers that be, but I would feel that the Yankees themselves would despise us, if we recanted our Southern principles. They would have no confidence in us and look with contempt on us, as they should do. I think a deserter on either side the most degraded human being that breathes. Yes, we hate them, and the Yankees do too, and they will hiss them.

Sunday, April 9th.

I went out and heard the deep toned cannon, carrying hundreds and perhaps thousands to that long sleep that knows no waking. Oh, how my heart went up for our great, our noble Lee, that God would give him strength in weakness to bring us out of battle a victorious people. If God does see fit to crush us and bow us down, because of our sins and the sins of this nation, I feel it will be in justice and mercy, and will even believe he doeth all things well; but there are hearts too noble to be conquered. Our Lee will stand out a *man* in all the nations of the earth, nobler and greater in adversity than any other man with a crown on his head. . . . I hear of fearful desertions. Poor craven spirits, — I hope the Yankee bullets will yet pierce their hateful hides. General Lee surrendered to superior numbers to-day at Appomattox Court House.

Headquarters Middle Military Division,
Winchester, Va., April 10, 1865.

The Major-General Commanding announces to the citizens in the vicinity of his lines that General Robert E. Lee surrendered with the Army of Northern Virginia yesterday to Lieut. General Grant near Appomattox Court House. . . . Officers and men were all paroled. . . .

(Signed) W. S. Hancock,
Maj. Genl. U. S. Vols.

Official,
E. B. Parsons,
Assistant Adjutant General,
A. P. M. G.

P. S. All detachments and stragglers from the Army of Northern Virginia will, upon complying with the above conditions, be paroled and allowed to go to their homes. Those who do not so surrender will be brought in as prisoners of war. The Guerilla Chief Mosby is not included in the parole.

W. S. H.

Headquarters Middle Military Division,
Winchester, April 11, 1865.

Colonel John S. Mosby,
Commanding Partizans,

Colonel:

I am directed by Major General Hancock to inclose you copies of letters which passed between Generals Grant and Lee on the occasion of the surrender of the Army of Northern Virginia. Major General Hancock is authorized to receive the surrender of the force under your command on the same conditions offered to General Lee, and will send an officer of equal rank with yourself to meet you at any point and time you may designate, convenient to the lines, for the purpose of arranging the details, should you conclude to be governed by the example of General Lee.

Very respectfully,
Your servant,
C. H. Morgan,
Bat. Brig. Genl.
Chief of Staff.

April 15, 1865.

Major General W. S. Hancock,
Commanding,

General:

I am in receipt of a letter from your Chief of Staff General Morgan, enclosing copies of correspondence between Generals Grant and Lee, and informing me that you would appoint an officer of equal rank with myself to arrange the details for the surrender of the forces under my command. As yet I have no notice through any other source of the facts concerning the surrender of the Army of Northern Virginia, nor, in my opinion, has the emergency yet arisen which would justify the surrender of my command. With no disposition, however, to cause the useless effusion of blood or to inflict upon a war-worn population any unnecessary distress, I am ready to agree to a suspension of hostilities for a short time, in order to enable me to communicate with my own authorities or until I can obtain sufficient intelligence to determine my future action. Should you accede to this proposition, I am ready to meet any person you may designate to arrange the terms of the armistice. I am,

Very respectfully,

Your obedient servant,

John S. Mosby,

Colonel C. S. A.

(This letter to Hancock, who was at Winchester, was written at Warrenton, Fauquier Co., Va., the home of the Washington family. It was sent by a flag of truce that was carried by Colonel Wm. H. Chapman, Dr. Monteiro, and my brother, Wm. H. Mosby, who was my adjutant. J. S. M.)

[Mosby's Farewell Address to his Command]

Fauquier County, April 21, 1865.

Soldiers —

I have summoned you together for the last time. The visions we have cherished of a free and independent

country have vanished, and that country is now the
spoil of the conqueror. I disband your organization
in preference to surrendering it to our enemies. I am
no longer your Commander. After an association of
more than two eventful years, I part from you with
a just pride in the fame of your achievements and a
grateful recollection of your generous kindness to
myself. And at this moment of bidding you a final
adieu, accept the assurance of my unchanging confidence and regard. Farewell!

Jno. S. Mosby,<br>Colonel.

Valley Farm, Aug. 27, '65.

My dearest Pauline:

I staid almost a week at Pa's and then returned to
Uncle John's, as the infernal Yankees were in Lynchburg, which made it dangerous to remain there longer.
Uncle John made John Hipkins go to Richmond, as
we were anxious to learn what were the designs of
the Yankees towards me. Mr. Palmer went to see
General Lee. General Lee sent me word by Willie
Cabell that he was waiting to see General Grant; he
also said that he entirely approved of everything I
had done. He is going to move up to Haymarket.
When I passed through Charlottesville there were
fourteen Yankee cavalry in the place. I met a lieutenant and one man in the street. They said nothing
to me. I went up to the University to call on Dr.
McGuffey. A short while after I left, it was sur-

rounded by two companies of Yankee cavalry. If you see Willie tell him Pa is anxious for him to return home. I want to find out what will be the course of the Yankees towards me before I return to Fauquier.

[Extract from a Lynchburg, Virginia, paper of 1865]

Some little stir was created in the city yesterday by the report that Col. Mosby, the celebrated partisan chieftain, was in Lynchburg. Various reasons were expressed as to the cause of his appearance, but the following are, we believe, the facts of the case. Some days since Col. Mosby's brother came to Captain Swank, Provost Marshal of this city, to inquire if Mosby would be paroled on coming in and surrendering to the authorities. Capt. Swank replied that he would make inquiries upon the subject, and give him an answer in a few days. Day before yesterday, he again called to see the marshal upon the subject, and was told that Col. Mosby would be paroled if he would come in and give himself up. In accordance with this information, Mosby came into Lynchburg yesterday, and applied at the Provost Marshal's office for a parole. Capt. Garnett happened to be attending to the duties of the office at the time and, not being aware of the arrangement, sent to Col. Duncan for instructions. He was immediately ordered not to parole Col. Mosby until further orders from Col. Duncan. In the meantime a dispatch was received from Richmond, and Mosby was ordered to leave town immediately, while the Provost guard were instructed to see that he did so without molestation or hindrance. The dispatch is generally supposed to have been an order for his arrest, probably under a misapprehension of the facts, — and, as he had come here under an implied safeguard from the military authorities, they felt bound in honor not to take advantage of the act.

[Extract from the *Alexandria State Journal*, 1865]

We last night noticed the fact that Major [sic] Mosby was in the city, and his presence was much courted by his friends and admirers. An hour after his arrival there was hardly a sympathizer with the late Confederacy here who did not know of his presence. Wherever he went he was followed by a large crowd of friends. He seemed to make Harper's store his headquarters, and whenever stationed there large crowds, composed of a plentiful sprinkling of colored men and boys, gathered on the corner and blockaded the sidewalk, sometimes almost obstructing the street. This became so annoying that about four o'clock P.M. last evening, the military authorities ordered his arrest. He was arrested by Capt. McGraw at the residence of Mrs. Boyd Smith, on St. Asaph Street, and taken before Genl. Wells, who held him until he communicated with headquarters at Washington and received orders for his release.

Leesburg, January 8, '66.

Dearest Pauline :

I was just in the act of starting home this morning when an order came for my arrest. I am now under arrest here, awaiting orders from General Ayres. Don't be uneasy. . . .

Yours affectionately,

John S. Mosby.

[From the *Baltimore Sun*, February 6th, 1866]

Col. Mosby has been released upon parole by Genl. Grant, he being included in the terms of Genl. Lee's surrender.

Thus it was nearly a year after Lee's surrender that the war closed for Mosby.

# CHAPTER XVIII

## IN RETROSPECT

[IN December, 1899, Colonel Mosby wrote the following letter to John S. Russell — his chief scout in the war — which throws valuable sidelights on many of the episodes connected with his command, and sums up his deliberate opinion of many of the controversial points connected with his partisan life. In this survey of the past, Colonel Mosby stated many of his final conclusions.]

San Francisco, Dec. 16, 1899.

Mr. John S. Russell,
Berryville, Va.

Dear John :

I have mailed you a set of photographs of the Berryville raid that made Sheridan retreat fifty miles down the Valley to the place where he started from. In 1867 Captain McAleer, of Baltimore, visited the scene, made sketches, and procured photographs of many of our men. He then went to Paris and had the pictures painted by two distinguished artists.[1] . . .

[1] Beaucé and Philippoteaux. Photographic reproductions of these paintings were widely circulated in France, England, and America shortly after the war.

Number 1 ("Mosby Planning an Attack on the Federal Cavalry") represents the battalion just as we reached the east bank of the Shenandoah — "the daughter of the stars." You are near me, listening intently to an order I am giving you to cross the river and find out what was in front. You returned after dark, when I was asleep enjoying a soldier's dream, "and the sentinel stars had set their watch in the sky", and told me that a long train, heavily guarded, was passing on the pike. In a few minutes all were mounted and moving to the attack.

Number 2 represents the Berryville fight and the stampede of the train guard. I am with Sam Chapman's company that was kept in reserve with the howitzer that is firing while Richards's squadron charge at one point on the line and William Chapman and Glasscock with their companies charge at another. Stockton Terry, of Lynchburg, is near me with the battalion colors. A body of the enemy formed behind a stone fence and made some resistance. Here Lewis Adie, of Glasscock's company, was killed. I remember very well when Guy Broadwater rode up and reported it to me in the midst of the fight. All I said was, "I can't help it." He was a fine boy.

Do you remember how the yellow-jackets routed us, and were near spoiling all my plans of that day? The howitzer came up at a gallop and was unlimbered on a knoll that commanded the pike. The gun was put in a position right over a nest of yellow-jackets. They were home-rulers, like the Boers, and instantly a swarm flew out to repel the invasion of their territory. My men had stood a volley from a body of infantry on the pike, but the sting of the yellow-jackets was too much for their courage. The horses reared and plunged, the men ran away from the gun. Whether the scene was sublime or ridiculous depends upon one's point of view at the time. My horse was frantic, and I felt a good deal like Hercules did when he put on the shirt of the Centaur and couldn't pull it off. We were on the verge of a panic — a few minutes' delay would give the enemy time to recover from their surprise. A shot from the howitzer was to be the signal for the squadrons to charge. They were waiting. But just then one of the men — Babcock I think it was — rushed forward, recaptured the howitzer, and dragged it off. The yellow-jackets returned in triumph to their hole in the ground. In a minute a shell burst among the wagons; it knocked off the head of a mule, the guard stampeded, while the braying of the mules could be heard above the roar of the gun. The mules we captured supplied General Lee's army with transportation, and the drove of fine beeves was sent as a present and furnished beefsteaks for his soldiers.

You will observe in the picture representing our return a figure on horseback playing a fiddle. It is Bob Ridley (Eastham). He got it from a headquarters wagon. Bob is playing a tune to which he had danced — "Malbrook has gone to the Wars."

Our object was to impede Sheridan's march.

I was sorry I could not be with you at the unveiling of the monument to our men at Front Royal, and I dissent from some historical statements in Major Richards's address. I do not agree with him that our men were hung in compliance with General Grant's orders to Sheridan. They were not hung in obedience to the orders of a superior, but from revenge. A man who acts from revenge simply obeys his own impulses. Major Richards says the orders were "a dead letter" after I retaliated, which implies that they had not been before. I see no evidence to support such a conclusion. In his letter in the *Times*, Major Richards says that Sheridan's dispatches about hanging our men were "visionary", *i.e.*, he never hung any. If so, the order had always been a "dead letter." No one ever heard of his hangings until his dispatches were published a few years ago; Sheridan was then dead, but his posthumous memoirs say nothing about hanging, although two pages are devoted to an account of the killing of Meigs and Custer's burning dwelling houses in Rockingham County in revenge. Meigs was not killed by my men; we never went that far up the Valley.

Sheridan's dispatches in the War Records about the men he hung were not even a revelation to me, — they revealed nothing. They were simply spectres of imagination, like the dagger in the air that Macbeth saw. If Sheridan had communicated Grant's dispatch of August 16th to any one to be executed, it would have been to Blazer, who commanded a picket corps that was specially detailed to look after us. In his report Blazer speaks of capturing some of my men; he never mentions hanging any. Those he captured were certainly not hung, for I saw them when they came home after the close of the war.

The following dispatches record the rise and fall of Blazer.

### [Sheridan to Augur]

August 20, 1864.

I have 100 men who will take the contract to clean out Mosby's gang. I want 100 Spencer rifles for them. Send them to me if they can be found in Washington.

P. H. Sheridan,
Major-General Commanding.

[Indorsement]

Approved: By order of the Secretary of War.

C. A. Dana,
Asst. Secretary.

### [Stevenson to Sheridan]

Harper's Ferry, November 19, 1864.

Two of Captain Blazer's men came in this morning — Privates Harris and Johnson. They report that Mosby with 300 men attacked Blazer near Kabletown yesterday about 11 o'clock. They say the entire command, with the exception of themselves, was captured or killed. I have ordered Major Congdon with 300 Twelfth Pennsylvania Cavalry to Kabletown to bury dead and take care of wounded, if any, and report all facts he can learn. I shall immediately furnish report as soon as rec'd.

Exit Blazer!

Richards commanded in the Blazer fight. I was not there. As an affair of arms it passed anything that had been done in the Shenandoah campaign and recalled the days when Knighthood was in flower. When we sent Blazer and his band of prisoners to Richmond, they would not have admitted that they ever hung anybody.

Major Richards refers to Grant's orders to destroy subsistence for an army so as to make the country untenable by the Confederates, and pathetically describes the conflagration. He ought to know that there had been burning of mills and wheat stacks in Loudon two years before Grant came to Virginia. Grant's orders were no more directed against my command than Early's. Augusta and Rockingham were desolated, where we never had been. But I can't see the slightest connection between burning forage and provisions and hanging prisoners. One is permitted by the code of war; the other is not.

After General Lee's surrender I received a communication from General Hancock asking for mine. I declined to do so until I could hear whether Joe Johnston would surrender or continue the war. We agreed on a five days' armistice. When it expired nothing had been heard from Johnston. I met a flag of truce at Millwood, and had proposed an extension of ten days, but received through Major Russell a message from Hancock refusing it and informing me that unless I surrendered immediately he would proceed to devastate the country. The reply I sent by Russell was, "Tell

General Hancock he is able to do it." Hancock then had 40,000 men at Winchester. The next day I disbanded my battalion to save the country from being made a desert. If any one doubts this, let him read Hancock's report. If it was legitimate for Hancock to lay waste the country after I had suspended hostilities, surely it was equally so for Grant to do it when I was doing all the damage in my power to his army. Stanton warned Hancock not to meet me in person under a flag of truce, for fear that I would treacherously kill him. Hancock replied that he would send an officer to meet me. He sent General Chapman. The attention Grant paid to us shows that we did him a great deal of harm. Keeping my men in prison weakened us as much as to hang them.

Major Richards complains of the "debasing epithets" Sheridan applied to us. I have read his reports, correspondence, and memoirs, but have never seen the epithets. In common with all northern and many southern people, he called us guerrillas. The word "guerrilla" is a diminutive of the Spanish word "guerra" (war), and simply means one engaged in the minor operations of war. Although I have never adopted it, I have never resented as an insult the term "guerrilla" when applied to me.

Sheridan says that my battalion was "the most redoubtable" partisan body that he met. I certainly take no exception to that. He makes no charge of any act of inhumanity against us. The highest compliment ever paid to the efficiency of our command is the statement in Sheridan's "Memoirs", that while his

army largely outnumbered Early's, yet their line of
battle strength was about equal on account of the
detachments he was compelled to make to guard the
border and his line of communication from partisan
attacks. Ours was the only force behind him. At
that time the records show that in round numbers
Early had 17,000 present for duty, and Sheridan had
94,000. I had only five companies of cavalry when
Sheridan came in August, 1864, to the Shenandoah
Valley. A sixth was organized in September. Two
more companies joined me in April, 1865, after the
evacuation of Richmond. They came just in time to
surrender.

I don't care a straw whether Custer was solely responsible for the hanging of our men, or jointly with
others. If we believe the reports of the generals,
none of them ever heard of the hanging of our men ;
they must have committed suicide. Contemporary
evidence is against Custer. I wonder if he also denied
burning dwelling houses around Berryville.

I once called at the White House in 1876 to see
General Grant; sent him my card, and was promptly
admitted. When I came out of his room, one of the
secretaries told me that General Custer had called the
day before, but that General Grant had refused to see
him. The incident is related in the "Life of Custer."
A few weeks afterward Custer was killed in the Sitting
Bull Massacre.

Major Richards further says "that there was
scarcely a family in all that section that did not have
some member in Mosby's command." If that is true,

I must have commanded a larger army than Sheridan. I didn't know it. He describes the pathos of the scenes that might have been if the "severe and cruel order" had been executed to transfer the families from that region to Fort McHenry, and says it would have "paralyzed" my command. If so, that would have been a more humane way of getting rid of it than killing the men. Now I have never considered women and children necessary appendages to an army; on the contrary, I would rather class them with what Cæsar, in his "Commentaries", calls impedimenta. Homer's heroes were not paralyzed when Helen was carried off to Troy; it only aroused their martial ambition. Sheridan knew that if he did anything of the kind it would stimulate the activity of my men, so he didn't try it. As for our lieutenant-colonel, who, as Major Richards says, married in that section, I think that if Sheridan had captured his wife and mother-in-law and sent them to prison, instead of going into mourning, he would have felt all the wrath and imitated the example of the fierce Achilles when he heard that Patroclus, his friend, had been killed and his armor had been captured. "Now perish Troy," he said, and rushed to fight.

Very truly yours,

John S. Mosby.

# CHAPTER XIX

## MY RECOLLECTIONS OF GENERAL LEE

MY first meeting with General Robert E. Lee was in August, 1862, when I brought the news of Burnside's reinforcement of Pope, a story I have told in the preceding pages. The next time we met was at his headquarters in Orange, about two months after Gettysburg. He did not seem in the least depressed, and was as buoyant and aggressive as ever. He took a deep interest in my operations, for there was nothing of the Fabius in his character. Lee was the most aggressive man I met in the war, and was always ready for an enterprise. I believe that his interest in me was largely due to the fact that his father, "Light Horse Harry", was a partisan officer in the Revolutionary War.

After General Stuart was killed, in May, 1864, I reported directly to General Lee. During the siege of Petersburg I visited him three times — twice when I was wounded. Once, when I got out of the ambulance, he was standing near, talking to General Longstreet. When he saw me hobbling up to him on crutches, he came to meet me, introduced me to General Longstreet, and said, "Colonel, the only fault I have ever had to find with you is that you are always getting wounded."

Such a speech from General Lee more than repaid me for my wound.

The last time I saw him during the war was about two months before the surrender. I had been wounded again. He was not only kind, but affectionate, and asked me to take dinner with him, though he said he hadn't much to eat. There was a leg of mutton on the table; he remarked that some of his staff officers must have stolen it.

After dinner, when we were alone, he talked very freely. He said that in the spring of 1862, Joe Johnston ought not to have fallen back from the Rapidan to Richmond, and that he had written urging him to turn against Washington. He also said that when Joe Johnston evacuated his lines at Yorktown, in May of that year, he should have given battle with his whole force on the isthmus at Williamsburg, instead of making a rear-guard fight.

When I bade Lee good-by after our last interview, I had no idea that it was my final parting with him as my commander. I can never forget the sympathetic words with which he cautioned me against unnecessary exposure to danger.

The following is the last order he ever gave me. It was dated March 27, 1865, and put me in command of all northern Virginia:

Collect your command and watch the country from the front of Gordonsville to Blue Ridge, and also the Valley. Your command is all now in that section, and the general (Lee) will rely on you to watch and protect the country. If any of your command is in Northern Neck, call it to you.

W. H. Taylor,
Assistant Adjutant-General.

Lee was raised in the political school of Washington and Hamilton. In the Virginia convention of 1788, his father had voted against the imbecile confederation and for the Constitution which made the laws of the Union supreme law of the land, and in 1798 spoke and voted against the famous States-rights' resolutions. In the year 1794 he commanded the Virginia troops that were ordered to Pennsylvania to suppress the Whiskey Insurrection. It is difficult to distinguish in law between Washington's proclamation in 1794, calling out the military force to execute the laws of the United States, and Lincoln's in 1861.

As Lieutenant-Colonel of the Second Cavalry, Lee was stationed in Texas in February, 1861, but was ordered to Washington, arriving there about the time of the presidential inauguration. The commander-in-chief, General Scott, a Virginian, was too old for active service — there was then no retirement law — and he wanted Lee near him as an adviser and second in command. On March 16, Colonel Edwin V. Sumner was promoted to be a brigadier-general in place of Twiggs, who had been dismissed for treachery in surrendering the Union troops in Texas. A Virginia lady, who met Lee about that time, told me, many years ago, that he spoke to her with great indignation about General Twiggs's conduct. Lee now became colonel of the First Cavalry. His biographers do not seem to have heard of this promotion and have ignored the fact that he accepted a commission from President Lincoln. Lee was with his family at Arlington and on confidential relations with the War Department up to the day of his resignation, April 20, 1861. As the command of the U. S. Army was offered to him, Scott must have thought that he would stand by the Union, and Lee's purpose to resign in the event of Virginia passing an ordinance of secession had not been disclosed.

Lee was forced by circumstances to take the side for which he fought in the war. On the subject of slavery and the right of secession, he agreed with Abraham Lincoln. Five years before, in writing about slavery, he had said, "It is a moral, social, and political evil."

Writing at Fort Mason, Texas, on January 23, 1861 — after seven States had passed ordinances of secession — Lee said :

The framers of our Constitution would never have exhausted so much labor, wisdom, and forbearance in its formation, and surrounded it with so many safeguards and securities, if it was intended to be broken by every member of the confederacy at will. It was intended for "perpetual union", so expressed in the preamble, and for the establishment of a government, not a compact, which can only be dissolved by revolution, or by the consent of all the people in convention assembled. It is idle to talk of secession. Anarchy would have been established, and not a government, by Washington, Hamilton, Jefferson, Madison, and all the other patriots of the Revolution.

When Lee resigned his commission to join the forces of his native State, he acted, as nearly every soldier acts, from personal sympathy with the combatants, and not on any legal theory of right and wrong. On the day when he resigned, he wrote his sister that he could not draw his sword against his family, his neighbors, and his friends.

On the previous day, he happened to go into a store in Alexandria to pay a bill. His heart was burdened with a great sorrow, and he uttered these words, which the merchant wrote down in his journal — they still stand there to-day: "I must say that I am one of those dull creatures that cannot see the good of secession."

Below this entry the merchant wrote, "Spoken by Colonel R. E. Lee when he paid this bill, April 19, 1861."

A few days later, Lee was made commander-in-chief of the forces of the State of Virginia. There was no competition for the position. The late Judge John Critcher represented Westmoreland, Lee's native county, in the secession convention, and was one of the committee sent to notify him of the appointment. The judge told me that when Lee returned with the committee to the convention hall, in the Capitol at Richmond, they had to wait for a few minutes in the rotunda. Looking at Houdon's statue of Washington, Lee said, very gravely, "I hope we have seen the last of secession."

He evidently feared that the seceding States

would soon separate from one another. "The Life of Alexander Stephens" shows that the apprehension was not unfounded, and that the members of the Confederacy were held together only by the pressure of war and by the despotic power of the central government at Richmond.

I once heard General John C. Breckenridge say, at a dinner in Baltimore, soon after he returned from his exile in Canada, that if the Southern Confederacy had been established, "there would have been such a spirit of local self-assertion that every county would have claimed the right to set up for itself."

I met General Lee a few times after the war, but the days of strife were never mentioned. I remember the last words he spoke to me, about two months before his death, at a reception that was given to him in Alexandria. When I bade him good-by, he said, "Colonel, I hope we shall have no more wars."

In March, 1870, I was walking across the bridge connecting the Ballard and Exchange hotels, in Richmond, and to my surprise I met General Lee and his daughter. The general was pale and haggard, and did not look like the Apollo I had known in the army. After a while I went to his room; our conversation was on current topics.

I felt oppressed by the great memories that his presence revived, and while both of us were thinking about the war, neither of us referred to it.

After leaving the room, I met General Pickett, and told him that I had just been with Lee. He remarked that, if I would go with him, he would call and pay his respects to the general, but he did not want to be alone with him. So I went back with Pickett; the interview was cold and formal, and evidently embarrassing to both. It was their only meeting after the war.

In a few minutes I rose and left the room, together with General Pickett. He then spoke very bitterly of General Lee, calling him "that old man."

"He had my division massacred at Gettysburg," Pickett said.

"Well, it made you immortal," I replied.

I rather suspect that Pickett gave a wrong reason for his unfriendly feelings. In May, 1892, at the University of Virginia, I took breakfast with Professor Venable, who had been on Lee's staff. He told me that some days before the surrender at Appomattox, General Lee ordered Pickett under arrest — I suppose for the Five Forks affair.[1] I think the professor said that he carried the order.

[1] Battle of April 1, 1865.

I remember very well his adding that, on the retreat, Pickett passed them, and that General Lee said, with deep feeling, "Is that man still with this army?"

I once went to see the tomb of Montcalm in the chapel of the Ursuline Convent at Quebec. When I read the inscription — "Fate denied him victory, but blessed him with a glorious immortality" — it recalled General Robert E. Lee.

# CHAPTER XX

## My Recollections of General Grant

I FIRST met General Grant in May, 1872, after Mr. Greeley had been nominated for the presidency by a convention whose members called themselves Liberal Republicans — although, as a matter of fact, many of them had been the most radical element of the party, but had seceded on account of personal grievances. My home was then at Warrenton, Virginia, where I was practising law. As it was only fifty miles from Washington, I was frequently there, but I had only once seen General Grant — one evening at the National Theatre, when he was in a box with General Sherman. Both men seemed to enjoy the play as much as the gods in the gallery.

In common with most Southern soldiers, I had a very kindly feeling towards General Grant, not only on account of his magnanimous conduct at Appomattox, but also for his treatment of me at the close of hostilities. I had never called on him, however. If I had done so, and if he had received me even politely, we should both have been subjected to severe criticism, so bitter was the feeling between the sections at the time.

No doubt, in those days, most Northerners believed the imaginative stories of the war correspondents and supposed that my battalion fought under the black flag. General Grant was as much misunderstood in the South as I was in the North. But time has healed wounds which were once thought to be irremediable; and there is to-day no memory of our war so bitter, probably, as the Scottish recollection of Culloden. Like most Southern men, I had disapproved the reconstruction measures and was sore and very restive under military government; but since my prejudices have faded, I can now see that many things which we regarded as being prompted by hostile and vindictive motives were actually necessary, in order to prevent anarchy and to secure the freedom of the newly emancipated slave.

I had given little attention to politics and had devoted my time to my profession, although I was under no political disability. As we had all been opposed to the Republican party before the war, it was a point of honor to keep on voting that way.

When Horace Greeley was nominated, I saw — or thought I saw — that it was idle to divide longer upon issues which we acknowledged to have been legally, if not properly, settled; and that if the Southern people wanted reconciliation, as they said they did, the logical thing to do was to vote for Grant. I have not changed my opinion, nor yet have I any criticism to make of those who differed with me. We were all working for the same end. Some said they couldn't sacrifice their principles for Grant's friendship; I didn't sacrifice mine.

Not long before the death of the late General M. C. Butler, United States Senator from South Carolina, I met him on the street in Washington.

"We ought to have gone with you for Grant," he said.

My views and opinions of that period are set forth in the following interview published in the *Richmond Enquirer*, in January, 1873.

Reporter: "I see it stated generally that you have some influence with General Grant, — is this true?"

Colonel Mosby: "I don't know what amount of influence I may have with the President, but General Grant knows the fiery ordeal I have been through here in supporting him, and I suppose he has some appreciation of it."

Reporter: "What is the policy that you have advocated for the Virginia people?"

Colonel Mosby: "The issues that formerly divided

the Virginia people from the Republican party were those growing out of the reconstruction measures. Last year the Virginia people agreed to make no further opposition to those measures and to accept all questions growing out of them as settled. There being no longer any questions, then, on principles separating Virginia people from General Grant, it became a mere matter of policy and expediency whether they would support him or Horace Greeley. I thought it was the first opportunity the Southern people had had to be restored to their proper relation and influence with the Federal administration. In other words, I said the Southern statesmen ought to avail themselves of this opportunity and support General Grant for re-election, and thereby acquire influence and control over his administration. That was the only way I saw of displacing the carpetbag crew that represented the Government in the Southern States. I think that events have demonstrated that I was right.

"General Grant has certainly accorded to me as much consideration or influence as any one man could have a right to expect. I know it is the disposition of General Grant to do everything in his power for the relief of the Southern people, if Southern politicians will allow him to do it. The men who control the policy of the Conservative party combine with the extreme Radicals to keep the Southern people arrayed against General Grant. As long as this course is pursued, the carpetbag crew who profess to support the administration get all the Federal patronage. This is the sustenance, the support of the carpetbag party in the South. Deprived of that, it would die to-morrow. I admit, as every Southern man must admit, the gross wrongs that have been perpetrated upon the Southern people. I am no apologist for them, but neither party proposes any atonement or indemnity for the past. I propose at least to give security for the future by an alliance between the Southern people and General Grant's administration." . . .

Reporter: "Has the President ever tendered you any position under his administration?"

Colonel Mosby: "Shortly after the presidential election the President said something to me on the subject of giving me an office. I told him while I would as lief hold an office under him as under any other man who had ever been President, yet there was no office within his gift that I desired or would accept. I told him that my motives in supporting him had been assailed, and my accepting a position under his administration would be regarded as a confirmation of the truth of the charge that I was governed by selfish motives. But my principal reason for not accepting anything from him was that I would have far more influence for good by taking nothing for myself." . . .

Reporter: "Colonel, I have heard that you are now promoting claims against the Government, — is that a fact?"

Colonel Mosby: "It is not. I have filed one claim for a citizen before the Southern Claims Commission. I shall turn this over, however, to a claim agent. I have had hundreds of claims of all sorts for prosecution against the Government offered me, but have declined them all, as I have no idea of bartering my political influence. . . . I do not think that any man nominated at Lynchburg will stand the most remote chance of success, because he will only be supported by the negroes of the State, led by a few white men. No matter what my relations to the administration may be, I wouldn't assist in putting this set in power."

I had strong personal reasons for being friendly with General Grant. If he had not thrown his shield over me, I should have been outlawed and driven into exile. When Lee surrendered, my battalion was in northern Virginia, on the Potomac, a hundred miles from Appomattox. Secretary of War Stanton invited all soldiers in Virginia to surrender on the same conditions which were offered to Lee's army; *but I was excepted*. General Grant, who was then all-powerful, interposed, and sent me an offer of the same parole that he had given General Lee. Such a service I could never forget. When the opportunity came, I remembered what he had done for me, and I did all I could for him.

Early one morning, a few days after the election of 1872, I had to go to the Treasury Department on business. The Secretary, Mr. Boutwell, had not come, and I was waiting in an ante-room. To my surprise, General Grant walked in. He shook hands with me, and said, "I heard you were here, and came to thank you for my getting the vote of Virginia." That is the only time I ever saw a President in any of the departments. Of course, I appreciated General Grant's compliment, although he gave me credit for a great deal more than I deserved.

General Grant had also done another thing which showed the generosity of his nature. A few weeks before the surrender, a small party of my men crossed the Potomac one night and got into a fight, in which a detective was killed. One of the men was captured and sent to Fort McHenry. After the war he was tried by a military commission and sentenced to be imprisoned. The boy's mother went to see President Johnson, to beg a pardon for her son; but Johnson repelled her roughly.

In her distress, she went over to the War Department to see General Grant. He listened patiently to her sorrowful story, then rose and asked her to go with him. He took her to the White House, walked into the reception room, and told the President that there had been suffering enough, and that he would not leave the room without a pardon for the young Southerner. Johnson signed the necessary paper.

In spite of the parole that I had taken, after I had settled down to the practice of law, I was several times arrested by provost-marshals stationed at the court houses where I went on the circuit. This was both annoying and unfair. My parole was a contract with the government that was binding on both parties. To arrest me before I had violated it was a breach of it.

As my wife passed through Washington on her way to Baltimore, she determined to go to the White House, not to ask for a pardon, but to make a complaint. She had not intimated her purpose to me. Her father and President Johnson had served in Congress together, and had been friends; so she told Johnson whose daughter and whose wife she was. Instead of responding kindly, he was rude to her.

She left him and went to see General Grant at the War Department. He treated her as courteously as if she had been the wife of a Union soldier, and then wrote the following letter, which he gave to her. He did not dictate the letter to a clerk; the whole is in his small, neat handwriting. It gave me liberty to travel anywhere unmolested as long as I observed my parole.

Headquarters of the Armies of the United States,
Washington, D. C., Feb'y 2nd, 1866.

John S. Mosby, lately of the Southern Army, will, hereafter, be exempt from arrest by military authorities, except for violation of his parole, unless directed by the President of the United States, Secretary of War, or from these headquarters.

His parole will authorize him to travel freely within the state of Virginia, and as no obstacle has been thrown in the way of paroled officers and men from pursuing their civil pursuits, or traveling out of their States, the same privilege will be extended to J. S. Mosby, unless otherwise directed by competent authority.

(Signed) U. S. Grant,
Lieutenant General.

When General Ewell was captured by the Federal forces, on the retreat from Richmond, he was sent to Fort Warren. Mrs. Ewell — who had married the general during the war — was from Nashville, and had known Johnson when he was Governor of Tennessee. She, too, called on the President, presuming on their old acquaintance, to ask that her husband be released on parole. Ewell was in a feeble condition; he had lost a leg in the war. Johnson treated her just as he had treated my wife, and asked her why she had "married a one-legged man."

Mrs. Ewell then went to see General Grant, who expressed great pleasure at being able to do something for "my old friend Ewell", and ordered that the poor fellow should be released from prison. He did hundreds of similar things.

As I have said, my first interview with General Grant was in May, 1872, when I was introduced to him by Senator Lewis of Virginia. He immediately began telling me how near I came to capturing the train on which he went to take command of the Army of the Potomac in 1864. I remarked, "If I had done it, things might have been changed — I might have been in the White House and you might be calling on me."

"Yes," he said.

In our talk I became convinced that he was not only willing but anxious to lift the Southern people out of the rut they were in, but he couldn't help them without their coöperation. If they insisted on keeping up their fire on him, he had to return the fire. I knew that he was in favor of relieving Southerners of the disabilities imposed by the Fourteenth Amendment, as he had recommended in his message. Such a bill had passed the House, but in the Senate, Sumner had insisted on tacking to it his Civil Rights Bill, which made it odious, and the measure was defeated.

I suggested that if he could get such a bill passed, it would be construed as an olive branch, and would create such a reaction in his favor in Virginia that we could carry the State for him.

"We will see what can be done," he replied.

As I was under no disability myself, it would have been hard to discover a selfish motive in what I urged Grant to do. A few days afterwards, a bill removing political disabilities was reported in the House; the rules were suspended, and the bill passed. It was sent to the Senate; there was a night session; Sumner went to his committee room to take a nap, and while he was asleep, the bill was called up and became a law. He was furious when he awoke and found out what had been done. Many Confederates who had been excluded from public position were then sent to Congress or received appointments from Washington. Among them was the Vice-President of the Southern Confederacy.

I crossed the Rubicon when I paid my first visit to the White House, and I never recrossed it. My son Beverly, who was about twelve years old, was with me. He had been with his mother six years before, when she called on Andrew Johnson. That night, when he knelt by her to say his prayers, after getting through the usual form, he turned to her and said, "Now, mamma, may I pray to God to send old Johnson to the devil?"

I told the story to Grant.

"A great many would have joined in Beverly's prayer," he said, laughing.

As many people in the South regarded me as a connecting link between the administration and themselves, I had to pay frequent visits to the White House, either to ask favors or to carry complaints. Such a duty is a shirt of Nessus to any one who wears it. Although I declined to take office from General Grant and exerted all the influence I had with him for the benefit of the Virginia people, this did not save me from the imputation of sordid motives.

It is generally believed that Grant appointed me consul at Hong Kong. He did not; I was appointed by Mr. Hayes.

Often as I went to the White House during Grant's second term, I never failed to see him except once, when he was in the hands of a dentist. In those days hundreds went to him for appointments, who would now be sent to the Civil Service Commission. In spite of all this pressure, he never seemed to be in a hurry. He was the best listener I ever saw, and one of the quickest to see the core of a question.

I once called at the White House about seven o'clock in the evening, with a telegram I had received from General Hampton. The door-keeper said that the President was at dinner. I gave the man my card and told him I would wait in the hall. He returned with a message from General Grant, asking me to come in and take dinner with the family. I replied that I had already dined. Then Ulysses S. Grant, Junior, came out and said, "Father says that you must come in and get some dinner."

Of course, I went in. At the table, the General spoke of having called that evening on Alexander Stephens, who was lying sick at his hotel. It looked as if our war was a long way in the past when the President of the United States could call to pay his respects to the Vice-President of the Confederate States.

A few weeks before the close of Grant's second term, I introduced one of my men to him.

"I hope you will not think less of Captain Glasscock because he was with me in the war," I said.

"I think all the more of him," the President promptly replied.

I once said to General Grant, "General, if you had been a Southern man, would you have been in the Southern army?"

"Certainly," he replied.

He aways spoke in the friendliest manner of his old army comrades who went with the South. Once, speaking of Stonewall Jackson, who was with him at West Point, he said to me, "Jackson was the most conscientious being I ever knew."

I saw Grant on the day when he signed the Electoral Commission Bill to decide the Hayes-Tilden dispute. He was in an unusually good humor, and said that the man in whose favor the commission decided should be inaugurated. He talked a good deal about his early life in the army and gave a description of his first two battles — Palo Alto and Resaca de la Palma.

A few days after he left the White House, I called on General Grant at the home of Mr. Hamilton Fish, where he was staying. I did not ask him to recommend me to the new administration, as some members of the Cabinet were not friendly to him.

President Hayes, however, appointed me United States Consul at Hong Kong; and it was there, in 1879, during Grant's tour of the world, that I last saw him. I went in a boat to meet him, and, as I was the official representative of the United States, the other craft that surrounded the steamship as soon as it anchored gave me the right of way. As I went up the gangway, I recognized him, with his wife and eldest son, standing on the deck. It did look strange that I should be there representing the government, while General Grant was a private citizen.

There was with me an old Virginian who had gone to Hong Kong before the war. When I introduced him, I told General Grant that when I arrived I had found this fellow countryman of mine in about the same temper that I was in when the general was fighting in the Wilderness; but that he was willing to surrender to the man to whom General Lee had surrendered. Mrs. Grant spoke up and asked liberal terms for him, and Grant said that he paroled him, and hoped he would be a loyal citizen.

The Governor of Hong Kong met General Grant's party at the wharf, and they went to the Government House. Next morning the general paid his respects to me at the American Consulate. He was the guest of the governor for about ten days. On several days I breakfasted with him, and we had many free and informal talks. Once he was giving a description of his ride on donkey-back from Jaffa to Jerusalem.

"That," he said, "was the roughest road I ever traveled."

"General," I replied, "I think you have traveled one rougher road than that."

"Where?" he inquired.

"From the Rapidan to Richmond," I answered.

"I reckon there were more obstructions on that road," he admitted.

I went with the general, Mrs. Grant, Colonel Fred Grant, and the governor, in a launch, to the United States man-of-war which carried his party up the China coast, and bade him my last farewell. When we started ashore, the ship began firing a royal salute of twenty-one guns, in honor of the governor, and the launch stopped. When the firing was over, General Grant lifted his hat, and we responded. I never saw the great soldier again.

Some time afterwards, I sent the general a Malacca cane which I had had lacquered for him. It bore the inscription, "To General U. S. Grant from John S. Mosby, Hong Kong."

He was in very poor health when he received it, but Colonel Fred Grant wrote me that his father was pleased at my remembrance of him.

When I heard that President Cleveland had removed me as consul, in 1885, I wrote to General Grant and asked him to secure me employment from some corporation, by which I could make a living. I did not then know how near he was to his end. My letter was forwarded to him at Mount McGregor, and on the day before I sailed from Hong Kong a dispatch announced his death. I felt that I had lost my best friend.

I did not suppose that my letter would have any result, but on arriving in San Francisco, I learned that he had dictated a note to Governor Stanford, of the Southern Pacific, asking him, as a personal favor, to take care of me. I was made an attorney in the company and held that position for sixteen years.

I have given as faithful an account as Æneas did to Dido of events — all of which I saw and part of which I was. No one clung longer to the Confederacy than I did, and I can say with the champion of another lost cause that if Troy could have been saved by this right hand even by the same it would have been saved.

# INDEX

Abingdon, Virginia, 11, 14, 15, 27.

Adams, Charles Francis, 13.

Aldie, Virginia, 159, 160.

Aldridge, West (Mosby's company), 317.

Alexander, General, in battle of Manassas, 63, 81, 82, 83; quoted, 65, 72, 75, 76–77, 78, 82.

Alexandria, Virginia, 55, 306, 379.

Alexandria pike, 50.

*Alexandria State Journal*, quoted, 363.

Amelia County, Virginia, 29.

Ames, Sergeant, adventure in Mosby's company, 170–171, 172–174; deserted from Fifth New York Cavalry, 168.

*Amy Warwick*, The, seized, 96.

Anderson, Major Robert, at Fort Sumter, 18.

Appomattox, 252, 388; Lee's surrender at, 28, 84, 356, 381.

Aquia Creek (on Potomac), 130.

Archer's brigade in Gettysburg campaign, 249, 250.

Arlington, Lee's home, 55.

Army of Potomac, at Frederick City, 224; commanded by Meade, 86, 223; finest regiment in, 286.

Ashby's Gap (Blue Ridge), Virginia, 212.

Ashby's regiment in battle of Manassas, 57, 85.

Ashland, Virginia, 28, 112.

Augur, General C. C., 307, 310; at Washington, 286, 290; dispatch to Lazelle, 295; dispatch to Sheridan, 287, 288, 294, 350; dispatch to Waite, 288, 289.

Averell, General W. W., 25.

Ball's Ford, 47.

Baltimore, Maryland, 85, 209, 224, 227, 233, 325, 326, 390.

Baltimore *Sun*, quoted, 6–8, 364.

Banks, General N. P., 59.

Barker, Captain, capture of, 174, 179.

Bartow's brigade at Manassas, 71, 78.

Bealeton Station, Virginia, 106.

Beattie, Ab., Major, 27.

Beattie, Fount (Mosby's company), 30, 48, 99, 320.

Beauregard, General P. G. T., 39, 43, 46; address by, 97; dispatch to D. R. Jones, 70, 73; dispatch to War Department, 62; in battle of Manassas, 56–58, 60–68, 72–79, 81–85; quoted, 75; report on battle, 68; strength of army, 84.

Beaver Dam Station (Chesapeake and Ohio R. R.), 126, 136.

Beckham, Mr. (citizen), 182.

Beckham's battery in battle of Manassas, 79.

Bee, General B. E., at Manassas, 71, 78.

Bell and Everett Meeting, 16.

Bernhardi, General, quoted, 208, 229–230.

Berryville, Virginia, 290.

Beverly's Ford, 204, 205, 207.

Blackburn's Ford (Bull Run), 70, 74.

Blackford, Captain William, 11, 99.

Blackstone's "Commentaries", 8.

Blackwell, Joe, visited by Mosby, 335.

JOHN SINGLETON MOSBY (1833–1916) was born in Powhatan County, Virginia, and grew up on a farm near Charlottesville in the Virginia Piedmont. After studying at the University of Virginia, and reading law while serving a jail sentence for shooting a fellow student, he was admitted to the Virginia Bar in 1854. In the election of 1860 he was a Douglas Democrat and a supporter of the Union, but upon the secession of Virginia he entered the Confederate military service under cavalry Colonel J. E. B. Stuart. With the consent of Stuart and R. E. Lee he subsequently formed an independent cavalry unit which operated behind Union lines in Loudoun and Fauquier Counties, which region became known as "Mosby's Confederacy." The history of his war experiences is found in the *Memoirs,* finished near the end of his life and published in 1917. Always of an individualist temperament, Mosby became a friend of U. S. Grant after the War, and a Republican. He held several U.S. Government posts, including a consulship in Hong Kong. He died in Washington, D.C. in 1916.

J. O. TATE, a native of Georgia, attended Swarthmore College and Columbia University. He is currently a Professor of English at Dowling College in Oakdale, Long Island, New York. Tate has written extensively on such prominent Southerners as Nathan Bedford Forrest, Jubal Early, Flannery O'Conner, Walker Percy, Allen Tate and Andrew Lytle.